A HISTORY OF MALAYA

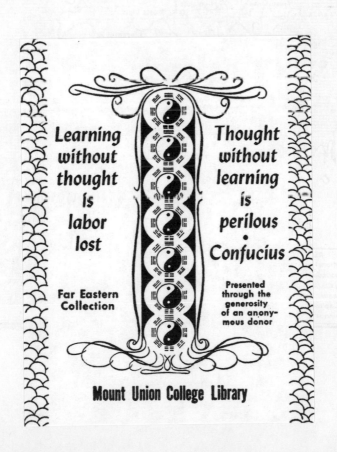

Learning without thought is labor lost

Thought without learning is perilous

• Confucius

Far Eastern Collection

Presented through the generosity of an anonymous donor

A
HISTORY OF MALAYA

A.D. 1400–1959

BY

J. KENNEDY, M.A.

Senior Lecturer in History
Malayan Teachers' Training College, Kirkby

ST MARTIN'S PRESS

1962

MACMILLAN AND COMPANY LIMITED
London Bombay Calcutta Madras Melbourne

THE MACMILLAN COMPANY OF CANADA LIMITED
Toronto

ST MARTIN'S PRESS INC
New York

PRINTED IN GREAT BRITAIN

PREFACE

THE aim of this book is to present a concise and reasoned account of the main trends of Malayan history during the last five and a half centuries. Before A.D. 1400 the southern part of the Malay Peninsula is seen largely in relation to archaeology, and to the records and claims of other political centres, including the maritime empires of Funan, Srivijaya, Suk'ot'ai, and Majapahit. The rise of the port-kingdom of Malacca has been taken as a starting-point because at this stage Malaya began to have its own written history. Malacca also gave to other Malay states in the Peninsula some measure of political unity, and this theme is repeated again near the end of the book in the independence of Malaya and the achievement of internal self-government by Singapore.

I am very much indebted to the works of Sir Frank Swettenham, Sir Richard Winstedt, R. J. Wilkinson, W. Linehan, W. G. Maxwell, L. A. Mills, C. C. Brown, V. Purcell, C. E. Wurzburg, D. G. E. Hall, C. D. Cowan, J. M. Gullick, C. A. Gibson-Hill, G. C. Allen and A. G. Donnithorne, together with those of other scholars mentioned in the footnotes and Select Bibliography.

My thanks are also due to Malayan student-teachers, past and present, at Kirkby, who have contributed in many ways to my work.

I hope that the book will help to increase interest in the study of Malayan history.

J. KENNEDY

Malayan Teachers' Training College,
Kirkby, Nr. Liverpool
August 1960

v

ACKNOWLEDGMENTS

I wish to record my thanks to Messrs. George Allen and Unwin, Ltd., and the Syndics of the Cambridge University Press for permission to quote from copyright works.

I am grateful also to the publishers, institutions, and organisations who have supplied illustrations and whose names are recorded in the List of Illustrations.

I am indebted to Miss B. Mather for her careful work on the typescript.

Last, but not least, I must thank my wife for much general help and for assistance with the maps.

J. K.

CONTENTS

LIST OF PLATES

MAPS

Chapter 1

THE MALAY KINGDOM OF MALACCA

A.D. 1400–1511

Parameswara, the founder of the Malay Kingdom of Malacca remains a shadowy figure. It is easier to trace his movements than his motives and to see the consequences of his actions rather than the man behind them.

We know him by a title meaning 'prince-consort'. He was apparently a prince of Palembang who had married a princess of Majapahit in eastern Java. He may have been a descendant of those Sailendra kings who had once ruled Srivijaya and, before that, central Java and, possibly, Funan.

'When he realised how nobly he was married, and how great was his power in the neighbouring islands,'[1] Parameswara announced his independence of Majapahit. This proved to be a rash step, for a Javanese expedition attacked and laid waste the island of Bangka and the region of Palembang, and Parameswara escaped by sea, a political refugee. By chance or design, he and his followers landed on the island of Tumasik, or Singapore. The year may have been about 1390.

The next episode in Parameswara's career reflects perhaps both his ambition and his impulsive nature. The reigning chief on the island of Singapore welcomed Parameswara and his followers; possibly, he was not strong enough to act otherwise. Within eight days, according to Pires's account, Parameswara had him murdered, and claimed the island and the neighbouring sea-passages as his own. Political ambition, aided possibly by feelings of personal rivalry, would seem to have been the motive for murder.

[1] Tomé Pires, *Suma Oriental.*

1

Parameswara's success was comparatively short-lived. As time went on, he feared an invasion directed by the Siamese state of Suk'ot'ai, which claimed overlordship of all the settlements in the Malay Peninsula as far south as Singapore. The murdered chief had been related by marriage both to the Siamese king and to the ruler of Patani, which was a vassal state of Siam. When he received news of the approach of a war fleet from Patani, Parameswara decided that it would be wise to be on his travels again, and he embarked with his followers. Pires puts the length of Parameswara's stay in Singapore as five years.

Muar provided Parameswara with his next home. Here, with about a thousand followers, he established a river settlement which engaged in a mixture of fishing, farming, and piracy. After six years at Muar, Parameswara took the advice of a group of his fishermen and sailed northwards to a more promising settlement with which they had made contact at Malacca.

The combination at Malacca of river, hill, and wide hinterland, offered a better prospect than Muar for trade, agriculture and defence. Parameswara's arrival here, about the year A.D. 1400, marked the beginnings of a change from a small settlement of fishermen-pirates to a busy and wealthy *entrepôt* port and the capital of a Malay empire.[1]

All this, of course, did not happen in a year or two. It seems true to say, however, that the foundations were laid during Parameswara's lifetime. He made Malacca his permanent home and was accepted by its people as their ruler. Earlier glimpses of his life showed him as a rebel and adventurer; age and experience now seemed to bring from him the qualities of a shrewd business-man and statesman.

Perhaps his first wise measure was to grasp the hand of friendship offered to him by Ming China. Parameswara's arrival at Malacca coincided with a period of rare but spectacular Chinese naval activity in the seas of South-East Asia and westwards via the Indian Ocean to the Red Sea and the coasts of East Africa. The presence of Ming fleets in South-East Asia acted both as a deter-

[1] The possibility of a much earlier port of Malacca has received some attention recently.

rent to the expansion of larger states like Suk'ot'ai and Majapahit and as a protection to small princedoms like Malacca. By encouraging the aspirations of small states and engaging them in direct diplomacy with China, the early Ming rulers hoped to prevent the appearance of any all-powerful state in the vast area of peninsulas and islands which lay to the Chinese south, or 'Nanyang'.

Parameswara's ready acceptance of Chinese help and protection brought him valuable presents and recognition of his title by the Chinese Emperor. These diplomatic exchanges had, for Malacca, other consequences of equal importance to the growth of the infant kingdom. Chinese trading-junks, laden with valuable cargoes, began to arrive at Malacca each year, borne on the north-east monsoon. This Chinese trade acted as a magnet for other merchants and shipping from near and far, and thus Malacca became an international market.

Although Parameswara could hardly have lived in great state during his early years in Malacca, there were, at times, touches of pageantry and ceremonial. Among the colourful events in early Malacca must be counted the visit of Chinese Admiral Cheng Ho in 1409, and the departure of Parameswara and his retinue, on board Chinese vessels, for a state visit to Peking in 1411.

Protected against the Siamese by his good relations with China,[1] Parameswara now sought to make both trade and political agreements in Java and Sumatra. Majapahit, torn by internal wars, was less promising than northern Sumatra. By a shrewd judgment, Parameswara allied himself in politics and trade with the Muslim state of Pasai in northern Sumatra, and this alliance was symbolised by the marriage, in 1414, of Parameswara to a Muslim Princess of Pasai. Already Pasai had a lively trade in produce from many parts of India and from Java, as well as specialising in locally grown pepper. Malacca's links with Pasai brought more Indian and Javanese traders to Malacca, where they found also the added attraction of bargaining for the luxuries of Chinese silk, gold thread, porcelain, and pottery.

[1] Parameswara and his successors seem to have reinsured sometimes by sending tribute to the Siamese until the reign of Muzaffar Shah.

When he allied Malacca with Pasai, and took a Muslim wife, Parameswara accepted also the religion of Islam. Most scholars think it likely that, at this stage in his life, Parameswara adopted the name Iskandar Shah. Muslim merchants from India — especially from Gujerat — and from northern Sumatra now came in increasing numbers to Malacca. The port-kingdom could offer not only a varied and expanding trade, but also the opportunity of practising and spreading the tenets of Islam under the favourable influence of a Muslim court.

The port was still growing — and much further development lay ahead — when Iskandar Shah died, in 1424. The main features of Malacca's trade with India, China, and the kingdoms of South-East Asia were, however, already apparent. Freedom from foreign attack still rested mainly on the reputation of a strong China, but, with increasing wealth and population, the port was gradually moving into a position where it was capable of taking charge of its own defence.

Malacca attracted a tremendous variety of trade and traders. The fullest descriptions which we have of this trade are to be found in Portuguese accounts written after the Portuguese conquest of Malacca in 1511.[1] From these accounts we get a vivid picture of a flourishing business, but we are unable to trace its growth through the century of Malay rule. Malay stories contained in the *Sejarah Melayu* give us glimpses of the town of Malacca at this time, and describe incidents concerned with the keeping of law and order and the protection of merchants' property.

Large ships anchored just south of the Malacca river estuary, and small craft swarmed in the river itself. On the north bank of the river stood godowns, which were protected by a high fence, and policed at night. Close to these stood the market-place. Much of Malacca's cosmopolitan population lived on this side of the river, the merchants having large houses set among gardens and orchards. The ruler's palace and the main mosque and burial ground lay on the south side of the river in the vicinity of St. Paul's Hill. On this side, too, lived, in all probability, some of the

[1] Especially in Tomé Pires, *Suma Oriental,* written in 1512–15.

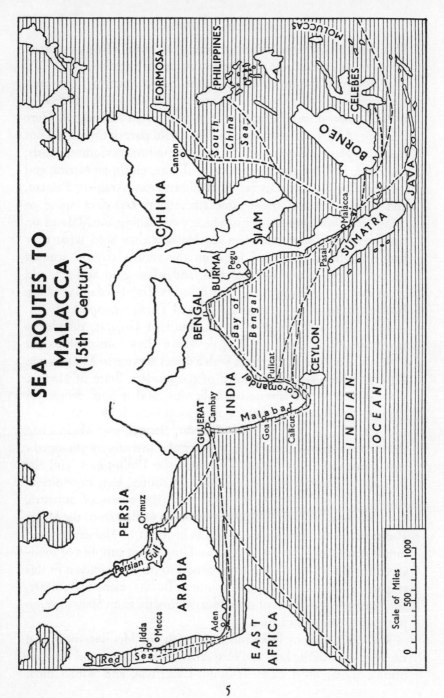

SEA ROUTES TO MALACCA
(15th Century)

FORMOSA

PHILIPPINES

MOLUCCAS

CELEBES

BORNEO

JAVA

CHINA

Canton

South China Sea

SIAM

BURMA

Pegu

Malacca

SUMATRA

Pasai

BENGAL

Bay of Bengal

CEYLON

INDIA

Pulicat

Coromandel

Malabar

Goa

Calicut

Camby

GUJERAT

INDIAN OCEAN

PERSIA

Ormuz

Persian Gulf

ARABIA

Jidda

Mecca

Aden

Red Sea

EAST AFRICA

Scale of Miles

0   500   1000

5

Malay nobles. A wooden bridge across the river, a likely resort of street-sellers, linked the two parts of the town together.

A complex system of trade routes led to Malacca from both west and east. From the Red Sea and the Persian Gulf, ships sailed to the Indian port of Cambay, in the kingdom of Gujerat. Here Persians, Arabs, Armenians, and Turks sold part of their stocks of Venetian glass and metal ware, Arabian opium, perfumes, pearls, and dyes, and bought, among other things, cloth, tapestries, and incense. With mixed cargoes of Mediterranean, Arabian, Persian, and Indian origins, these same traders booked deck-space or cabin-space on Gujerati ships which were sailing for Malacca on the next south-west monsoon. In Malacca they sold what they had brought, and carried back on the return voyage scented timber, spices, porcelain, damasks, and silks, gold and tin, and other items, including even birds from the Banda Islands, whose feathers found a market among Arab and Turkish peoples.

From the west coast of India, south of Gujerat, merchants sailed first to Calicut or Bengal, where they joined ships for Malacca. Another Indian port with a direct service to Malacca was Pulicat, which lay in the north of the modern State of Madras. This served as an alternative collecting and export centre for Gujerati products as well as for more locally-made cloths.

These regular sailings from Gujerat, Bengal, and Madras had their counterparts from the east in regular arrivals by the north-east monsoon from China, Formosa, the Philippines, and the Moluccas. These were the big shipping routes, but, in addition, smaller craft of many kinds came from the coasts of Sumatra, Java, Borneo, and their adjacent islands, as well as from the Malay Peninsula itself. The shorter sailings brought to Malacca tin and jungle produce, pepper and gold, and important supplies of food-stuffs for a port which had soon ceased to be self-sufficing in this respect. Finally, from Pegu in southern Burma, came teak, silver, and rice, whilst rice was obtained also indirectly from Siam through ports in northern Sumatra.

Malacca was thus linked in trade with the Mediterranean and Europe, the Middle East and East Africa (via Gujerat and Red Sea ports), India, most parts of South-East Asia, and with China.

'Men cannot estimate the worth of Malacca,' wrote Pires very soon after the Portuguese conquest, 'on account of its greatness and profit. Malacca is a city that was made for merchandise, fitter than any other in the world; the end of monsoons and the beginning of others. Malacca is surrounded and lies in the middle, and the trade and commerce between the different nations for a thousand leagues on every hand must come to Malacca.'

This Malacca trade was handled by a great number of merchants. The large vessels from India and China were divided into storage sections, which were hired out at fixed prices to merchants and groups of merchants. Travelling merchants and agents of many races accompanied their cargoes to and from Malacca, and others settled in the port itself. The result was a colourful, cosmopolitan, population of many languages and cultures, to match the almost endless variety of merchandise loaded and unloaded, sold and resold, on ships and sampans and in the godowns and the market. The most prominent and influential single group of traders were the Gujeratis, though this name in itself may have covered a number of racial groups, all Muslims, who came to Malacca from the port of Cambay.

The congregation in Malacca of experienced traders from many lands must have helped the development of what became an orderly and efficient business organisation. Groups of Malacca merchants combined to bid for the incoming cargoes, which they then divided up among their number in proportion. The incoming trader could be paid quickly, and the Malacca merchants could resell or store what they had bought, as it suited them. By this practice a standard system of wholesale and retail trade was achieved, for, wrote Pires, 'the law and prices of merchandise in Malacca are well-known.'

Port charges were also standardised. Shipping from a westerly direction paid tolls equivalent to six per cent of the value of the cargo. Shipping from Sumatra (apart from northern Sumatra which was regarded as 'western'), Java, the east coast of Malaya, and further east to the Moluccas, the Philippines, and China, paid presents instead of a percentage on the cargo, but these presents were of a 'reasonable amount'[1] and represented a similar payment to that made by shipping from the west. The Chinese junk trade was an exception to this, for the Chinese, as in political diplomacy, gave larger presents than anyone else. Locally settled traders paid charges of three per cent.

Gold, silver, and tin were all used for currency in Malacca. Gold and silver were valued according to quality, and the usual small coinage was in the form of tin 'cashes', which bore the name of the reigning king. There was also a standard system of weights and measures based upon 'bahars', 'cates' and 'taels'. There were different weight systems for different categories of merchandise. Malacca did not lack the arithmetical complexities of a centre of international trade.

Precautions were taken against favouritism and the corruption of officials. In particular, the six per cent dues were based on valuations made by independent committees set up for the purpose under the chairmanship of a Customs Judge. Moreover, four port officials, known as Shahbandars, were appointed to supervise the trade and to look after visiting merchants. For this purpose the Gujeratis formed one group, the Bengalis and the merchants of Pegu and Pasai (northern Sumatra) another; a third region included southern Sumatra, Java, and the Moluccas, and the fourth group included shipping from Indo-China and China. The Shahbandars themselves were nationals of one of the countries with whose trade they were concerned. They found transport and lodgings for visiting merchants, and acted as welfare and liaison officers in cases of personal problems and complaints. They must have played an important part in the smooth running of international relationships.

Although much of the profit from this trade went to the merchant class, the ruler of Malacca and his leading noblemen also derived large incomes from it. The nobles held high offices of state, and these may have carried some rewards from the royal treasury. In addition some of them at least received the customary presents from the incoming cargoes.

It was the ruler, however, who was in the best position to raise

[1] Tomé Pires, *op. cit.*

money. First, he had the revenue from port charges and presents. All the weighing of merchandise entering and leaving Malacca was subject to a royal tax of one per cent, and secretaries and receivers were specially appointed to supervise and collect it. Through his officials the king of Malacca ventured some of his resources as a private trader. Chinese junk-owners, for example, gave the king specially favourable terms for handling his cargoes, and the king exempted his own agents from paying dues in Malacca.

To these sources of income should be added a number of smaller charges, such as licences for the sale of property or land, rents from street vendors, and the proceeds of fines and confiscations in the administration of justice. From the middle of the fifteenth century onwards another very important source of income developed — the receipt of tribute in one form or another from an increasing number of vassal states.

The king was, of course, faced with expenses of administration, but these could be reduced in various ways. Many officials and nobles received presents and perquisites in the course of their work.[1] In other cases, the king could give special honours or exemptions in lieu of (or part-payment of) a salary. The king also had the right to conscript labour and to demand military service, and this provided him with another source from which he could grant favours and rewards.

The commercial rise of Malacca and the increasing wealth of its kings was reflected in its political development. The king came to live in great state. He was shielded by an array of dignified officials, and he could be approached only with due ceremony and ritual. It is to these Malacca rulers that we now turn our attention.

Iskandar Shah's successor bore a Hindu title, Sri Maharajah, though the *Sejarah Melayu* later calls him Muhammad Shah. Though he reigned for twenty years, we know even less about him than about Parameswara, except for his alleged organisation of the offices of state. It would seem likely that his reign was constructive, because very shortly after his death Malacca was strong

---

[1] The income from street-sellers seems to have been directly apportioned to some of the nobles.

B

enough to refuse tribute to Siam at a time when China had withdrawn from her former active foreign policy and was not likely to give effective help.

Sri Maharajah's death was followed by one of those struggles for succession which became such a feature of the subsequent history of the Malay States. In this instance, the main parties concerned were not the claimants themselves, but their supporters. The case concerned two sons of Sri Maharajah, one, Raja Ibrahim, by marriage with a princess of Rokan in Sumatra, the other, Raja Kasim, by marriage with the sister of a Tamil Muslim merchant named Tun Ali who had settled in Malacca from northern Sumatra. Raja Ibrahim, who was only a child, was installed with the title Sri Parameswara Deva Shah,[1] under the guardianship of his uncle, the Raja of Rokan. This regency was overthrown about a year later by a *coup d'état* in favour of the older half-brother, Raja Kasim. The young king and his uncle were both killed in an attack on the palace led by Tun Ali and Raja Kasim, with the implicit approval of the Chief Minister (Bendahara), who had been pressed or persuaded to accompany the rebels. The attack may have been based partly on personal animosity to the Raja of Rokan, but it also furthered the interests of Tun Ali's family and secured a Muslim dynasty on the Malacca throne.

The new ruler took the name Muzaffar Shah, and became the first of the Malacca kings to use the title of Sultan.[2] He refused to send tribute to Siam. A Siamese army was despatched to Malacca in 1445, via the difficult overland route from Pahang. The Siamese force, possibly weakened already by the long approach to Malacca, was defeated, and it withdrew. Malacca was showing itself capable of resisting foreign invasion.

In this fighting a high reputation was won by Tun Perak, who was destined to play a leading part in Malacca's politics for the next forty years. Tun Perak was a son of the Bendahara Sriwa Raja who had been implicated in the plot against Raja Ibrahim and the Raja of Rokan. The high office of Bendahara, ranking normally next to the Sultan, seems to have been created very

[1] An ingenious combination of Hindu and Muslim titles.
[2] Possibly in 1456.

early in the era of the Malacca kings, and it was established in one family.

Tun Perak's father had less influence with the new ruler, Muzaffar Shah, than Tun Ali, who had led the revolution which secured the throne for his nephew. Whether from disappointment, frustration, or remorse, the old Bendahara poisoned himself. Tun Ali was now appointed Bendahara and the overlooked Tun Perak withdrew to Klang. With these moves, a complete change of Bendahara family had taken place — in fact, a second *coup d'état* had occurred with the exiled Tun Perak as its main victim.

Tun Perak soon became headman of the small community at Klang, and it was in this capacity that he led the Klang contingent in the defence of Malacca against the Siamese in 1445. Now the Sultan decided to keep Tun Perak in Malacca, and to confer on him honours and titles. Sharp friction arose between Tun Perak and the elderly Tun Ali, which was resolved only by an act of the greatest diplomacy on the Sultan's part. The Sultan had married Tun Perak's sister Tun Kudu. This may have been an attempt to placate Malay opinion when the office of Bendahara was transferred to a Tamil family. Tun Kudu may also, of course, have used her influence to gain the Sultan's favour for Tun Perak. Muzaffar Shah now persuaded Tun Ali to resign his Bendaharaship in return for a new wife whom the Sultan would find him. Tun Ali insisted on the choice of Tun Kudu, wife of the Sultan and sister of Tun Perak, and this was agreed to.[1] Tun Ali married the Sultan's ex-wife, and thus became Tun Perak's brother-in-law. In this way the Sultan avoided the civil war which threatened when his court was divided into two factions. Tun Perak came into his family inheritance as the new Bendahara of Malacca about 1456. From this time until his death in 1498 he remained Bendahara, serving in turn four Sultans, all of whom were his relatives. He remained a power behind the throne, and 'the brain of Malacca's imperialist policy in Malaya and Sumatra for more than three reigns'.[2]

The emergence of Tun Perak as Bendahara coincided with the

[1] Tun Kudu's views about her change of husband have not been recorded.
[2] R. O. Winstedt, *History of Malaya*, p. 46.

second Siamese attack on Malacca in 1456. This was an attempt at a sea-borne invasion via the southern tip of Malaya and the Malacca Straits. The Malacca fleet met the invaders off Batu Pahat, and a show of force was sufficient to make the Siamese lose heart and retreat.

The defeat of this second Siamese invasion marked a turning-point in Malacca's history. So far the port-kingdom had been building up resources, and now the defences had been tested and had remained intact. From 1456 onwards Malacca pursued an active, and often aggressive, foreign policy and built up a loosely-held empire of her own in Malaya and eastern Sumatra.

Much of this empire-building took place in the reign of Sultan Mansur Shah. The Sultan himself, however, does not appear to have been a very strong character, and the direction of policy came from the Bendahara Tun Perak, who was his cousin. Soon after his appointment as Bendahara, Tun Perak commanded a fleet in a successful invasion of Pahang, a vassal state of Siam. The Siamese governor was taken prisoner, and a Malay chief was appointed Viceroy of Pahang, owing homage to the Malacca Sultan.

About this time Tun Perak despatched two embassies. One went to Siam on a mission of peace but not subservience; the other went to China to restore the old Malacca custom of seeking Chinese recognition for the ruler. Both missions achieved their purpose.

Malacca now embarked on a policy reminiscent of that of the early South-East Asian empires of Funan and Srivijaya. Expeditions sent across the Straits to Sumatra conquered Siak and Kampar, but failed in an attempt to subdue Pasai. At, or before, this time,[1] Indragiri and Rokan in Sumatra were forcibly added to the list of Malacca vassals, and the small states of the Malay Peninsula from Kedah on the west coast down to Johore and the Rhio Archipelago, and northwards via Pahang to Trengganu and Kelantan, all made their allegiance to the growing power of Malacca. The Malacca empire had almost reached its full extent by the time of Mansur Shah's death.

The next Sultan, Ala'ud'din, was a younger son of Mansur

---

[1] It is impossible to date some of these events exactly; the *Sejarah Melayu* and Tomé Pires place some events in different reigns.

THE MALACCA EMPIRE in A.D. 1500

Scale of Miles
0   40   80   120   160

— — — — Boundary of Malacca Empire

Shah, and a nephew by marriage of Tun Perak, and his title to the throne was, to say the least, doubtful. In all probability, Tun Perak's influence decided the matter. Ala'ud'din, however, showed more individuality and strength of character than any of the later Malacca Sultans.[1] He dealt with attempts by his elder half-brother in Pahang to thwart his authority, and he took a personal interest in the maintenance of law and order in his capital. On one occasion, patrolling the market area in disguise late at night, he challenged and killed three of a company of five thieves and recovered their booty. Ala'ud'din also reasserted Malacca's authority over Siak.

[1] The *Sejarah Melayu* describes him as 'a man of such strength that he had no rival in those days'.

This able and energetic Sultan died, a comparatively young man, in rather mysterious circumstances. Suggestions of poisoning have been made, with the self-styled Sultan Mahmud Shah of Pahang (the elder half-brother) as one of the conspirators. The evidence, however, would not appear to be sufficiently conclusive for a verdict of murder to be returned.

Again a second son (and a young boy) succeeded to the throne under the title of Mahmud Shah, and again he was a relative — this time a grand-nephew — of the ageing Tun Perak. Mahmud Shah was destined for a career of losses and bitter disappointments. He was also unfortunate in the chroniclers of his twenty-three years' reign in Malacca. The compiler of the *Sejarah Melayu* was biased against him because he ordered the execution of a Bendahara, Tun Mutahir. The Portuguese had no sympathy for a Sultan whose conduct they regarded as treacherous. The least that can be said of him is that he was not a very effective ruler, and that his court was a centre of intrigue and favouritism. It was unfortunate for the Malay Kingdom of Malacca that it was Mahmud and not Ala'ud'din who had to face the dilemma presented by the arrival of the Portuguese.

The early years of Mahmud's reign saw Malacca at its zenith, with its suzerainty over the peninsula extending as far north as Patani. An attempt by the Raja of Ligor, vassal of the King of Siam, to conquer Pahang was repulsed with the help of forces from Malacca. But there was weakness as well as strength. Foreign merchants began to complain of oppressive practices and, at the court, there were plots and counter-plots. Some account of this will be given in the next chapter as background to the atmosphere in Malacca when de Sequeira's ships arrived in 1509.

Three further aspects of this century of Malay rule in Malacca call for some attention.

First there was the structure of the government, with its hierarchy of officials, which is said to have developed during the reign of Sri Maharajah (Muhammad Shah). In theory the ruler's word was law, and he certainly exercised great personal authority at times. Despite the influence of Islam, the rulers of Malacca were shrouded in an atmosphere of semi-divinity which owed much to Hindu traditions — as did the court ceremonial. There was great emphasis on etiquette in the Sultan's public appearances on an elephant or in a litter, and in his reception of envoys or his appointment of officials in the audience-chamber. Only the ruler could wear gold or yellow, unless he himself partially relaxed the rule in order to symbolise the granting of a particularly high honour in individual cases. Hang Tuah, the almost mythical Malay warrior-hero whose patron was Tun Perak, was allowed the extraordinary privilege of wearing what he liked.

In practice much depended on the ruler's personal character and ability. He had the alternative temptations of enjoying the luxuries which his position offered or of retiring into spiritual contemplation, without, in either case, carrying out his political duties.

The office of Bendahara stood next to royalty and it represented that of Chief Minister, and sometimes Viceroy, and Commander-in-Chief. The holder of this office was also Chief Justice and Premier Noble of the State. He was both a dignified and a powerful figure, and to displease him was little better than to displease the Sultan. From Muzaffar Shah's time onwards, the Bendahara was an older relative of the Sultan. As these Sultans were only boys at the time of their installations, the dominant position of the Bendahara was emphasised. One Bendahara, Tun Perak, actually held office, as we have seen, during the reigns of four Sultans. Only a very strong ruler could take any independent line with such a power standing behind the throne. Moreover, both Tun Ali and Tun Perak were kingmakers to whom the Sultans were indebted from the first.

However powerful the Bendahara, however, he had to be careful to avoid the trappings of royalty, and in matters of purely personal concern he was wise to listen to the Sultan. Bendahara Tun Mutahir was put to death on the orders of Sultan Mahmud partly, at least, because he had lived in a style too much resembling that of the Sultan and — what was worse — had refused to allow the Sultan an opportunity of asking for his daughter's hand in marriage.

After the Bendahara came the Temenggong, Laksamana, and Penghulu Bendahari. The Temenggong was Chief of Police and Master of Royal Ceremonies; the Laksamana was, technically at least, Admiral of the Fleet,[1] and the Penghulu Bendahari (or Sri Naradiraja) was the Royal Treasurer. Around the court there were many other minor officials and attendants — chamberlains, heralds and pages — and there were titles of nobility acquired both by family descent and by royal favour. Malacca nobility formed a pyramid of four great, eight lesser, sixteen small, and thirty-two inferior, chiefs. On the commercial side, the four Shahbandars have already been mentioned, and there were also customs officers, weighing inspectors, mint officials, secretaries, and auditors. There was probably as much consciousness of rank and seniority in this civil service as there was among the nobility.

Secondly, trade and politics by no means comprised the whole of life in Malacca. Perhaps the Malacca kingdom's greatest claim to fame in the fifteenth century could be based on the part which it played in the conversion of Malay peoples to Islam.

Like Hinduism and Buddhism, which had preceded it in South-East Asia by many centuries, Islam made its first impact in the royal courts; only later, and very gradually, did it spread to the mass of the people. The path of Islam to South-East Asia lay via India, and Indian Muslims played a very prominent part in its spread. The first Muslim states were established in northern Sumatra towards the end of the thirteenth century, and it was through marriage to a princess of one of these states, Pasai, that the first king of Malacca adopted Islam at his court. How far Islam was the court religion of the second king is debatable, but the accession of Muzaffar Shah, following the palace revolution of 1445, ensured a Muslim succession. Muzaffar's mother and his uncle, Tun Ali, were members of a Tamil Muslim trading family who had been settled in Pasai before coming to Malacca.

Hindu traditions lingered on in court ceremonial,[2] and Sanskrit words were used for some of the titles of rank, together with Sanskrit announcements at the investitures. Islam had, however,

---

[1] Hang Tuah was the most renowned Laksamana.
[2] They still do today in the Malay States.

become the religion of the royal family, and the nobility, no doubt, followed their example. By its political contacts with other states, Malacca helped the spread of Islam in at least two ways. One was by marriage between members of the royal house of Malacca and members of other ruling families; in this way a Muslim court was established at Kedah, and marriages with the ruling houses of Kelantan and Indragiri also helped to spread Islam at court level. The other way was by conquest and the replacement of the local ruler by a Muslim prince of the Malacca family. This happened, for example, in Pahang and Kampar. The prestige which Malacca enjoyed in the vassal states, and the authority it had over them, must, in some courts at least, have created influences favourable to the religion of Malacca.

The town of Malacca had had from its early years a very considerable and influential foreign Muslim population. This included Turks, Arabs, Persians, and Muslim Indians from both Tamil India and Gujerat. The open practice of Islam by these wealthy traders, and the high prestige which surrounded them, helped to interest other peoples in their religion. Javanese traders and mercenary soldiers are said to have been converted to Islam in Malacca, and to have taken their new religion back to Java. Muslim merchants also married into the non-Muslim population, thus creating new Muslim families.

It is interesting also to note that there were Muslim mystics and theologians in fifteenth-century Malacca, and that theological questions passed with great formality between Malacca and Pasai, with much reference to texts from the Koran.[1] For the Malay Peninsula and eastern Sumatra, Malacca was a very important diffusion-centre of Islam. It also contributed to some extent, through Javanese settlement in the port, and the comings and going of trading boats, to the spread of Islam in Java.

Finally, a brief mention may be made of the literary work, *Sejarah Melayu*, which provides us with colourful details of this period. Much of it is thought to have been written about A.D. 1535 but it was compiled, with later additions, by a descendant of the

---

[1] The questions, written and sealed in a special way, were transported by elephant and boat with great ceremony.

Malacca Bendaharas about A.D. 1612. It looks back from Johore to a 'golden age' in the Malacca kingdom, and, in particular praises its Bendaharas. The *Sejarah Melayu* is lacking both in dates and in time sense. It can often be shown to be absurdly inaccurate about events for which there are more reliable sources. Yet, with all its shortcomings, it presents a pattern of life and a series of vivid character sketches without which our impressions of Malay Malacca would be very much the poorer. Like the *Iliad* and the *Odyssey* of Ancient Greece, the *Sejarah Melayu* is full of brave deeds and wonders, but may still represent a faithful portrayal of the way life was lived in the royal courts with which it deals.

Among many other topics, the reader can sense the great emphasis on titles and etiquette, the admiration for physical bravery and skill with weapons, and, with few exceptions, the

KINGDOM OF MALACCA
Table of Rulers and main Bendaharas

Ruler	Dates A.D.	Bendahara	Dates A.D.
Parameswara ⎱	c. 1400		
Iskandar Shah ⎰	−1424		
Sri Maharajah ⎱	1424		
'Muhammad Shah' ⎰	−1444		
Sri Parameswara	1444	Sriwa Raja	?−1445
Deva Shah	−1445		
Sultan Muzaffar Shah[1]	1445	⎧ ,, ,,	
	−c. 1456	⎨ Tun Ali	1445−c. 1456
		⎩ Tun Perak	c. 1456−1498
Sultan Mansur Shah[1]	c. 1456	,, ,,	
	−1477		
Sultan Ala' ud'din	1477	,, ,,	
	−1488		
Sultan Mahmud Shah	1488	⎧ ,, ,,	
	−1511	⎨ Tun Puteh	1498−1500
	(died 1528)	⎪ Tun Mutahir	1500−1510
		⎩ Paduka Tuan	1510−1511

[1] The dates of Muzaffar Shah's death and Mansur Shah's accession are not established beyond doubt. They both fall within the period A.D. 1456−9.

sense of loyalty to the ruler. We can be grateful for the descriptions of dress used on formal occasions, for the homely metaphors, and for the detailed accounts of many incidents, one including the costly palace of Sultan Mansur Shah and the fire which destroyed it. Last, but not least, the *Sejarah Melayu* has many delightful touches of humour to remind us that, then as now, Malay formality was often relieved by a keen eye for an amusing situation or a keen ear for a witty word.

Chapter 2

THE PORTUGUESE AND THE
DUTCH IN THE MALACCA STRAITS

A.D. 1509–1641

A mixture of circumstances and motives led the Portuguese to pioneer the long sea route from Europe to the East. They were a people bred on the shores of the Atlantic, with sea-fishing as one of their traditional occupations. Lisbon, the Portuguese capital, was a fine river-port, linked in trade with many parts of Europe. At Sagres, on Cape St. Vincent, in the south-west corner of the kingdom, Prince Henry the Navigator (1394–1460) had established a scientific research centre for the study of winds, tides and currents, the preparation of maps and routes, and the building of ships. Mariners from many countries were welcomed at Sagres, where their skill and knowledge was pooled with that of the Portuguese.

Prince Henry despatched expeditions to chart routes southwards along the west coast of Africa, and, after his death, this practice was continued. Bartholomew Diaz rounded Africa in 1488; ten years later Vasco da Gama reached Malindi in East Africa, where he secured the services of an Indian pilot to guide him across the Indian Ocean to Calicut. For the next few years the Portuguese were engaged in attempts to establish a firm trading base on the Malabar coast of India.

Skill in shipbuilding, advanced knowledge of navigation, and royal patronage, all contributed to placing Portugal in the lead in the exploration of uncharted seas during the fifteenth century. From Portugal a natural route, not without dangers, of course, followed the western outline of the African continent. It was long a belief in Portugal that if you continued sailing south you would

20

eventually reach a 'land's end' where you could change to an easterly or north-easterly course. Diaz proved that this was possible, and da Gama eventually completed the link to India.

The desire for knowledge and the reward of new discoveries only partly explains the Portuguese enterprises. A strong motive was the wish to make contact with a Christian kingdom or kingdoms which lay in East Africa, India, or even on the route to China. In particular, the Portuguese had a myth about a legendary Christian priest-king in the East, known as John the Priest, or Prester John. This myth was by no means confined to Portugal. With great variety of detail, it occurred at different times and places in Western Europe throughout the Middle Ages.[1] The Portuguese had also a very strong missionary spirit. Their country had been the first Christian kingdom to emerge independent of Muslim rule in the Iberian Peninsula. It was not surprising, therefore, that they felt an urge to be the first to establish relationships with whatever Christian kingdoms existed in the East.

Linked with this enthusiasm for Christianity was an anti-Muslim attitude which had become almost second nature to the Portuguese in their long history of revolt against Muslim rule. Portugal was not unwilling to extend her traditional campaign against a Muslim state to attacks upon other Muslim areas beyond her own frontiers. In 1415, for instance, Prince Henry the Navigator had himself taken part in the capture from the Moors of the port of Ceuta in Morocco, on the southern side of the Straits of Gibraltar. The Portuguese were conscious of a land barrier of Muslim states in North Africa, and at the eastern end of the Mediterranean, which barred the way to contact with non-Muslim regions in the East.

These Portuguese feelings based on religion, politics, and prestige, were reinforced by economic reasons. Produce from India and the East Indies reached European ports, including Lisbon, by very devious routes. In this east-west trade, Muslim rulers controlled the overland routes which led from the ports of the Red Sea and the Persian Gulf to the eastern Mediterranean,

[1] A short summary of the legend of Prester John is given in Sonia E. Howe's *In Quest of Spices*, pp. 46–52.

and Muslim traders bought, sold, and transported, all along the routes. These traders included, for example, Indian Gujeratis who linked Malacca with Cambay, and Arabs, Turks, Persians, and Egyptians, who linked Cambay with Cairo, Alexandria, or Aleppo.

It was not only Muslim princes and merchants who profited from this trade in spices, silks, cloths, and other commodities. At the European end, the Venetians had a monopoly of the purchase of eastern products in the eastern Mediterranean ports. They paid high prices, but with the monopoly of distribution they held in Europe they could sell dearly and thrive on middleman profits.

Thus, for Portugal, a direct sea route to the East symbolised many things. Access to eastern trade-markets would damage Muslim trade and break the monopoly of Venice. A break-through might be achieved to Christian, or at least non-Muslim, kingdoms beyond the Muslim barrier. National prestige would be enhanced, and Lisbon might become a second Venice.

Vasco da Gama traded at Calicut on his first arrival in India, but the Portuguese were soon driven to find another base, further south, at Cochin. In the first decade of the sixteenth century Muslim and Portuguese fleets struggled for supremacy in the Indian Ocean. The Muslim powers quickly recognised the dangers to their interests in the coming of the Portuguese, while, for their part, the Portuguese aimed at cutting the Muslim trade routes to the Red Sea and Persian Gulf. This would enable the Portuguese to divert trade to Europe in their own ships, via the Cape. The issue was in the balance until 1509, when the Portuguese defeated a combined Egyptian and Indian fleet off Diu on the coast of Gujerat. This victory gave to Portugal naval supremacy in the Indian Ocean.

Earlier, King Manoel of Portugal had decided to maintain a large, permanent, force in the East, and had appointed Francisco de Almeida as its commander. Almeida left Lisbon in 1505 and established his headquarters at Cochin, assuming the title of Viceroy. He had great faith in sea power alone, and it was he who won the battle of Diu. About two months before Almeida handed over office to his successor, a Portuguese fleet of four or five ships under Diogo Lopes de Sequeira anchored off Malacca. Sequeira brought credentials and presents from King Manoel, who had despatched him from Lisbon in the previous year; he sought permission from the Sultan to land and engage in trade.

The Portuguese were well aware of the importance of Malacca. As early as 1506 King Manoel had ordered Almeida to go and build a fort there, as there were rumours that a Spanish fleet was proceeding to Malacca from the opposite direction.[1] A no less urgent reason was to establish a 'factory' in this *entrepôt*, especially to take part in its spice trade. The arrival of the Portuguese at Malacca caused some excitement even in that multi-racial port, but it also presented a dilemma for the Sultan and his advisers.

Bendahara Tun Perak had died in 1498, and had been succeeded by his brother Tun Puteh, already an elderly man, who died about two years later. From 1500 to 1510, the Bendahara was Tun Mutahir, son of the Tamil Tun Ali and uncle of Sultan Mahmud. The sons of Tun Perak were overlooked. This was a curious repetition of the situation in Sultan Muzaffar Shah's reign. Mutahir's appointment was certainly not acceptable to Tun Perak's family and their supporters, and his conduct gained him further enemies. He had a great love of dress and show, he was haughty in his manner; he received gifts which looked suspiciously like bribes; he engaged in trade and became very wealthy. He thus became a target for jealous and envious feelings from the Malacca courtiers, and from the traders who were oppressed by his demands. He was, however, still secure in office when the Portuguese arrived in 1509.

At first Sequeira received a friendly reception, and he was able to land men and stocks, and to begin to trade. No agreement about a 'factory' was reached, however, and opposition to the Portuguese soon showed itself. Muslim traders in Malacca saw the arrival of the Portuguese as an intrusion into their economic sphere and as a first move in the extension of Portuguese sea power from the Indian Ocean to the Malacca Straits. The Gujeratis formed the vanguard of this opposition, and they gained the support of the Bendahara, who already had trading commit-

[1] E. Prestage, *Afonso de Albuquerque*, p. 46 (footnote).

ments with them, for a plan to destroy the Portuguese expedition.

This plan was only partly successful, which, in a sense, was worse than complete failure. The Portuguese may, in any case, have been sufficiently wary not to allow a majority of their men on shore at the same time. An attempt to seize the Portuguese ships was foiled by quick action on Sequeira's part. He withdrew, leaving two ships, which would have been undermanned, on fire. Some of the shore party were killed and nineteen were taken prisoner. Sequeira sailed back to India with a bitter story to tell. By destroying the Portuguese expedition, the Gujeratis had hoped to make it the first and last attempt at such an enterprise in Malacca. But even if the attack on the Portuguese had been a complete success, it seems likely that, sooner or later, there would have been retaliation. Sequeira's report on Malacca and on his treatment there ensured that this retaliation would not be long delayed.

Nearly two years passed before the next Portuguese ships sailed down the Straits to Malacca. During this time Almeida had been succeeded in India by Afonso de Albuquerque. Albuquerque's policy was to safeguard Portuguese trade by building strong fortresses at key coastal sites. He captured and fortified Goa in 1510. Among the ships which he used for the attack on Goa was a small squadron which had been sent by King Manoel to conquer Malacca. Albuquerque, on his own authority, delayed these ships until he could merge them into a much bigger fleet under his own command. He told Diogo Mendes, their commander, that with such a small fleet he would return from Malacca, like Sequeira, with a 'broken head'.

Albuquerque sailed from Goa in April, 1511, with eighteen ships and upwards of a thousand men, including some Malabar auxiliaries; he anchored off Malacca at the beginning of July.

In the interval between Sequeira's withdrawal and Albuquerque's arrival, life in Malacca court circles had been by no means uneventful. The main sensation was the fall of Bendahara Tun Mutahir. The Bendahara's love of money and his neglect of the Sultan's personal interests combined to bring about his condemnation and death. By his high-handed manner, he offended a

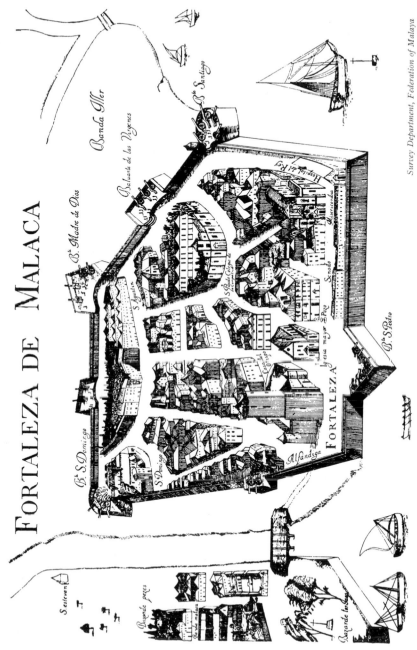

FORTALEZA DE MALACA

Banda Iler

Bª Madre de Dios

Baluarte de las Virgenes

Sta Santiago

S. Agustin

Bª S. Domingo

S. Domingo

S. Paulo Colegio de la compañia

Hospital del Rey

Misericordia

Senado

Iglesia mayor El Paço

Casa del Obispo

Bº S. Pedro

FORTALEZA

Alfandiga

S estevan

De prsis pees

Banda malaca

Razar de la Iaya

Survey Department, Federation of Malaya

PORTUGUESE MALACCA

wealthy Tamil merchant who was subsequently due to appear before him in a law case. The Tamil, hearing that Mutahir had received a large sum in gold in order to judge the case against him, feared for his life and property, and proceeded to the Laksamana with a large gift in money and jewels on his own behalf. The Laksamana was already hostile to Mutahir, and, according to one account, he had opposed the plan for attacking the Portuguese in 1509.[1] He was now persuaded to tell the Sultan that Mutahir was conspiring against him.

Sultan Mahmud was in the right frame of mind to listen to such an accusation. His personal grievance against Uncle Mutahir concerned Tun Fatimah, Mutahir's daughter. While Mahmud was looking for another consort, Mutahir had married Tun Fatimah to another cousin, leaving no opportunity for Mahmud to see the girl until the day of the wedding. On seeing Fatimah, Mahmud felt that his Chief Minister had treated him very badly.

In one of the most memorable phrases of the *Sejarah Melayu*, the Laksamana's accusation against Mutahir was as welcome to Mahmud as 'the offer of a pillow to a man half-asleep'. The *Sejarah Melayu* describes the formal execution as traitors of Mutahir and his family, but it seems more likely that they were attacked and massacred.[2] A son of Tun Perak, the aged Dato' Paduka Tuan was appointed Bendahara.

Albuquerque had come to Malacca to make demands rather than requests, and to back these, if necessary, by the use of force. He demanded the surrender of the Portuguese prisoners, and the payment of compensation for loss of Portuguese life and property two years earlier. In his reply Mahmud put the blame for the events of 1509 on Bendahara Mutahir, who was now dead. He retained the prisoners at first because they were useful hostages whose presence in Malacca might deter or delay Albuquerque from making an attack. Mahmud's advisers pressed him to defend the town, and he tried to temporise with the Portuguese. Albu-

[1] Tomé Pires, *Suma Oriental*, Vol. II, p. 257.
[2] R. J. Wilkinson, 'The Malacca Sultanate', *JRASMB*, Vol. 13, pt. 2, p. 67.

querque now became more aggressive. He set fire to some Cambay vessels in the harbour, whereupon the captives were released. Demands were now made not only for trading rights but also for the site of a fort which could protect the 'factory'. In this increasingly emotional atmosphere both sides prepared for war. In Malacca, the stockades were manned; on board the ships, preparations were made for a landing under cover of ships' artillery.

Albuquerque's first attack gained a footing on the river-bridge which linked the two sections of the town, but a withdrawal was ordered at nightfall. Three weeks later, a second landing was effected with the aid of a modified Chinese junk which, loaded with men, was rammed against the bridge to serve as a huge landing-craft. The bridge and the town centre were taken on August 15th, after some hard fighting, but pockets of resistance held out for several days. Finally, the town was systematically sacked. The defenders took refuge in the hinterland, or fled with Mahmud and his son Ahmad, who eventually reached Pahang.

For the Portuguese it had not been an easy victory. In manpower, they were greatly outnumbered, and the landing operation was a difficult one. The defenders of Malacca used a variety of weapons from firearms to bows and arrows and poisoned darts. Yet certain advantages lay on the Portuguese side. Their strategy was helped by a description of the Malacca site sent to Albuquerque earlier by one of the Portuguese prisoners through a friendly merchant. They were well armed and they employed ships' cannon. Their morale was high. Many of the merchants in Malacca stood aside from the fighting, and were prepared to accept a change of political masters provided that they and their properties were not molested. Some merchants, including the Chinese, had at that time positive grievances against the Malay administration. It may be, also, that Malacca had become too secure in the long years of freedom from foreign attack, and relied too much on Javanese mercenaries whose pay was in arrears when Albuquerque arrived. A particularly decisive factor was that of leadership. Neither the Sultan nor Ahmad, his eldest son, was a military leader; the Bendahara was an old man and a cripple.

On the other side, Albuquerque, was a military leader of proved ability and had the confidence of his men, even, in the end, of the ships' captains, who had a reputation for rejecting higher authority.

Once the town had been secured and booty collected, Albuquerque organised the building of a stone and mortar fortress near the seashore, south-east of the river estuary. This had a high tower, it could be reinforced from the sea in time of danger, and it had its own water-supply from two wells. It marked the beginning of the elaborate fortifications which were built in the years that followed. These were in the shape of a rough quadrilateral, and consisted of walls of stone and mortar on the sides facing the river and the Straits, and ramparts of earth on the sides facing inland. Strong towers or bastions with gun emplacements were built at key points along the walls, each named after the Virgin Mary or one of the saints. The original fort played the part of an inner stronghold within this rectangle of defences which encompassed the hill. Four gateways pierced the walls, the ones most commonly used being the Customs Gate, which gave access to the bridge and the north side of the river, and the gate by St. Anthony's Church, which led to the hinterland.

Such local lime and stone as was available was used for these building operations, including, in the first instance, stone from buildings and tombs in what had been the royal sector of Malacca. A harder type of stone was transported from an island to the north-west of the Malacca river estuary which some Portuguese accounts named 'Ilha des Pedras', or Island of Stones.

Within the walls and ramparts was built, with local modifications, a late medieval European town of stone buildings. These included churches and religious houses, and civic buildings such as a Governor's House, Town Hall, and two hospitals. There were no less than five public churches, one of which was raised to the rank of a Cathedral in 1557, while another conspicuously crowned Our Lady's Hill, which was to be known later as St. Paul's Hill. The Jesuit College of St. Paul was founded on the hill in 1548. The rest of the town consisted mainly of dwelling-houses and gardens for the Portuguese community of soldiers, administrators, and merchants.[1] Other churches and religious houses were built outside the walls.

On the north bank of the river the same kind of township as had existed under the Malay rulers continued, though with differences of detail. Here, there were communities of Malays, Tamils, Javanese, and Chinese, and a central market-place where the Javanese took a leading part in supplying Malacca with food. The houses in this part of the town were built of wood, but roofed with tiles as a precaution against fire. On the northern boundary, a long earth rampart was constructed in an east-west direction between the Malacca River and the sea. This rampart or 'tranqueira' had a gateway at either end, the one on the coast being defended by a stone bastion and a gun-site.

Since the military and administrative centre of Portuguese Malacca lay within the walls and adjacent to the hill, Portuguese writers sometimes used the term 'suburb' to describe that which comprised the old township of Malacca on the north bank of the river, and which was now bounded by the rampart. It was known as Upè, or Tranqueira. In time of danger from external attack its inhabitants could cross the river and take refuge within the walls. The other two 'suburbs' were Sabac (Bunga Raya), which lay inland, a little further up-river, and Yler (Banda Hilir). Sabac, with its wooden houses built right over the Malacca River, was a village whose people were engaged in fishing in the river and adjacent swamps, and in the collection of timber and charcoal from the hinterland. The people of Yler in their wooden houses with thatched roofs were probably occupied in fishing and agriculture. A solitary guard-house seems to have been the only military protection on this side.

Albuquerque sailed back to India after a few months. He had waited to see the building of the fort and the beginnings of a system of administration. He also minted a new coinage in tin, silver, and gold. Malacca came to be governed by a Portuguese Captain of the Fortress, who, from 1571, had the title of Governor of the South. This official was appointed by the King of Portugal

[1] According to Eredia, in 1613 there lived within the walls three hundred married Portuguese men with their families and a garrison of soldiers.

for a tour of three or four years, and he was usually a nobleman whom the king was rewarding. He was subject to the Viceroy at Goa, but except on matters of long-term policy he inevitably acted on his own initiative. The military garrison was under the orders of a Captain-General, who was again usually a nobleman, and who was appointed by the Viceroy for three years. A Chief Justice, or Ouvidor, was also appointed by Goa. His powers were limited to the town of Malacca, and important civil cases in which large sums of money were involved were subject to appeal to the High College of Justice at Goa. In criminal cases the Ouvidor was required to seek advice and confirmation from the Governor. Below the Ouvidor were seven magistrates, elected from the leading citizens, who presided over civil and criminal cases, subject to rights of appeal to the Ouvidor. In theory, at least, this system laid some check on those administering the law.

These seven magistrates also formed part of a municipal council whose rights and privileges were based on those of Evora, a provincial town in Portugal. The Bishop of Malacca and the three leading officers of the confraternity which supervised works of mercy in the town were also members of this local government, which dealt with matters of finance, public works, local trading regulations, and the cleansing of the town.

Three of the Malay titles from the former régime were preserved. The Viceroy appointed a Temenggong to have authority over the Malays settled inland; this office was held, at least in the latter part of the period, by a Portuguese. Over the various Asian communities in the township of Malacca, a Bendahara presided. He was appointed for life by the King of Portugal. To assist him there was a Shahbandar, whose work was to supervise non-Portuguese shipping and to receive foreign envoys and take them to the Governor. The first Bendahara was a Hindu merchant named Ninachatu, who had rendered assistance to the former Portuguese prisoners. He was succeeded by Abdullah, the ruler of Kampar, who served for a short time under the Portuguese with a title equivalent to Viceroy or Governor. Abdullah was ex-Sultan Mahmud's son-in-law, and his acceptance of office under the Portuguese caused a feud between the two men. Through

Mahmud's intrigues the Portuguese were led to accuse Abdullah of treachery and to order his execution.

The main Asian groups had their own headmen, or 'Capitans', who acted as their representatives with the Portuguese authorities, and who were responsible for law and order within their own communities.

The trade of Malacca was now handled on terms favourable to the Portuguese. All ships passing through the Straits were required to call at Malacca and pay the appropriate duties. Portuguese patrols at times took drastic measures to enforce this rule. Large presents were expected from foreign traders in addition to import duties ranging, in normal conditions, between six and ten per cent on the value of the goods.

Portuguese trade was carried on in the name of the King of Portugal, but Portuguese officials at Malacca succumbed increasingly to the temptation to supplement their salaries by using their official positions in order to engage in private trade. This conflict of loyalty and self-interest often led to the making of individual fortunes at very considerable loss to the Portuguese government. It also caused an increasing element of bribery and corruption to spread through the ranks of the Portuguese administration from top to bottom. As early as 1530 it was reported that the King of Portugal would not have any profit from Malacca while the trade was in the hands of officials who bought and sold their own goods and not the King's.

The policy of high tolls and presents, the use of force, and the unfair competition created by the special privileges of Portuguese trade, both official and private, tended to make Asian traders seek other ports. This was especially true of Muslim traders, who had once been the main strength of the Malacca trade. The Muslim trade between India and the Malacca Straits tended, as at a much earlier date, to concentrate in northern Sumatran ports, especially Acheh, Pasai, and Pedir.

From Malacca eastwards, the Portuguese carried trade to Java and the Moluccas, Siam, China, and Japan. This sometimes involved a complicated range of cargoes from Europe, India, and South-East Asia, in the same ship, which might also engage in some carrying from China to Japan. The policy was one of selling where there was most demand, and exchanging bullion or currencies where the most favourable rates could be obtained. In island South-East Asia the Portuguese were opposed by the spread of Islam. Some of the new Muslim rulers were hostile to the Portuguese, and in other states the Portuguese found themselves competing unsuccessfully against Muslim trade. They obtained only a limited and temporary share in the Javanese trade, though Javanese boats brought much of Malacca's food supplies. In the Moluccas they were forced to defend one base after another on Amboina, Ternate, and Tidore. By 1523 attempts to gain a lasting foothold in northern Sumatra were foiled by the Achinese conquest of Pasai and Pedir, and a bitter enmity developed between Acheh and Portuguese Malacca. In the Malay Peninsula the main trade commodities which interested Portuguese Malacca were tin from Perak and pepper from Kedah. At some periods the tin trade was particularly flourishing, but even these west coast trade links broke at times through hostile Malay alliances, or the invasions of the Achinese from the other side of the Straits.

In some cases, too, the Portuguese were their own worst enemies. Especially in the Moluccas, they gained a bad reputation for greed and oppression. Only one Portuguese governor, Antonio Galvao (1536–40), seems to have been respected and admired by the local people. St. Francis Xavier, the well-known Spanish-born missionary of the East, was one of the harshest critics of the conduct of Portuguese officials, both in the Moluccas and in Malacca itself. He has been depicted as an angry man shaking the dust from his feet as he was about to leave the wicked city. He advised his brother Jesuits to ask the Portuguese officials how they gained their living:

> 'Ask if they pay taxes, if they make monopolies, if they help themselves with the King's money, and so on. They will answer you that they owe nothing to anybody. . . . Really they are under obligation to restore much to many.'[1]

Tomé Pires, writing during the first two or three years of

[1] R. O. Winstedt, *A History of Malaya,* pp. 92–3.

Portuguese administration at Malacca, was very critical of his fellow-countrymen. Commenting on the arrogance and lack of discipline shown by young Portuguese officials, he put in a plea for older men, 'expert traders and lovers of peace'. 'Courteous youth and business life do not go together,' he added, 'and since this cannot be had in any other way, at least let us have years, for the rest cannot be found.'

It must be remembered that the Portuguese were very fond of indulging in self-criticism; it was a national trait. What, then, was the relationship between the Portuguese ruling class in Malacca and the Asian communities who lived outside the walls?

In the first place, minority rule was not new. The Malays had represented a ruling class in a merchant town whose predominant religion may have been Islam, but whose racial composition was marked by several large non-Malay groups. To some extent the Portuguese lived apart, and the other peoples lived life much in their own way under their own leaders. After the first few years there is little or no evidence of serious friction between the ruling and subject classes of Portuguese Malacca. Several factors may help to explain this.

Early opposition which came from the Javanese quarter was ruthlessly dealt with, a lesson that rebellion could not be lightly undertaken. It was among the Muslim sections of the population that the strongest anti-Portuguese feeling could be expected, and potential leaders of Muslim resistance tended to move away from Malacca. Some had fled with Sultan Mahmud; others, especially the traders, sought new centres in northern Sumatra, carrying, no doubt, bitter feelings with them. The execution of Abdullah, ruler of Kampar and Bendahara-Viceroy of Malacca, on the grounds of treachery and treason, may well have spread an impression abroad that Malacca was 'a city dangerous for Muslims to inhabit'.[1]

The Portuguese by no means held themselves completely aloof from the other races. The people living in the old township on the north bank could take refuge within the defences in time of danger. According to Eredia, 'the suburb of Upè ... when war-

[1] R. O. Winstedt, *A History of Malaya*, p. 71.

time organisation prevails . . . is entirely depopulated and abandoned, the whole population taking refuge within the walls of the fortress.'[1]

The greatest link between the Portuguese and other races lay in intermarriage. Throughout their history the Portuguese had absorbed many racial elements into their own race; they were 'accustomed as a people to the idea of racial admixture and to the practice of normal relationships with other races'.[2] Intermarriage, of course, normally meant marriage between a Portuguese man and an Asian woman. That this did not necessarily need any encouragement is shown by the case of the romantic marriage between Juan de Eredia and a Bugis princess from Celebes, one of whose three sons was Emanuel Godinho de Eredia, mathematician, explorer, and chronicler. Deliberate encouragement to such marriages was often given by both Church and State.

Governors of Malacca urged young Portuguese to marry in order to induce them to stay for longer terms of service, and perhaps permanently, and so increase the Portuguese element in the resident population. St. Francis Xavier, whilst in Malacca, also spoke strongly in favour of inter-racial marriage. He saw it as a means of creating a more settled life, and raising the moral standards of the Portuguese garrison and administration. At the same time it was a means of increasing the number of Christians in Malacca. By 1613 Eredia estimated the Christian population in a total of eight parishes in Malacca at 7,400. No doubt intermarriage, running through three or four generations, was the biggest single factor in this expansion. Marriage and subsequent family relationships, Christian and non-Christian, must also have played a part in harmonising social ties between the Portuguese town and its 'suburbs'.

The charges of greed, arrogance, and harshness, made against Portuguese officials were, unfortunately, not without foundation. National pride at a time of Portuguese greatness, and the attitude of young officials with unaccustomed powers, living thousands of miles from the home country, offer a part-explanation of these

---

[1] J. V. Mills (ed.), 'Eredia's Description of Malacca, 1613', p. 19.
[2] B. Harrison, *A Short History of South-East Asia*, p. 70.

traits. Added to this was the bribery and corruption associated with the contradictions of public and private trade. Perhaps, most of all, the insecurity of life in Portuguese Malacca for a small community, threatened by many enemies, led to a mixture of attitudes, including that of the braggart and of the 'get-rich-quick'.

On the other hand, Portuguese clergy administered parishes in the suburbs, and lived among the people there. In the walled town there was a hospital for the poor and a confraternity dedicated to works of mercy. In the time-honoured tradition of the East, the Asian population of Malacca had respect for a holy man, and they would have identified Francis Xavier as Portuguese. In 1553 they turned out in large numbers to walk in the funeral procession behind his body to the church on St. Paul's Hill.

The need for defence dominated all aspects of life. The fortifications were a daily reminder of the dangers which occurred with alarming frequency, even while Albuquerque was still in Malacca. A wealthy and powerful Javanese merchant named Utimutiraja led a movement against the Portuguese. He intrigued with ex-Sultan Mahmud, prevented the circulation of the new Portuguese currency in Upè, and tried to control all food-supplies in order to starve out the garrison. Albuquerque learned of these plans and had Utimutiraja arrested and executed. Further Javanese revolts were led by another 'Capitan Java', Patih Kadir, who was eventually driven out and forced to return to Java. Soon after these events, in 1513, a Javanese fleet of 100 ships, with a fighting force of many thousands,[1] attacked Malacca. The Portuguese inflicted a heavy defeat on this armada in the Straits.

The main power behind this attempted Javanese invasion of 1513 was Japara, a trading state in north-central Java. Even before the coming of the Portuguese, there existed a strong Javanese threat to the control of Malacca; Japara was aspiring to claims which Majapahit had never been able to enforce. Again, in 1574, Portuguese Malacca faced and defeated a dangerous fleet from the same Javanese state. But the more regular sources of danger to the Portuguese position lay at the northern and southern ends of the Malacca Straits, in the Sultanates of Acheh and Johore.

[1] Portuguese accounts give numbers varying between 12,000 and 100,000.

From Johore the ex-Sultan of Malacca and his descendants attacked Portuguese shipping and sent fleets against Malacca itself in efforts to restore the old Sultanate.

The island and river-capitals of Johore were also, in times of prosperity, rival trading centres to Malacca, where vessels could call without paying dues to the Portuguese. Portuguese shipping bound to and from China had to negotiate sea passages to the south of the Malay Peninsula, where Johore raiding craft might lie in waiting.

In the years between 1515–24, and again in 1551 and 1616, there were serious Johore attacks upon Malacca. Of these, the campaign of 1551 seems to have come nearest to success. The Johore Malays burned shipping in the harbour, captured the suburbs, and stormed the fortress itself, before settling down to a three months' siege in the hope of starving out the defenders.

At times the Portuguese counter-attacked vigorously, as in 1526, when they destroyed the Johore capital on the island of Bintang, and in 1587, when they destroyed a capital at Johore Lama on the Johore river. The threat of a more formidable Malay power, Acheh, which was liable to attack Johore as well as Malacca, enabled the Portuguese and the Johore Malays to enjoy periods of truce, and even of active alliance and co-operation. In 1582, for instance, Portuguese ships assisted in the defence of Johore against an Achinese attack, and the Johore Sultan went to Malacca to tender his thanks in person.

The spasmodic wars with Johore certainly caused losses in shipping and manpower to the Portuguese, as well as proving a constant drain on money and resources. Johore contributed in no small way to the uneasiness of life in the fortress-city. Yet the Achinese attacks were more bitter, more forceful, and more feared. Acheh, like Johore, was a rival trade-centre, especially for Indian goods and Straits produce. The Achinese forestalled a Portuguese attempt to obtain a footing in northern Sumatra when they conquered Pasai and Pedir in 1523. For Acheh the wars against Portuguese Malacca were part of a policy of expansion in the Malay Peninsula. They were aimed also at capturing a rival trade-base. They were accompanied by a bitterness which sprang

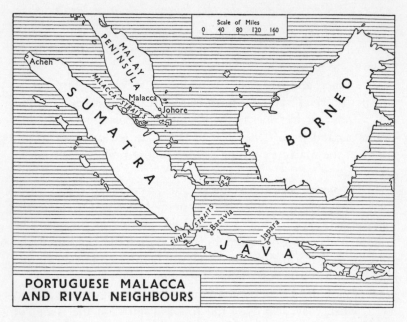

PORTUGUESE MALACCA
AND RIVAL NEIGHBOURS

mainly from the fact that Islam had deep roots in northern Sumatra and had there something of the spirit of a fighting movement.

The Achinese made many attacks on Malacca, and these were times of great concern and distress within the fortress. In 1547 an Achinese fleet sailed unmolested in the Malacca Straits to effect a brief landing at Malacca, and then proceeded to Perlis to erect a fort as a base for attacking Portuguese ships from India or Burma. The Portuguese averted this danger by sending out a fleet in pursuit to win a battle at sea, whilst a Johore Malay flotilla lay in the Straits to the south of Malacca awaiting events. In 1568 Malacca was surrounded by an Achinese army 15,000 strong, but the defenders repulsed a general assault with heavy losses. Again in 1615, and in 1616, there were sea battles between Acheh and Malacca off Muar, and another large-scale invasion attempt took place in 1628.

Malacca was saved sometimes by the arrival of a relief fleet from Goa; sometimes by a loss of heart on the part of the attackers at a critical moment, and always by the strength of the fortifications and the resolute courage of the small garrison. The failure of the Malay powers to form any effective and lasting alliance also gave the Portuguese the chance of fighting only one of them at a time and, sometimes, of playing off one against the other.

Eventually, it was the entry on the scene of a new European power, the Dutch, which doomed the Portuguese position.

A combination of economic and political circumstances brought the Dutch to South-East Asia. Their homeland was the northern part of the Low Countries or Netherlands; they were a people closely linked with the sea, and fishing and water-borne trade were important to their economy. Dutch merchants had established themselves as carriers from one port to another in the inter-European trade of the sixteenth century. They carried, for example, cargoes of cloth or fish from northern European ports to Portugal, Spain, and the Mediterranean, and they brought back, among other commodities, oriental produce — including spices — from Lisbon. Portuguese shipping was spread out along sea routes which extended westwards to Brazil and eastwards to China and Japan, and it became impossible, in practice, for the Portuguese to act as middlemen in Europe itself. The Dutch carrying-trade to and from Lisbon had mutual advantages for themselves and for the Portuguese. Dutch merchants bought up much of the available supplies of produce from India, the East Indies, China and Japan, and made their profit by reselling at other ports. After 1580 political complications began to put an end to this happy marriage, and to stimulate the Dutch to adventure on the sea route to the East.

It was in 1580 that Philip II of Spain successfully claimed the Portuguese throne on the death of King Henry, and united the Iberian Peninsula under his own rule. This forced union of the two kingdoms lasted for sixty years. Despite promises of recognition of constitutional rights, and the granting of favours to the Portuguese nobility, Spanish rule remained unpopular in Portugal, and it was only upheld by the employment of Spanish military forces.

The Netherlands, of which Holland was a northern province, were also under the government of the Spanish Habsburg kings through an appointed Governor and a Council representative of the seventeen separate states or provinces. Misguided policies from Spain met with opposition, and from 1566 onwards this opposition merged into open warfare. The war between the Netherlands and Spain continued with fluctuations of fortune and periods of truce until the northern provinces were recognised as independent by the Peace Treaty of Westphalia in 1648. It is significant for our purpose to note that the Dutch played a major part in this long fight against Spain.

When Portugal became, politically speaking, Spain in 1580, the Netherlands Revolt had long been an open war. It is therefore remarkable that Dutch merchants could still trade with Lisbon, and Dutch agents could still live in Portugal. The Portuguese wished this trade to continue; it was in their interests, though not in those of Spain. Again, from the Spanish point of view, the war in the Netherlands was a civil war against rebels rather than a war against a foreign state. Finally, it would be a mistake to judge sixteenth-century warfare by twentieth-century standards and imagine that, in a war between two regions, everyone was involved, to some degree, all the time.

Nevertheless, it became increasingly difficult for the Dutch traders to operate in Portugal. They became 'subject to arrests and all manner of unbearable tyrannies by the King of Spain',[1] and finally, in 1594, Lisbon was closed to Dutch trade altogether. It was no mere coincidence that the very next year the first small fleet of Dutch ships sailed via the Cape, under van Houtman, to reach north-west Java. Deprived of their middleman trade from Lisbon, the Dutch came to trade in Eastern markets themselves.

The story of the development of Dutch trade and shipping routes does not concern us here, apart from one or two essential facts. Dutch merchants soon realised the necessity to form some kind of association. This would enable larger fleets to sail at regular intervals, and provide resources for arming ships and, if necessary, building and manning land forts. It would also make possible a common policy of trade, so that Dutchmen would not be bargaining one against the other to the advantage of any ruler or trader in the East Indies with whom they were dealing. In 1602

[1] J. S. Furnivall, *Netherlands India*, p. 20.

this association took the form of a monopoly company with the name of the 'United East India Company'.[1] It had strong support from the governments of six important merchant towns.

The Dutch concentrated in their early voyages on north Javanese ports, both as centres of trade in themselves, and as calling-points en route for the Moluccas. By 1619 they had a permanent headquarters at Jakarta (renamed Batavia), and they began to make this a centre for the trade of Java, southern Sumatra and the Malay Archipelago.

The Dutch East India Company was prepared for war as well as for trade. A blow against Portugal was a blow against Spain, and from the profits of the East Indies trade contributions could be made to the fighting for independence at home. The Dutch made agreements for exclusive trade rights as Europeans with South-East Asian rulers, and formed alliances with the enemies of Portuguese Malacca, including Acheh and Johore. At the same time, whenever circumstances allowed, attacks were made on Portuguese shipping. As early as 1606 the Dutch delivered a main attack on Malacca itself, although not, as it had been hoped, with the support of Johore. Between 1607 and 1640 the Dutch campaign for the control of Malacca was based more on a policy of destroying Portuguese trade and cutting off Malacca from the great sea routes than on frontal attack. Throughout the 1620s and 1630s the trade of Malacca grew less and less, and Dutch ships sailed openly in the Straits. Little help came from Goa; in fact, Goa itself was sometimes blockaded by Dutch fleets. Food in Malacca became scarce as Dutch patrols watched for rice boats from Java and Sumatra.

In 1637 the Dutch made a further treaty with Johore for combined operations against Malacca, and, three years later, the time was considered opportune for an all-out attack. Malacca had been virtually sealed off from Goa, the Portuguese garrison was thought to be sufficiently weakened to surrender easily, and no subsequent trouble would be expected with Acheh, which was now quiet.

A large Dutch-Johore fleet, with a landing-force of about 4,000, arrived off Malacca in 1640 and began landing operations at

[1] In Dutch, 'Vereenigde Oostindische Compagnie' (V.O.C.).

the beginning of August. The siege lasted for a further six months. Inside the walls there was starvation; outside, death came quickly from dysentery, cholera, and malaria. Earlier there had existed a Portuguese plan for strengthening and extending the fortifications on the land side, but this had never been carried out. It was on this side that a breach was made in January 1641, and the remnants of the garrison finally surrendered. The Dutch attributed the long siege to the lack of help from Acheh, their own failure to seal off the town completely, the toll of their own forces taken by epidemics, and the valour of the last Portuguese Governor, Manoel da Sousa Coutinho.

The loss of Malacca was a symbol of the decline in Portugal's sea power which had been evident for many years. Too many enterprises had meant a great drain on ships and man-power for a small, and essentially poor, country. Inefficiency and corruption had deprived the home government of much of the profits of overseas trade. Portugal, too, had fallen a victim to the ambitions of Spain. Portuguese ships and harbours were used for naval expeditions planned from Madrid. The coming of the Dutch to the East Indies had itself been a direct result of Spanish policy.

In Malacca the Dutch restored the fortifications, replaced Portuguese crests with Dutch ones, and rebuilt the church on the hill in the style of the Dutch Reformed Church. A Dutch town hall (Stadthuys) was erected soon after the conquest, and other new buildings followed in the course of the next hundred and fifty years. Prominent among these was a new church (Christchurch) in the town to mark the centenary of Dutch rule in Malacca. During much of their long period of tenure there the Dutch forbade the Portuguese and their descendants to practice their religion openly. This was a reflection of the bitterness of religious controversy in sixteenth- and seventeenth-century Europe.

Dutch Malacca was mainly a fortress from which Dutch trading interests could be watched in the Straits. Only in a very secondary sense was it a centre of trade. For the Dutch in South-East Asia, Batavia remained the main *entrepôt* and headquarters, and Malacca was an outpost. Its importance lay in its strategic position on the

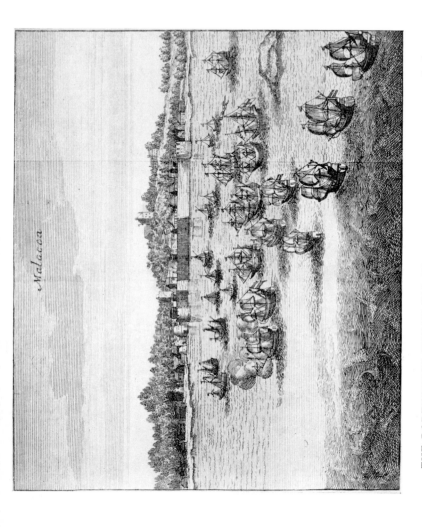

Malacca

THE PORTUGUESE-DUTCH SEA-FIGHT OFF MALACCA IN A.D. 1606

From 'Recueil des Voyages qui ont servi à l'établissement et au progres de la Compagnie des Indes Orientales, formée dans les Provinces unies des Païs-bas.' Translated by R. A. Constantin de Renneville, 7 vols. Amsterdam 1702–7

Straits, and the part which it could play in Dutch policies to secure as much of the trade of South-East Asia as possible, not only as between Europe and the region, but also in the carrying-trade between Asian ports. This policy was attempted by means of treaties with local rulers which gave the Dutch exclusive trading privileges in the purchase of valuable commodities such as spices, gold, pepper, and tin. By becoming sole purchasers, the Dutch could also hope to become sole distributors, notably of Indian textiles, from their own trade-bases.

This policy of a monopoly trade was in keeping with European commercial practices in the sixteenth and seventeenth centuries, but the Dutch encountered many difficulties in their efforts to sustain it in South-East Asia. Treaties, sometimes made under pressure, were easily broken by the local rulers, and there was keen competition from Asian traders. To take only two examples of this, the Bugis from Celebes competed for the spice trade, while at the western end of the region Indian Muslim traders brought cloth and took away tin and other Straits produce from ports on the Malacca Straits.

To enforce the carrying out of their agreements, and to exclude what they considered to be illegal trade, the Dutch became committed to a policy of patrol-ships and forts or fortified 'factories'. From Malacca they made treaties, first for the purchase of half the tin supply of Perak and Kedah, and, considerably later, for tin from Selangor and Sungei Ujong. They also secured a monopoly of gold and pepper from Indragiri, and later of tin from Siak, in Sumatra. In practice they were never able to gain the full benefit of these agreements, despite patrols in the Straits and the building of forts and 'factories' near river mouths in Kedah and Perak. At different times, Kedah, Perak, and even Acheh, were blockaded by Dutch fleets.

From Malacca attempts were made to force shipping to call at the port and pay dues, on receipt of which permits would be issued for the vessels to continue their voyages. Although many vessels called at Malacca, the cargoes unloaded there were small, apart from essential stores and food supplies requisitioned for the Dutch garrison. Dutch efforts to use Malacca as a centre for the

D

distribution of Indian cloth in the region of the Straits also met with disappointment. Indian Muslim merchants traded successfully in Acheh, Kedah, and even Perak, and, from the end of the seventeenth century, the Bugis from Selangor entered the keen but limited markets for Straits produce.

The Malacca trade in Dutch times, therefore, never reached impressive proportions, and the population remained small. Despite the new Dutch buildings, Malacca had only a slight resemblance to a Dutch city transported to the East. In this respect Batavia, planned with a neatness and symmetry characteristic of Dutch enterprise, and distinguished by its wide, tree-lined streets and quays, and its canals, was the supreme example. Yet some atmosphere of old-world glory clung to Malacca, and what its Governors lacked in circumstance, they sometimes made up in pomp; gilt coaches and velvet coats seem to have been in fashion for formal occasions.

DATES OF EVENTS

(As viewed from Malacca)

1509	Sequeira's arrival at Malacca.
1511	Albuquerque's capture of Malacca.
1512–13	Javanese rebellions. Attack from Java (Japara).
1515–19 1523–4	Attacks from Johore.
1526	Destruction of Johore capital (Bintang).
1547	Defeat of Achinese at Perlis.
1551	Attack from Johore.
1557	Malacca named a bishopric.
1568	Attack from Acheh.
1571	Malacca Captain named 'Governor of the South'.
1574	Attack from Java (Japara).
1580	Portugal politically joined to Spain, under Philip II.
1586	Attack from Johore.
1587	Destruction of Johore capital (Johore Lama).
1594	Dutch trade banned from Lisbon.
1595–6	First Dutch voyage to East Indies.
1602	Dutch United East India Company.
1606	Dutch treaty with Johore.

1606–7   Attacks from the Dutch.
1615–16   Attacks from Acheh and Johore.
1628   Attack from Acheh.
1629   Defeat of Achinese in the Straits.
1637   Dutch treaty with Johore.
1640–1   Siege and capture of Malacca by the Dutch and Johore Malays.

Chapter 3

THE MALAY KINGDOM OF JOHORE

A.D. 1512–1812

Mahmud, last Sultan of Malacca, cherished for a time the idea of a Malay counter-attack on the Portuguese, either from the Malacca hinterland or from Muar. When this came to nothing, he and his followers made the slow and painful overland journey by track and river valley to Pahang, where Mahmud's relatives Abdul Jamil and his son, Mansur, were joint-Sultans.[1]

Here, in Pahang, Mahmud was glad to accept the hospitality of a prince who had hitherto paid him tribute in gold. Relations between the Sultan and his former vassal seem to have been cordial, and further links were forged by a marriage between Mansur and one of Mahmud's daughters.

But Mahmud, once he had recovered from his recent ordeals, was restless. Compared with Malacca, Pahang was a backwater. Moreover, he was a guest there rather than a free agent. Optimistically, he despatched an embassy to China, recalling in his message the great friendship which had existed between Ming China and Malacca, and asking for Chinese aid to restore him to his former throne. The reply was disappointing. The Ming Emperor sent his sympathy, but was unable to send practical help on account of his own preoccupation with the defences of the northern frontier of China against marauding Tartars. It might have been added that the Chinese court at this time had no quarrel with the Portuguese. Chinese traders had not been unwilling to witness a political change-over in Malacca, and had continued to trade there peacefully under Portuguese rule. A little later Portu-

[1] The exact relationship varies in different sources. Both were descended from Sultan Mansur Shah of Malacca.

guese traders made a favourable impression in their first contact with Chinese ports.

After a stay of rather less than a year in Pahang, Mahmud and his followers sailed south to seek a new home in Johore. The first site lay possibly on a tributary of the Johore river, but this was abandoned after a short stay in favour of the island of Bintang to the south-east of Singapore. Here Mahmud began to develop a new centre of trade, and from this island-capital to create a new Malay state eventually based on the Johore river basin and its neighbouring islands. If Mahmud has the misfortune to go down in history as the last Sultan of Malacca, he may perhaps have the credit for being the first Sultan of Johore.[1]

The question arises — why did Mahmud choose Bintang? It may not be possible to give an exact answer, but Bintang did provide Mahmud with certain advantages for the policy which he intended to pursue. From Bintang it was possible to make attacks on Portuguese shipping passing slowly through the island groups immediately south of the Malay Peninsula, either outward-bound for the Moluccas or China, or homeward-bound for Malacca. The capture of a Portuguese ship meant booty and prestige, and represented a first step in the long drawn-out counter-attack on Malacca itself.

Secondly, Bintang provided a convenient centre from which Mahmud could despatch messengers by boat to his former vassal states, especially to Pahang, and to the river-states of eastern Sumatra which faced the west coast of Malaya.

Tribute and allegiance were due in a very personal sense to a Malay ruler, and Mahmud's misfortune in Malacca did not prevent him from requiring that the customary tribute and tokens of allegiance be submitted to him at Bintang. Moreover, he could pose as a leader of a Malay and Muslim confederacy united in opposition to the Portuguese.

Finally, Bintang could serve as an assembly-point for the ultimate attack on Malacca. With the growth of trade, revenue, and prestige, at Bintang, Mahmud awaited the day when a Malay fleet would sail from his island-capital to recapture Malacca. By

[1] Mahmud's son, Ala'ud'din, is sometimes called the founder of Johore.

1517 an advance force from Johore held a stronghold on the Muar river, and Johore fleets had begun to raid Malacca itself.

Between 1515–19, and again in 1523 and 1524, Johore attacks were repulsed by the Portuguese in Malacca. The nuisance of these raids, together with the increasing dangers to Portuguese shipping in the southern part of the Malacca Straits, led to reprisals from Malacca. First, the fort at Muar was attacked and captured; then, in 1526, a sea-borne invasion of Bintang took place, and Mahmud's capital was destroyed. The unfortunate Mahmud sailed away from his second capital, landed in Sumatra, and made his way painfully to the court of the prince of Kampar, where he died about two years later. A Malay Shakespeare may yet portray Mahmud's career as a tragedy in five acts. He witnessed the Malacca scene at the height of its prosperity; then followed the Portuguese affair of 1509 and the invasion of 1511; exile in Pahang; a new kingdom at Bintang, and finally death in exile in Kampar. How far Mahmud's misfortunes were of his own making, and how far he was a victim of circumstances beyond his control, would make a good theme for characterisation.[1]

For more than a hundred years after this Johore's history was punctuated by the alternate appearance of new capitals and disappearance of Sultans to death in exile. At times no capital or Sultan can be perceived, yet the dynasty and the tradition of a Johore Kingdom somehow survived.

Mahmud's younger son, Ala'ud'din, founded a new capital, possibly at Johore Lama[2] on the Johore river, soon after his father's death, and continued the former policy of trying to attract trade and tribute, and assailing the Portuguese. A Portuguese raid on the Johore river in 1536 forced Ala'ud'din to submit to peace terms, and by this time Johore was beginning to realise the coming threat from the rising commercial and political power of Acheh in northern Sumatra.

Both Acheh and Johore were Malay and Muslim States; both

[1] Views on Mahmud's character are given in R. O. Winstedt's 'A History of Johore', *JRASMB*, Vol. 10, part 3, pp. 13–14.
[2] There is some doubt and confusion about the exact site and name. The capital may have been established at Johore Lama only from about 1540.

were opposed to the Portuguese tenure of Malacca and to Portuguese trade in South-East Asia. But fundamental rivalries and jealousies divided the two states. They were rival trade-centres. For Johore, the capture of Malacca would have represented a return of the Sultan to the kingdom of his fathers. An Achinese conquest of Malacca would have meant a strategic outpost of Acheh on the other side of the Malacca Straits. Moreover Acheh, with increasing sea power, began to menace small states in eastern Sumatra which Johore regarded as her vassals. In a curious combination of alliances, Johore called on the help of Malay states in the Peninsula and in Sumatra, and even joined at times with the Portuguese in order to avert destruction by Acheh. This kind of situation lasted to a greater or lesser degree for about a hundred years (*c.* 1539–1636).

No attempt will be made here to examine these alliances and wars in detail. The alliances were based on convenience and expediency, and the wars consisted of sharp and bitter attacks from the sea, particularly on Malacca and the river-capitals of Johore. Acheh was almost always the attacker. At times a trial of strength took place on the open seas, as in 1540, in the Malacca Straits, when a combined Malay fleet from Perak, Siak, and Johore, defeated an Achinese fleet of 160 vessels. The rivalries of the Malay states, and the ambitions of Achinese rulers to dominate both politically and economically the Malay world in the vicinity of the Malacca Straits form the true basis of events between 1540 and 1640, and give a clearer picture than would a mere account of the hostile fleets as seen from the Portuguese fortress at Malacca.

In 1564 the Achinese sacked Johore Lama, and Sultan Ala'ud'din was taken prisoner to die in Acheh, according to most accounts.[1] Yet once again the dynasty survived, through a son, and the capital was rebuilt. These capitals were built mostly of wood and protected by a mixture of stone walls, wooden palisades, earth ramparts, and ditches. Unless they were completely destroyed, they could be quickly rebuilt. Twenty-three years later, after various changes of sides, Johore Lama was destroyed once again,

---

[1] The *Sejarah Melayu*, however, holds that he died in Johore Lama.

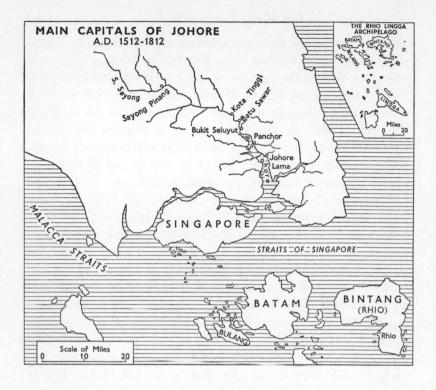

MAIN CAPITALS OF JOHORE
A.D. 1512-1812

THE RHIO LINGGA
ARCHIPELAGO

this time by the Portuguese in retaliation for Johore attacks on Portuguese merchant ships and on Malacca itself.

Successive Johore capitals began to move further up-river, presumably for greater security against enemies who made their appearance at the Johore estuary. Johore Lama was replaced by a new centre at Batu Sawar, near the modern Kota Tinggi. The Batu Sawar period (*c.* 1587–1615) was marked by the first negotiations between the Dutch and Johore, and later by the most devastating of the attacks from Acheh.

The Dutch policy was to make as many anti-Portuguese alliances as possible; in return they sought trading privileges from the South-East Asian rulers. Dutch prestige rose high in Johore when, in 1603, Dutch ships captured a Portuguese carrack heavily laden with a rich cargo from China while she lay at anchor in the Johore River. In 1606 a Dutch-Johore treaty was signed for combined operations against Portuguese Malacca. By this treaty the

Dutch Admiral (Matelief) promised to help the Sultan of Johore 'conquer the town of Malacca and take it out of the hands of the Portuguese, their common enemy . . .'.[1] In return the Dutch were to have free trading rights in the Johore river. The captured Malacca would be divided into two, the walled town going to the Dutch and the remaining territory to the Johore Sultan. There was to be a division of booty, and the Dutch were to have a monopoly of the European trade.

How this arrangement would have worked in practice is only a matter for speculation, because the treaty never became really effective. A Dutch historian has described it as 'selling the skin of the bear before it had been caught'. The Dutch made attacks on Malacca in 1606, but received no support from Johore. This may have been partly due to a distracting family feud between the rulers of Johore and Patani, but the Johore Malays may also have had second thoughts about the advantages which this treaty would bring them. Discouraged by the failure of Johore to implement the treaty, and by the equal lack of interest shown by Johore Malays in Dutch suggestions for forts on the Johore river estuary, the Dutch gradually withdrew from involvements in the Johore river[2] for many years.

The weakness of the Johore defences was soon proved by the war fleets of Sultan Iskandar Shah (1607–36) of Acheh. Iskandar (also known to history by the title Mahkota 'Alam[3]) was the most feared and the most successful of the Achinese rulers.

In many attacks on the Malay Peninsula, he destroyed Batu Sawar in 1613, and proceeded to extend his control over Pahang in the east, and Kedah and Perak in the west. Throughout his reign he cast a menacing shadow over Portuguese Malacca.

The familiar story of destruction and exile was thus repeated in Johore. Some Malays were deported as prisoners to northern Sumatra, others, in large numbers, sought new homes in Jambi (eastern Sumatra), Macassar (Celebes), and the Moluccas. For

---

[1] R. O. Winstedt, 'A History of Johore', p. 27.

[2] There was a second treaty of a face-saving nature in 1606, which left out the plan for Malacca.

[3] Crown of the World.

many years the Johore scene remained confused, and it is a remarkable tribute to Malay conservatism that a dynasty survived
at all. Johore forces took part, on the Portuguese side, in a successful sea battle against the Achinese in 1629, and by 1641, if not
earlier, a new river-capital existed at Makam Tauhid, also in the
Kota Tinggi area.

The power of Acheh declined after the naval defeat in 1629, and
the death of Iskandar Shah in 1636 symbolised the end of an era of
Achinese aggression. Meanwhile the Dutch had been playing a
very careful game for long-term results. They had for some thirty
years avoided commitments in the Acheh-Malacca-Johore wars,
while building for themselves a strong position in north-west
Java. At the same time, they had largely succeeded in driving out
the Portuguese (and the English) from trade in the Moluccas, and
they were gradually severing the Portuguese trade routes and
destroying Portuguese shipping.

By 1637 the political scene along the Malacca Straits was beginning to change. Acheh was quiet. The Dutch were negotiating
an alliance with Johore for the seizure of Malacca, and Dutch
patrols in the Straits were beginning to seal off Malacca from sea
communication with the outside world.

The Dutch-Johore treaty of 1637 did not repeat the idea of a
two-part Malacca. At first sight, it would seem that the Johore
Malays did not get a particularly good bargain. Johore forces took
an active part in assisting the Dutch to capture Malacca (1640–1).
In return they had the friendship of the Dutch, and were left alone
to build up their own trade *entrepôt* in the Johore River valley.
Perhaps, in the long view, this treaty gave Johore what it most
needed — a period of peace and recuperation. In any case, Malacca
was no longer a great port and, when one thinks of later Singapore, the possibilities of a Johore *entrepôt* were not inconsiderable.

The year 1641, in fact, marks a well-defined watershed in the
landscape of Johore history. 'Never', says Winstedt, 'had any
period in Johore history opened with brighter prospects.' The
Portuguese power was broken; the Dutch at Malacca were
friendly, and were to remain for a long time on peaceful terms;
Acheh had ceased to be a threat. By trade and diplomacy, Sultan

Abdul Jalil began to revive the spirit of the old Johore Empire. Pahang, together with Siak and Indragiri in Sumatra, came under his control, and friendly alliances were made with Patani in the northern part of the Peninsula, and Jambi across the Straits in Sumatra. With no enemy in sight, Johore seemed destined to lead a revived Malay Empire which might recall the days of Malacca. For some twenty-five years Johore prospered. By 1660 the Johore river-capital — once again at Batu Sawar — had a flourishing *entrepôt* trade. Then began a series of events, both external and internal, which brought the whole structure of empire down with a crash.

The first of these was a long and wasting war with Jambi, which broke out in 1666 and lasted for some twenty years. If it appeared in European history books, it would probably be called 'The War of the Breach of Promise'. Its outbreak, in fact, was due to a broken marriage contract. The Johore Sultan's nephew[1] was betrothed to a daughter of the ruler of Jambi. The marriage was intended to symbolise the political friendship of the two states, and probably to put an end to trade frictions also. Jambi, which produced pepper, was equally well-placed as a collecting and distribution centre of South-East Asian produce. But the marriage between the Johore prince and the Jambi princess never took place. With a view to his own advancement, the Johore Laksamana arranged instead a marriage between his own daughter and the betrothed prince.

A serious personal insult to the Jambi ruler and his daughter would thus seem to have been the reason for an outbreak of hostilities which were more easily begun than completed. Economic rivalries may have provided an underlying motive. The Johore capital at Batu Sawar was destroyed by a Jambi expedition in 1673, and the old Sultan died three years later in exile in Pahang.

Johore's history is full of ironies, and, by a strange turn of fate, Abdul Jalil's successor, Ibrahim (a nephew), chose the island of Bintang for the site of a new capital. Perhaps it was a conscious attempt to abandon the ill-fated sites in the Johore valley and to

[1] This relationship is given by C. A. Gibson-Hill, 'Johore Lama and Other Sites', p. 159.

return to the first fighting-base of the Malacca Sultan, Mahmud. For about seven years Ibrahim strove to hold together a tottering empire, while still engaged in war with Jambi. At his death in 1683 he was succeeded by a young son, Mahmud, and a regency government in which the Laksamana took a prominent part.

Mahmud, the young prince, was, by all accounts, mentally unbalanced and callously cruel. He tried out the efficiency of a pair of handsome English pistols which an adventurer, Alexander Hamilton, had presented to him, by shooting at the first Malay he met outside the palace. For his cruelty and capriciousness, he was hated and feared by the Malay chiefs, and when he met a violent death at the hands of an outraged father or husband[1] no one seems to have mourned for him. He died without an heir, and as he was the last in direct line of descent from the Malacca Sultans, a new dynasty arose.

This situation occurred in 1699, and it marks the second stage in the decline of Johore after 1666. The new Sultan was the former Bendahara, Abdul Jalil[2] His claim to fill the vacancy for a Sultan probably represented a solution which would divide the Johore Malays least, but it could never be a perfect one. For eight years or so he played his part wisely and well. Then he handed over effective rule to his younger brother, the Raja Muda, whose greed and ambition soon aroused the jealousy and hostility of the other Malay chiefs. Johore was in a state of unrest from about 1712. Apart from dissatisfaction with the Raja Muda, the influence of Bugis settlers at Rhio was already creating Malay and Bugis factions.

The weak position of the new Johore monarchy was clearly shown in 1717, when a Siak prince, Raja Kechil, led a Minangkabau force successfully into Johore (the capital was now at Johore Lama again), and deposed Sultan Abdul Jalil. Kechil became the new Sultan, and the deposed Sultan agreed to serve him as Bendahara. The Raja Muda had meanwhile killed his family and himself. Kechil had circulated a story that he was a son of the last Sultan Mahmud, born after his father's death and smuggled away

---

[1] There are two accounts, which vary in detail.
[2] The repetition of this name is confusing.

to Sumatra. The evidence of history — such as it is in this case — is not in Kechil's favour, but at a time of unpopular and, to some extent, upstart rule, the story was just sufficiently credible to reduce the Johore Malays to a token defence. Kechil also appeared to champion the Malay cause against Bugis elements in the state.

Having gained power by a show of force, Kechil (now Sultan Abdul Jalil Rahmat Shah) soon had to defend his title by force. The dangers came both from internal conspiracy and external attack. The internal conspirators included the Bendahara and his elder daughter. Kechil had offended Malay convention by marrying the younger of the Bendahara's daughters rather than her older sister, and legend has credited the elder daughter with a plot to induce the Bugis leader, Daing Parani, to invade Johore from Selangor.

Kechil had, in any case, made the fatal blunder of first asking Bugis aid from Selangor for his invasion and promising high offices of state in reward, and then carrying out the attack without Bugis help or knowledge. An air of intrigue must have surrounded Kechil's court at Rhio, on the island of Bintang. There was sufficient evidence for Kechil to order the death of the Bendahara, who was struck down while a fugitive at Kuala Pahang. This action increased rather than prevented the prospects of a counter-revolution.

In 1721 the blow fell. Daing Parani and his Bugis forces drove Kechil from Rhio and back to his homeland in Siak. Sulaiman, son of the late Bendahara, now became Sultan, but the new office of Yam-tuan-Muda was created whereby a Bugis chief, Daing Merewah, exercised effective control over a Malay puppet-Sultan. Bugis chiefs also married into the families of the leading Johore Malays. Kechil's intervention in Johore had unwittingly paved the way for a long period of Bugis domination.

Sulaiman remained Sultan until his death in 1760. Increasingly he tried to throw off the Bugis yoke, but where the Bugis once gained a foothold, they proved very tenacious. In 1745 Sulaiman made a treaty with Dutch Malacca in which he offered the Dutch control of Siak, free trade in Johore, and a restoration of the Dutch tin monopoly in states controlled by

Johore, in return for Dutch help against the Bugis. At this time the Bugis Yam-tuan-Muda cautiously withdrew from Rhio and established himself on the island of Lingga. This treaty had little real effect, not surprisingly, since much of Johore's offer was theoretical rather than practical. It presumed powers of control which Johore at that time did not possess.

However, a further, and similar, treaty in 1755 was followed by open warfare between Dutch and Bugis. A Bugis attack on Malacca was followed by a counter-attack on Lingga. In 1758 the Bugis agreed to peace terms by which the Bugis leaders acknowledged the lawful sovereignty of the Johore Sultans, and confirmed the Dutch claims of a monopoly in the tin trade. The Bugis had received a serious setback, but it was only a temporary one. Two years later Sulaiman died. His two younger brothers died soon after him — murdered, according to the Malay version. There followed a long regency during the boyhood of Mahmud Shah, Sulaiman's infant grandson. During this time the Bugis established effective control again, through the office of Yam-tuan-Muda.

From 1760 to 1784 the Bugis retained their dominant influence in Rhio. They were, however, driven out by the Dutch in the latter year, following Raja Haji's unsuccessful attack on Malacca.[1] The position of the Malay Sultan was no better, because Dutch control now replaced Bugis control. The Sultan turned for help against the Dutch to the Ilanuns of Borneo, who drove out not only the Dutch, but also the Sultan and his Malay chiefs as well! The Dutch soon restored their position, but Sultan Mahmud, still conspiring against them, remained a fugitive until 1795. In that year a British garrison took over the defence of Malacca by agreement with the exiled Dutch Government in England, and the Dutch garrison was withdrawn from Rhio. Mahmud Shah was restored to his throne, but he was still not destined to be a free agent. A Bugis leader, Raja Ali, successfully claimed the title of Yam-tuan-Muda in the face of Malay opposition, and Johore was back to the situation of 1722.

The consequences of this long period of Bugis influence in

[1] See Chapter 4, p. 65.

Johore were considerable. The power of the Malay Sultans of
Johore had been weakened beyond repair. First Minangkabaus,
and then Bugis and Dutch, had destroyed whatever prospects
there were of holding together a Johore empire, although the
Bugis had made an attempt to revive this by force in the decade

JOHORE   TIME CHART   A.D. 1512—1800

Sultan	Reign	Capital	Events	Date
Mahmud of Malacca	1512–28	Bintang	Attacks on Malacca	1515–19 1523–24
			Capital destroyed by Portuguese	1526
Ala'ud'din Riayat Shah	?1528–64	(i) Sayong Pinang	Attacked by Portuguese	1536
		(ii) Johore Lama	Attack on Malacca	1551
			Capital taken by Achinese	1564
Muzaffar Shah Abdul Jalil	c. 1564–9 } c. 1569–70 }	Bukit Seluyut	Assisted Malacca against Achinese	1568
Ali Jalla Abdul Jalil Riayat Shah	c. 1570–97	(i) Bukit Seluyut? (ii) Johore Lama (iii) Batu Sawar	Attack on Malacca Capital destroyed by Portuguese	1587 1587
Ala'ud'din Riayat Shah II	1597–1613	Batu Sawar	Treaty with Dutch	1606
			Treaty with Malacca	1610
			'Sejarah Melayu' compiled	c. 1612
			Capital taken by Achinese	1613
Abdullah Ma'ayat Shah	?1613–23	(i) Batu Sawar (ii) Lingga	Capital abandoned	c. 1617
			Capital destroyed by Achinese	1623
Abdul Jalil Shah II	1623–77	(i) Uncertain — many wanderings (ii) Makam Tauhid (iii) Batu Sawar	Treaty with Dutch	1637
			Attack on Malacca (with Dutch)	1640–1
			Trade revival	1641–66
			War with Jambi	1666–c.1690
			Capital destroyed by Jambi	1673
Ibrahim Shah	1677–85	Bintang (Rhio)	Negotiations for alliance with Dutch	c. 1682
Mahmud Shah	1685–99	Kota Tinggi	Treaty with Dutch	1685
			Assassinated	1699

END OF THE MALACCA LINE

Sultan	Reign	Capital	Events	Date
Abdul Jalil Riayat Shah III	1699–1718	(i) Panchor (ii) Rhio	Raja Muda in control Invasion by Raja Kechil	1708 1717–18
Raja Kechil (Abdul Jalil Rahmat Shah)	1718–22	Rhio	Abdul Jalil III (now Bendahara again) executed Bugis invasion; Kechil driven back to Siak	1719 1721–2
Sulaiman	1722–60	Rhio	Bugis under-kings (Yam-tuan-Muda) ⎧Daing Merewah ⎨Daing Chelak ⎩Daing Kemboja Treaties with Dutch Bugis withdrawal to Lingga Dutch-Bugis treaty	1722–8 1728–45 1745–77 ⎰1745 ⎱1755 1745 1758
Abdul Jalil Muadzam Shah	1760–1	Rhio	Bugis in control again	1760
Ahmad Riayat Shah	1761–?1770	Rhio	Bugis regency	
Mahmud Shah	?1770–1812	Rhio	Bugis under-kings (Yam-tuan-Muda) ⎰Raja Haji ⎱Raja Ali	1777–84 1795–1807
(Dutch rule at Rhio 1784–95)			Bugis attack on Malacca Dutch attack on Rhio Dutch garrison withdrawn from Rhio Bugis influence restored	1784 1795

1760–70. Former vassal states in Sumatra and Malaya no longer looked to Johore for leadership, especially after a spirited attempt by Mahmud to form a Malay coalition against both Dutch and English in 1787 had achieved no military success.

The Bugis policy of supporting younger candidates for the throne was to have an indirect result of some significance. In securing the succession for the younger son of Mahmud Shah in

1812, the Bugis deliberately overlooked an older brother who was the true heir to the throne. This situation was used by Raffles in order to obtain a treaty for Singapore in 1819.[1] It is hardly an exaggeration to say that among the consequences of Bugis control in Johore must be counted the founding of British Singapore.

[1] See Chapter 6.

Chapter 4

BUGIS INFLUENCE IN THE MALAY STATES IN THE EIGHTEENTH CENTURY

In dealing with the history of Johore, reference has been made to a Bugis invasion and to the establishment of Bugis control over Malay Sultans. During the eighteenth century the Bugis played a dominating part in several Malay states, and at some periods they exercised control, directly or indirectly, along the whole west coast of modern Malaya, with the exception of a Dutch bulwark at Malacca. To understand the origins and extent of this Bugis influence, it is necessary to consider briefly the situation, in the latter part of the seventeenth century, of what is today the island world of eastern Indonesia.

The Bugis homeland lay in the south-west corner of the octopus-shaped island of Celebes. Here the Bugis lived under hereditary chiefs, a vigorous, intelligent, and aggressive Malay people, skilled boatmen and shrewd traders. They had a particular flair for the art of fighting, and when European and local rivalries for the spice trade of South-East Asia were at their height, the Bugis were much in demand as hired troops for operations on land and sea. They had adopted from the Portuguese a form of European-type armour, and they were accomplished musketeers. Provided that they were well paid, they served their employers well, and at various times they were to be found fighting on behalf of the Dutch to punish a native ruler who had quarrelled with them, or braving Dutch hostility in order to convey spices to Portuguese merchants who feared to sail too close to the Moluccas.

Macassar, the main port of southern Celebes, was for years a great source of trouble to the Dutch, because it represented an open gateway in a wall which they had tried to build for themselves round the spice trade. Through and from Macassar, rice, gold, and produce from India, China and Europe, were smuggled by Bugis traders to the island of Ceram in return for cargoes of precious cloves. Both European and Asian traders resorted to Macassar as a market for spices.

When the Dutch East India Company was sufficiently free from other commitments, it concentrated its forces to bring Macassar into line with its policy of monopoly. In 1660 the ruler of Macassar was forced to sign a treaty promising to stop trading with the Spice Islands. This treaty was not kept, and seven years later a Dutch expedition captured Macassar, placed it under Dutch over-lordship, and installed a Dutch garrison. Four months after this, in 1668, the Dutch found it necessary to depose the ruler altogether and to place the area of south Celebes under a Dutch governor, with his headquarters at Macassar.

By these measures the Dutch not only aroused the hostility of the majority of the Bugis[1] but also, in effect, took away the liveli-hood of a considerable number of Bugis traders who had pre-sumably made a living from the spice trade. Rather than settle peacefully under Dutch rule, groups of Bugis, resourceful and well armed, sailed under the command of their traditional chiefs to start new enterprises and homes on other shores. Some of them founded settlements in northern Borneo and northern Java; others continued westwards as far as the Malacca Straits and the west coast of Malaya. About the year 1680 Bugis groups were settling not far from the coast, in the valleys of the River Klang and River Selangor.

Why did Bugis emigrants choose the swampy coastline of what is now the state of Selangor as one of their new settlement areas? A number of reasons suggest themselves. This coastline faced a main trade route which could offer opportunities for either legitimate trade or piracy. The Selangor river valleys, and the adjacent mangrove swamps, offered hideouts where an enemy might find it difficult to penetrate. There were no spices to be found here, but in small quantities there was another trading commodity — tin.

[1] Some Bugis, because of their own family feuds, had actually helped the Dutch to capture Macassar.

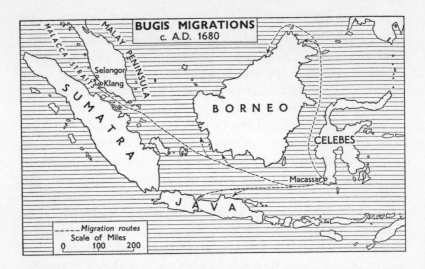

BUGIS MIGRATIONS
c. A.D. 1680

Migration routes
Scale of Miles
0   100   200

The Bugis themselves were enterprising enough to plant gambier, which they had grown in Celebes. Moreover, the Bugis were able to make their settlements without fear of serious opposition.

The small and scattered Malay settlements which may have existed in this area had little or no political unity. In theory, over-lordship would have been claimed by the Sultan of Johore, and any tin trade at Klang was, again in theory, a matter of agreement between the Sultan and the Dutch at Malacca. While the Bugis were settling in Selangor, Johore was wasting its energies and resources in a long, fruitless, war with Jambi. As for Dutch Malacca, the attention of its officials at this time seems to have been diverted by attempts to secure from Johore a monopoly of recently found tin at Siak, in Sumatra. The Bugis were to prove such a threat to Dutch Malacca in the eighteenth century that one is tempted to wonder whether the nearness of Selangor to the Dutch port was in itself an incentive to the settlement there of Bugis with old scores to pay?

Although they were of Malay stock, and were Muslims, the Bugis were regarded by Peninsular Malays as newcomers and intruders. Their ability as soldiers, however, caused the Malays both to fear them and to seek their services during times of Malay quarrels, as when Raja Kechil of Siak sought the help of a Bugis fleet from Selangor in his invasion of Johore in 1717. The Bugis were willing to fight in such circumstances, but they drove a hard bargain and demanded high prices. They were conscious of Malay opinion, and among their aims were social recognition and political authority for their chiefs. In return for Bugis help, Kechil promised that, when he became Sultan of Johore, one of the Bugis chiefs should act as his deputy, or under-King (Yam-tuan-Muda).

This was a dangerous arrangement, because it was easier to invite the Bugis than to dismiss them, and they were to show great persistence in holding political authority once they had seized it. Kechil seems to have had second thoughts. Possibly he decided that he could muster sufficient forces from his Minangkabau followers to take the throne of Johore. By sending no information of the invasion-date, he broke his part of the bargain with the Bugis and thus aroused their bitter hostility.

The rest of this story has been told.[1] Revenge against Kechil. ambition for high office in Johore, and encouragement from Malay elements intriguing against the new Sultan, all combined as motives for the Bugis invasion of 1721–2. Kechil was driven back to Siak; the new Sultan was the son of the late Bendahara, and Daing Parani, the Bugis victor, placed one of his five brother chiefs, Daing Merewah, in the office of Yam-tuan-Muda. Bugis leaders married Johore Malay princesses, Parani himself setting the example by marrying Tengku Tengah, sister of the new Sultan, a lady whom Raja Kechil had slighted when he married her younger sister, Tengku Kamariah.

The diplomacy of the Bugis showed a very shrewd grasp of the situation. There was no move to create a Bugis Sultan.

This would have outraged conservative Malay opinion and undoubtedly caused unrest and civil war. In Bugis eyes, however, the new office of Yam-tuan-Muda was to be the one which mattered, and the Malay Sultan was to take his orders from the Bugis under-King. Behind a Malay façade, Johore was to be a Bugis-controlled state. Moreover the marriages of Bugis chiefs to the daughters and sisters of Malay princes was aimed both at symbolising the links between Bugis Selangor and Johore, and

[1] See Chapter 3.

at giving the Bugis some social standing in their relationships with other Malay states. Bugis control in Johore lasted, with only relatively short breaks, throughout the remainder of the eighteenth, and into the nineteenth, century.

The Bugis had been in Johore less than two years when they were presented with an opportunity to intervene in Kedah. Succession disputes were particularly common in the history of the Malay States, and often they led to a civil war between two brothers, or half-brothers, and their respective supporters. In Kedah, Daing Parani secured the succession for the eldest son of the late Sultan, but this was soon challenged by a younger brother, who sought the help of Raja Kechil and his Minangkabau Malays. The result was a two-year war (1724–6) in Kedah between Minangkabaus and Bugis, each supporting a claimant to the Kedah throne.

As in Johore, but after far more fighting, the Bugis were successful, and Raja Kechil was once more driven back to his homeland in Sumatra. If it was any consolation to him, his great opponent, Daing Parani, was killed in the fighting. The older brother was now unchallenged as Sultan, but he had become indebted to the Bugis, who demanded money payments for their services in a long and costly war. The main victim of this war was, of course, Kedah itself. It had endured at the same time the bitterness of civil war and the miseries of military campaigns conducted by foreign fleets and armies. Its trade, to take only one aspect, was ruined.

The Kedah Sultan was, in fact, unable to meet the Bugis demands for ready payment, and he had to offer to pay his war debts on an instalment basis. Thus he not only owed his position as Sultan to Bugis support, but was also for many years their debtor. Forty-four years later, in 1770, the Bugis were still demanding payments from Kedah on the grounds that the amount agreed upon in 1726 had never been fully paid. Rightly or wrongly, the Sultan's refusal to meet these demands led to an invasion of Kedah by Raja Haji, and a temporary military occupation of the capital. It is significant that during this period, while an exile in what is today Perlis, the Sultan of Kedah talked to Francis Light about his problems, and was prepared to concede a trade base to a power willing to support him against Kedah's enemies, and strong enough to do so. Although the Siamese were seen as potential enemies, they were at war with Burma in 1770; it was the Bugis who were the immediate oppressors. Sixteen years were to pass before an English trading base was established at Penang, but, from the Kedah standpoint, that base was ceded in return for military support against enemies, actual and potential. The Bugis thus played no small part in the situation which led to the founding of British Penang.

In Perak there was a confused scene of struggles round the throne and of quarrels arising from the tin trade. The Bugis were present in both these spheres of activity. At least two Bugis invasions of Perak took place in the eighteenth century. These were caused, to some extent, by the infiltration into Perak of anti-Bugis elements, following the Kedah war. Minangkabau leaders and Kedah chiefs who had been defeated in Kedah tried to rally further support from the Malays of Perak. The Bugis invasion of 1728 seems to have been aimed at breaking up this Minangkabau movement, and at the same time securing the throne for a Sultan (Muzaffar Shah) who had enlisted Bugis support. A second Bugis invasion, in 1742, seems to have taken place in similar circumstances. Underlying both these successful attempts at preventing enemy invasion from north of the River Bernam may have been the economic necessity for maintaining a strong footing in the Perak tin trade. Despite treaties with the Perak Sultans and forts at Dindings and Pangkor, the Dutch were never secure in their monopoly of Perak tin. Bugis invasions of Perak, and the average Malay's fear of the Bugis, must surely have meant the shipping of tin to Selangor, and from there, perhaps, to Johore.

The Perak scene is blurred for us by incomplete accounts, but it is evident that Bugis interference was considerable. Perhaps this was shown most of all by the attendance of the Malay Sultan of Perak at the installation of a Bugis prince as Sultan of Selangor.[1] Raja Lumu, son of Daing Chelak, who was Yam-tuan-Muda of Johore, was elevated to the title of Sultan Salahu'd-din Shah. The

---

[1] The date still seems uncertain. 1740 or 1742 would seem to be the most likely, though a somewhat later date has also been suggested.

presence at this ceremony of the Malay Sultan of Perak was a typical Bugis move to legalise the proceedings in Malay eyes. This new Sultanate of Selangor not only confirmed the existing independence of the state; it also illustrated the nature of the relationships existing between Selangor and Perak.

Finally, there was Dutch Malacca. The Dutch attitude to the Bugis was shown in the instructions for rebuilding a Dutch fort at Pulau Dinding in 1745. The garrison was to consist of 30 Europeans and 30 Asians, but *no Bugis!* Dutch and Bugis had competed for the spice trade in the seventeenth century; in the eighteenth century, they competed for tin and other Straits produce.

The Dutch were worried about the extent of Bugis influence along the west coast of Malaya. To the north and south of Dutch Malacca, Bugis fleets sailed much as they wished. Perhaps it was only a healthy respect for each other's fighting strength which kept peace between the Bugis and the Dutch for long periods. Peace would often be a relative term, for it was punctuated by episodes of a long drawn-out trade-war.

The attempts by Johore Malays to weaken or drive out Bugis influence were watched with interest by Malacca. Little came of a Malacca-Johore treaty in 1745, but another alliance, ten years later, led to open warfare with the Bugis. The Bugis got the worst of this, and by a treaty of 1758 they conceded both the authority of the Johore Malay Sultan and the Dutch rights to a monopoly of the purchase of tin in what had once been part of the Johore dominions. This treaty merely served to give the Bugis a breathing-space; by 1760 the Bugis had regained their power behind the Johore throne.

For many years, however, the Bugis avoided a further open clash with the Dutch. Under Raja Haji they attempted a revival of Johore authority in eastern Sumatra; they put further pressure on Perak, and they carried out a successful invasion of Kedah. With this fresh outburst of Bugis activity, tensions between Dutch and Bugis were bound to increase. It is remarkable that open hostilities did not break out until 1782, when Raja Haji quarrelled with the Dutch over the distribution of the cargo of a ship captured from the English, in which the Bugis wanted a share.

Malacca faced a Bugis attack in 1784 as it had faced one in 1756. Raja Haji was killed in the fighting, and the Dutch pressed their counter-attack successfully against Selangor and Rhio. The Bugis Sultan was temporarily driven out of Selangor, but he restored his position, though still on the defensive, in 1785.[1] The Bugis were driven out of Rhio by the Dutch, but they returned in 1795, when the English East India Company took over the Dutch position there during the Napoleonic Wars.

One further state must be briefly mentioned. Inland from Malacca, Minangkabau Malays had made settlements in the fifteenth and sixteenth centuries. Because this took place gradually and peacefully, their history is obscure. The weakening of the Bugis position in Selangor and Rhio gave these little states an opportunity to make their first loose coalition, and, in 1773, to establish a dynasty. Late in the nineteenth century, this coalition reached its present union as Negri Sembilan.

DIAGRAM TO SHOW BUGIS INFLUENCE IN THE EIGHTEENTH CENTURY

KEDAH	Bugis intervention, 1724–6. Bugis invasion, 1770–1.
PERAK	Bugis invasions, 1728 and 1742. Bugis involved in tin trade. Sultan of Perak attended Raja Lumu's installation in Selangor, *c.* 1740.
SELANGOR	Early settlements from 1680. Bugis Sultanate, *c.* 1740.
DUTCH MALACCA	Faced competition of Bugis traders. Bugis attacks, 1756 and 1784.
JOHORE	Bugis invasion, 1721–2. Creation of Bugis Yam-tuan-Muda with real political power. Bugis driven out, 1784; returned, 1795.

[1] In 1786 Sultan Ibrahim was compelled to acknowledge Dutch suzerainty and to grant Malacca a monopoly of tin.

By the end of the eighteenth century the heyday of the Bugis was over. Their influence represented a passing phase, but one which lasted a considerable time, and had far-reaching results. The Bugis weakened the Malay Sultanate of Johore beyond repair. They helped to weaken Malay authority in Kedah and Perak. They created a new state and dynasty in Selangor, a dynasty from which its present ruler is descended. They weakened Dutch power and influence in Malacca, and possibly prevented its extension in other Malay states. In Kedah and in Johore, they unconsciously created situations which led to the founding of British Penang and British Singapore.

In the long-term view, by intermarriage and a more settled way of life the Bugis element merged into the Malay population. Well into the nineteenth century, however, a Bugis aristocracy was discernible in Selangor.

Chapter 5

THE ENGLISH EAST INDIA COMPANY'S SETTLEMENT AT PENANG

A.D. 1770–1805

The story of the founding of the English East India Company's Settlement at Penang can be viewed from three different angles, first from that of the Sultan of Kedah, who was the hereditary ruler of the island of Penang before 1786; secondly, from that of the English East India Company, with its eastern headquarters first in Madras, later in Calcutta, and its home office in London; and thirdly, some attempt should be made to assess the aims and ideas of Francis Light, who saw the possibilities of Penang, and worked to bring the other two interested parties together.

Kedah was an old Malay state; its history, in fact, from earliest times, illustrates the typical settlement and culture patterns of well-situated and fertile regions of South-East Asia. Since 1474 Kedah had been a Muslim state, and its ruling house was linked in marriage with that of Malacca.

Kedah had been a trading region since the early centuries of the Christian era, and probably even earlier. Its river mouths had been used for centuries as ports-of-call and collecting centres by shipping from India, and they also attracted traders from northern Sumatra and the west coast of the Malay Peninsula. Kedah's early trade-centre lay in the valley of the Merbok, but by the fifteenth century the Kedah River itself had become the focus of political and economic life.

The main export commodity from Kedah was tin, but there was also a steady trade in elephants, ivory, timber, and rattans. In

67

the seventeenth century Kedah also had successful pepper plantations, which added another valuable item to the export market. In
return, Muslim merchants brought to Kedah the produce of
India and the Middle East — Indian cloths from the Coromandel
and Bengal coasts, metalware, glassware, drugs, and spices.
Overland routes from Patani and Ligor brought elephants and
ivory to Kedah, and carried back to the east coast of the Peninsula
a considerable proportion of Kedah's imports.

The economic advantages of Kedah attracted, over the years,
many external influences. In the fifteenth century Kedah owed
allegiance to Malacca and from there, subsequently, the Portuguese, and after them the Dutch, put pressure on the rulers of
Kedah to cede them a monopoly of the tin trade. The Achinese
invaded Kedah in 1619 during their attacks on the Malay Peninsula,
partly to control Kedah's trade, and partly to destroy the pepper
plantations, which constituted a threat to the rival production
centre in northern Sumatra.

The tolls and taxes on trade, and the profits of private trade
conducted by his agents, were the main sources of income of the
Sultan of Kedah. Yet, for one reason or another, Kedah seldom
achieved political security to match the wealth, real or potential,
of her rulers. The earliest claims for some sphere of influence in
Kedah were made by the kings of Siam, Kedah's northern
neighbour. They dated back to about A.D. 1300 when the first
Siamese kingdom in the Menam valley successfully demanded
tokens of tribute from the small settlements in the Malay
Peninsula.

It is very difficult to be precise about what these Siamese claims
actually amounted to by the eighteenth century. In normal times,
the Sultan of Kedah despatched, once in three years, envoys to the
royal court of Siam at Ayuthia, and later at Bangkok, bearing
with them a costly present of gold and silver, which Malay
craftsmen had fashioned into two ornamental plants of branches
and leaves. These 'Golden Flowers' (Bunga Mas) were presented
to the king during a ritual ceremony and he regarded them as a
payment of homage and a token of submission by a vassal to an
overlord. The Malay Sultan, on the other hand, did not necessarily

think of the gift in this way. From his point of view, it was merely a token of alliance and friendship with a powerful northern neighbour. He would normally have considered himself as having sovereign rights within his own state of Kedah. The significance of the gift — and even its dispatch — depended very much upon circumstances. During times of Siamese weakness, or when the king was distracted by foreign wars, the Sultan of Kedah could forget about sending his 'tribute'; when Siam was strong, the 'Bunga Mas' offering was sent, and sometimes further demands for men, money, and supplies, had to be met. The real test was whether Siam was in a position to enforce her demands.[1]

When Sultan Muhammad of Kedah first discussed with Francis Light a scheme for sharing his own trade with a foreign power which could protect him from hostile threats and attacks, he had in mind this question of the relationships between Kedah and Siam. No ruler of Kedah at that time (*c.* A.D. 1770) could be sure that his reign would be free from Siamese pressure, or even from Siamese invasion. Yet it was not the Siamese problem which was then the most urgent.

In 1771 the Bugis from Selangor invaded Kedah after making demands for money which Muhammad refused to meet. The Bugis claim was that Kedah had never completed payments for Bugis services rendered in a civil war forty-five years previously.[2] Thus Sultan Muhammad was driven from his capital, and took refuge further north in what is today Perlis. He had not only lost his capital for the time being; he was also cut off from his source of income, for Bugis leaders were collecting the debts due to their fathers by seizing the Kedah trade. In these troubled circumstances, the Sultan was prepared to make trade concessions in return for a military alliance which would at least give him some prospects of security.

We have now to consider the point of view of the English East India Company. As the name suggests, the Company had been

[1] Burma had also, at times, demanded tribute from Kedah; sometimes Kedah had sent 'Bunga Mas' to Burma, sometimes to Siam; even, on occasion, to both at once.
[2] See Chapter 4.

formed, in 1600, for trade with the East Indies, and its early expeditions, like those of the Portuguese and the Dutch, had been concerned with the spice trade. In the early seventeenth century the English Company had gained a number of bases for this trade, including a 'factory' at Bantam in north-west Java, and another at Patani in the Malay Peninsula. The pressure of Dutch competition, and the greater resources of the Dutch East India Company, gradually caused English trade, apart from isolated private ventures, to withdraw from South-East Asia and to concentrate itself upon India. The failure of the English East India Company in South-East Asia was, in fact, a prelude to its long history in the trade and politics of India.

One 'factory', however, remained in the English Company's hands from 1685 onwards, and this was at Bencoolen, on the west coast of Sumatra. It has been described as 'one of the most costly and unprofitable stations which the Company ever possessed'.[1] Bencoolen's main purpose was to serve as an outlet-port for pepper plantations. Its site was unhealthy; it was often inefficiently run, and the morale of its officials was low. It was situated on the wrong side of Sumatra, away from the Malacca Straits, and it never developed as a wider trade-centre. In addition, even its pepper trade was greatly hampered by rival ports controlled by the Dutch.

The history of the English East India Company in South-East Asia in the seventeenth century had thus so far been made up of a series of disappointments and frustrations, and this partly explains the great caution which its Directors showed about any later ventures into the same vast region beyond India.

The idea of an East India Company port to the east of the Bay of Bengal came up for discussion, investigation, and even implementation, many times in the course of the eighteenth century.[2] Two main reasons underlay these efforts to find and secure a new base. The first one, chronologically, was the need for an English naval base where men-o'-war could be supplied and

---

[1] L. A. Mills in 'British Malaya, 1824–1867', *JRASMB*, Vol. 3, pt. 2, p. 13.
[2] A summary of this search for a base is given in D. G. E. Hall's *A History of South-East Asia*, Chapter 26, pp. 421–42.

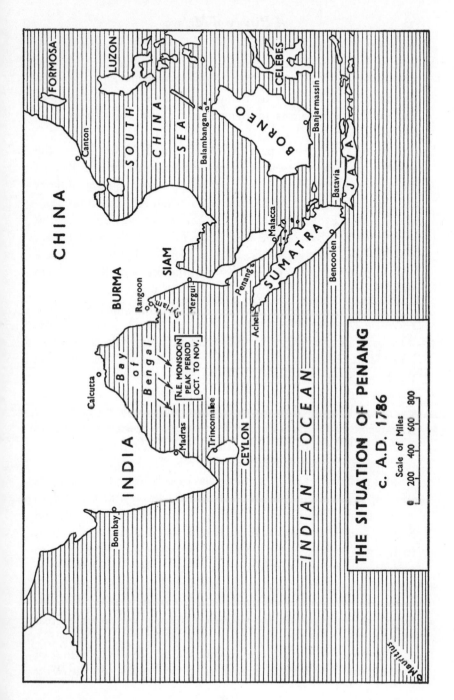

THE SITUATION OF PENANG

c. A.D. 1786

Scale of Miles

0 200 400 600 800

CHINA

FORMOSA

LUZON

Canton

SOUTH CHINA SEA

CELEBES

BORNEO

Balambangan

Banjarmassin

Batavia

JAVA

BURMA

Rangoon

SIAM

Tenasserim

Mergui

Malacca

SUMATRA

Penang

Bencoolen

Achen

Calcutta

Bay of Bengal

N.E. MONSOON
PEAK PERIOD
OCT. TO NOV.

INDIA

Madras

Trincomalee

CEYLON

INDIAN OCEAN

Bombay

Mauritius

repaired. This need arose from the strategy of the Anglo-French wars in India and the adjacent seas. The main scene of naval warfare was the Bay of Bengal. Naval supremacy achieved by one side or the other in the Bay of Bengal could be a decisive factor in the military campaigns in Bengal, and along the Coromandel coast.

During the greater part of October and November — the north-east monsoon season — naval operations in the Bay of Bengal were impossible on account of hurricanes. The rival fleets then retired to their own bases for repairs and refitting in preparation for the next encounter. For English ships, this meant a long voyage to Bombay on the west coast, for the Coromandel coast was exposed to the north-east monsoon, and offered no safe anchorage during this period. By the time the refitted ships from Bombay were back again in the Bay, it was April.

It was often a matter of some importance to have a fleet back in action in the Bay by January, before the enemy had appeared. This gave an opportunity of blockading enemy ports and patrolling the trade routes without interference. For this reason, both the English and the French sought to secure convenient naval stations as bases for movements in the Bay of Bengal. The English Company attempted at first to find a suitable harbour on the Indian side of the Bay, but without success. The areas of special interest now became the west coasts of Burma and Siam, and the north coast of Sumatra.

This problem of naval strategy was evident from as far back as the last two decades of the seventeenth century, and it led to Anglo-French competition for dockyards at Mergui in Siam, and Syriam in Burma. Neither Burma nor Siam gave easy concessions to European traders, and both countries were subject at times to violent political upheavals and civil wars. Mergui, while under Siam, was used only for a very short period by either the English or the French. Syriam was used as a repair depot for English ships from 1689 to 1743 but, for various reasons, it was never a great success.

Three wars in the eighteenth century, before the founding of Penang, saw English and French as opponents both in the West

EARLY PENANG WITH THE HILLS OF PROVINCE WELLESLEY IN THE BACKGROUND

and in the East.[1] The naval clashes in the Indian Ocean illustrated many times the importance of sheltered bases and repair stations. The French obtained permission to open a dockyard at Rangoon in 1768. On the other hand, two English embassies to Acheh, in 1762 and 1764, met with no success. In the last of these three wars, the French Admiral de Suffren used Acheh successfully for refitting his ships in 1782, and was back in the Bay of Bengal months before the English Admiral Hughes, whose fleet had withdrawn for repairs to Bombay. Again, in 1783, French cruisers were able to make effective use of Mergui (which was now a Burmese port) and Trincomalee in Ceylon. The disadvantages of the English with regard to a naval base could not have been more clearly shown.

In the case of Penang, however, the naval aspect should not be overstressed, as, in the second half of the eighteenth century, another important argument for a new East India Company port east of India was advanced, based on commercial reasons only. The English East India Company had never completely given up the idea of trade in the East Indies. For this purpose, of course, Bencoolen was retained, though it was not a success. Banjarmassin, in southern Borneo, had a Company 'factory' and fort about A.D. 1700. This lasted only seven years, but it was revived again between 1738 and 1756. In the latter year the Dutch obtained a pepper monopoly from the local Sultan, and the English interest came to an end. Finally, Balambangan, an island off the north of Borneo, was granted to the Company by the Sultan of Sulu in 1762, but it was not until 1773 that a settlement was actually made there. This was destroyed by pirates in less than two years.

The Company's desire to have some part in the trade of the East Indies was one reason for the continued, if intermittent, interest in a South-East Asian port. In the second half of the eighteenth century the increased trade carried in East Indiamen between India and China raised another issue — the need for an English-controlled port-of-call between Bombay, Madras (or Calcutta), and Canton. Before 1786 English shipping sailing

[1] The War of the Austrian Succession (1740-8); The Seven Years' War (1756-63); The War of American Independence (1775-83).

F

between India and Canton, when in need of supplies or repair, had to use either Dutch ports or the ports of native South-East Asian rulers. The Dutch authorities charged high tolls, and in time of war between the English and the Dutch, English ships would have to give these ports a wide berth. The main danger about using the Asian ports was that political conditions might change between one voyage and the next, and this led to uncertainties about the reception one might receive. The plan for a settlement at Balambangan was very closely linked with an alternative route to China, discovered by Commodore Wilson in 1757–8, by which shipping could sail eastwards of the Philippines, and arrive at Canton by sailing from the New Guinea coast northwards between Luzon and Formosa.

Three factors, therefore, entered into the consideration of a new English East India Company port in South-East Asia, namely, the need for a naval base, the desire to enter the South-East Asian market, and the need for a port-of-call for English shipping between India and China. An ideal choice would be one port which could fulfil all three requirements.

Francis Light was an ex-naval officer, discharged at the age of twenty-three at the end of the Seven Years' War, who took service as a ship's captain for the European firm of Jourdain, Sullivan, and de Souza, in Madras. Light's voyages took him to the west coast of the Malay Peninsula and to northern Sumatra, and he learned to speak Malay and Siamese well enough for the purpose of conducting trade negotiations.

Light was in Kedah in 1771, and it was to him that the Sultan made his proposal about a trade settlement in return for military help and protection. Light advised the Sultan to write to the East India Company, and at the same time wrote letters to his own firm in Madras, suggesting that Penang might suit the East India Company better than it suited his employers. Two months later, in January 1772, he wrote directly to Warren Hastings, urging that the Kedah Sultan's offer should be accepted.

Before proceeding further, there are one or two points here which call for comment. The East India Company was in close touch at this time with private firms which might be able to give them useful information, and Light must have known of the Company's interest in securing a new settlement. Also, as it happened, the Company was then focusing its attention on the Malacca Straits. By 1770 efforts to find a suitable harbour in the vicinity of the Straits of Sunda had been abandoned and in 1771 the Company, despite previous disappointments, decided to send another mission to Acheh. It is interesting to note too that the Sultan's offer was merely concerned with a trade-base on the Kedah River; it was Light who mentioned Penang, because he had noticed its possibilities. These included, according to Light, an excellent harbour, with facilities for refitting ships bound for China, together with the likelihood of a useful local collecting trade in tin, pepper, rattans, and other jungle produce.

The Company sent its own agent, Edward Monckton, to negotiate with the Sultan of Kedah in 1772, at the same time sending its third mission in ten years to Acheh. Both sets of negotiations ended in failure. In Kedah there were certain difficulties at the outset. Monckton, young and inexperienced, and speaking no Malay, did not make a favourable impression on the Sultan. Light himself had no powers to act on behalf of the Company, though he took part in some agreement drafting. The fundamental reason for the breakdown of the talks was, however, the unwillingness of the Company to give any promises which might involve military commitments. In the view of the Madras Council of the Company, a new settlement which might involve a strong and costly garrison and participation in wars in the Malay Peninsula might well prove to be more of a liability than an asset. After some months the talks were broken off, and the Kedah Sultan drily informed Monckton that, in any case, the Siamese would have opposed such a move as they had been discussing.

It was true, of course, that the Sultan was taking risks. He not only risked offending Siam, whose King had not been consulted; he also risked offending the Muslim traders who conducted the Indian trade, and who regarded a proposal for an English (or any European) trade-base in Kedah as a dangerous intrusion into their own economic activities.

Twelve years passed without any further progress being made in the Penang project. In fact, it must have seemed, in 1772, that this had now very little chance of fruition. Light spent much of this long interval in trading with the island of Ujong Salang (Junk Ceylon), which lies off the west coast of Siam. Meanwhile the Company attempted to establish a settlement at Balambangan, which was destroyed within two years. Between 1775 and 1783 came the War of American Independence, when the governing body of the East India Company was fully occupied with matters other than experimental settlements. Light wanted the Company to occupy Ujong Salang, and discussed this with Warren Hastings in Calcutta in 1780; Hastings was impressed, but the time was not opportune for such a move.

By 1784 another war was over, and once again the idea of the new eastern port was under consideration by the Company. Two missions were sent by Warren Hastings, one to Acheh, the other to Rhio. It was not for want of trying that the Company failed to gain a base at Acheh, but, once again, the Achinese would not come to terms. At Rhio, the Dutch had just driven out the Bugis and taken their place as the power behind the throne; there was no hope of an English base there now.

By a curious repetition of circumstances, Light was in Kedah again in 1784, and friendly with the young Sultan, Abdullah, whose father had received Monckton in 1772. Knowing of the failure of the missions to Acheh and Rhio, Light put forward to the Company once again the case for Penang. He did this in very favourable circumstances.

From the Company's point of view, the need for a naval station to the east of the Bay of Bengal had been emphasised once again by the tactics of the French navy in 1782 and 1783. The trade with China was increasing, and the loss of the American colonies was stimulating English commerce to seek new and expanding markets in the East.[1]

If Penang should prove not only a useful port of call for ships' supplies, but also a centre of trade in its own right, it might help to solve the problem of what could be sold in China in exchange

[1] In Britain, duties on Chinese tea were greatly reduced from 1784.

for tea and silk. When Penang was founded, the Directors of the Company defined the reasons as being 'for extending our commerce among the Eastern islands, and indirectly by their means to China'. Another favourable point was that the Dutch had suffered a number of defeats at sea in the course of the recent war, and the Dutch government conceded to Britain in the peace settlement an acknowledgment of the right of British trade in the East Indies, even in the Moluccas. Dutch policy in 1784-5, however, seemed aimed at strengthening rather than relaxing Dutch interests in South-East Asia. Penang seemed to offer a chance to check the restoration of Dutch power before this had gone too far.

The new Sultan of Kedah was also well disposed to the revived Penang scheme. Although the Bugis had long since withdrawn from Kedah, the young Sultan's position was not very secure. Support for him among the Kedah princes was divided, and several were unfriendly. To the north, Siam was less distracted by wars and becoming a powerful state.[1] The chance of outside help was attractive to Kedah.

In this favourable atmosphere Light obtained draft proposals from the Sultan of Kedah, and these he took to Calcutta early in 1786. The Acting Governor-General, Macpherson, agreed to Light's scheme, and persuaded the Company to make a 'factory' at Penang with Light as its Superintendent. The Company accepted Penang for commercial reasons; the question of its suitability for a naval base was still left undecided. Light returned from Calcutta to Kedah with three ships, a small garrison of troops, and stocks and stores for the base camp which would mark the beginning of the new settlement. He had an audience with the Sultan, and some days later proceeded, with the Sultan's consent, to Penang. A short ceremony was held on the island about a month later (August 11th, 1786) by which Light formally took possession of it. He named it Prince of Wales' Island, after the eldest son of the reigning British sovereign, George III, and named the new port Georgetown after the King himself.

Underlying these successful negotiations, however, was the same fundamental difference of approach as had marked the talks

[1] This was clearly shown in the early nineteenth century.

of 1772. The Kedah Sultan still wanted military support 'whenever any enemy from the interior shall attack us'. The Company, willing to agree on most other points,[1] limited its immediate commitments to an armed vessel guarding the island of Penang and the adjacent coast of Kedah. The question of attacks on Kedah from the interior was to be referred back to London for a final decision.

Thus, Light's occupation of Penang took place while the vital issue, as the Sultan saw it, remained in the balance. The Company, in fact, never committed itself beyond the protection of the island and the opposite coastline. Light did his best to impress on Calcutta the importance of sending at least a token force to Kedah which would probably be sufficient to deter enemies from attacking. In January 1788 the Governor-General in Council informed Light of a decision against any measures which might involve the Company in military operations 'against any of the Eastern princes', though in any other way Light could use the influence of the Company for the security of the King of Kedah.

This, of course, placed Light in an extremely uncomfortable position; no one was more aware than he of the Sultan's views. He was now paying the price for having taken the initiative, and for having hoped that at least sufficient promises of military support would be given to satisfy the Sultan and discourage his enemies. An attitude of growing mistrust developed between the Sultan and Light, and the Sultan refused to reply to offers of annual payments in return for loss of trade.

This whole question of the terms on which Penang was ceded has been the subject of much controversy, especially as Kedah needed help very badly against Siamese pressure early in the nineteenth century. The East India Company was not legally wrong, because it broke no agreement or promise, but it was morally wrong for holding on to Penang on terms which never, as they stood, satisfied the Sultan. Light's intentions were honest, but he did 'jump the gun' with the vital question still outstanding. The Sultan acted in good faith, and regarded the 'reference-back' of the military-support clause as a formality. The East India

[1] Compensation for loss of trade to Kedah was not definitely fixed.

Company's decision against military help was in keeping with its normal policy, and based on bitter experience. At the same time, it showed a cool lack of concern for the Kedah-Penang situation. From Light's point of view, as a man of action, the whole matter could have been settled successfully and amicably by the sending of a few troops and guns to Kedah to show the Company's good intentions. This would, in Light's opinion, have satisfied the Sultan and kept away his enemies.

After five years the Sultan gave up hope of any further assurances by the Company, and prepared to take Penang by force. A war fleet was assembled at Prai, but Light, who knew well enough what was happening, attacked first and scattered the invasion force. The Sultan now agreed to sign a treaty ceding the island of Penang to the East India Company in return for an annual payment to him and his successors of 6,000 Spanish dollars a year. This treaty of 1791 became the legal basis for the Company's tenure of Penang; it included nothing about military protection, although, in the view of a later British administrator in Malaya,[1] the Sultan of Kedah still regarded this as part of the bargain.

In 1800 Sir George Leith, then Lieutenant-Governor of Penang, negotiated a further treaty with the Sultan for the cession of a strip of mainland Kedah, which was renamed Province Wellesley after the Governor-General in India. The Company's purpose was to give greater protection to Penang by having command of both sides of the strait which divided the island from the mainland, and also to develop a food-producing area, especially for rice, which could supply Penang and make it largely self-sufficing. The addition of Province Wellesley to Penang had a later counterpart in the addition of Kowloon to Hong Kong. By the treaty of 1800, the Sultan's annuity from the East India Company was increased to 10,000 dollars a year.

Light remained Superintendent of Penang until his death in 1794. His was largely a one-man government; he was short of trained assistants, and he himself had had no training in adminis-

[1] F. Swettenham, *British Malaya*, p. 46.

tration. He did what seemed best in a situation full of problems and difficulties, but there were many administrative mistakes. To make things worse, the Company gave Light only half-hearted support. No decision was taken at this stage about a naval base at Penang; in fact, the permanence of the settlement itself was by no means assured. Light's own salary was small, and he was told to practice the strictest economy; no trade taxes were to be levied, and Penang was to be a free port.

There was no regular procedure for the granting of land and titles to land. Settlers were allowed to occupy such land as they could clear, with the promise of a future title. No land was reserved for public use, and both Europeans and Asians were granted land without reference to how they would employ it. Light himself and his business partner, James Scott, acquired large tracts of land. There was no government fund which could be used either for loans, or for the repurchase of lands which came on the market, and it was the adventurer or speculator who profited most from this state of affairs.

Land was one source of trouble; revenue was another. Light and his immediate successors had the very difficult task of trying to balance the budget in a pioneer settlement where free trade was practised and where there were no external subsidies. The inevitable 'farming-out' of taxes to individuals often meant that the tax-farmers made a large profit at the expense of the government. Some small import duties were introduced on Straits produce in 1801, but these were abandoned after one year, and in their place an export duty was placed on pepper and other locally grown produce. All these duties were 'farmed' to the highest bidder, as there were no regular customs officers before 1805. Expenses greatly exceeded income even twenty years after the founding of the settlement.

Light attempted to grow cloves, nutmeg, and cinnamon; but these failed; pepper — also introduced by Light's efforts — proved to be a much more successful plantation-crop, and one of real economic value to the island. Further attempts to grow spices after Light's death met with only moderate success.

In the early years little was done about roads or public buildings, and the township round the port grew up in a haphazard way on swampy land which bred sickness and disease. The early community included a large adventurer element, and law and order were maintained by a system of Captains or headmen for the Asian groups. Serious cases of civil complaint or crime were tried by the Superintendent or his assistants, and some decisions had to be confirmed by the Bengal Government. Europeans charged with serious crimes were sent for trial to the Bengal courts. No law-court or clear system of law was established before 1807.

By 1788 the population of Penang was about 1,000, and it increased to 12,000 in 1804, by which time Province Wellesley had been included. The main racial group was Malay, but there were large Chinese and Indian communities, and a mixture of many other Asian races, together with a European minority, mainly British, in trade and administration.

Penang's trade kept pace with this increase in population. From Britain and India cloth, metalware, and opium, were high on the list of imports, whilst from Burma, Siam, the Malay Peninsula, and Sumatra, came rice, tin, spices, rattans, gold-dust, ivory, ebony, and pepper. Some of this 'Straits produce', as it was called, was useful to the Company in providing a balance of payments, other than in silver, for the China trade.

As head of the administration, Light was succeeded by Major Macdonald (1795–9), Sir George Leith (1799–1804), and Mr. R. T. Farquhar (1804–5). Until 1805 the Government was still largely a one-man affair, though his title had been changed from Superintendent to Lieutenant-Governor. In the latter year, the Company showed a complete change of heart and endowed Penang with a lavish administration of more than fifty officials, a Governor, and the name of 'Presidency'. This placed Penang on an equal footing with the three great Presidencies in India — Calcutta, Madras, and Bombay. Mr. Philip Dundas was the head of this new government, which soon occupied itself with schemes of road-making and drainage.

The Company, which had previously been parsimonious and pessimistic concerning Penang, now indulged in over-optimism.

The growth of Penang's population and trade had led to the belief that it would become both a great trade-centre and a naval harbour. By 1800 the idea of a naval base at Acheh, Trincomalee, the Andamans, or the Nicobars, had been given up, and the future in this respect seem to lie with Penang.

The trade and the population of Penang increased steadily, but it did not show the same spectacular growth as Singapore, which began in 1819 and soon overtook the older settlement. The naval dockyard never became a reality. There was a lack of suitable hard timber from any source nearer than Burma. The British naval victory over the French at Trafalgar in 1805, the very year of the Penang Presidency, greatly reduced the dangers of French sea power for the future. Although Penang had a good harbour, it was found to be unsuitable for the construction of dockyards. There was a lack of skilled engineers and craftsmen, and in any case there was the question of expense. This new administration in itself was a top-heavy burden on Penang's economy.

Among the new officials who arrived at Penang in 1805 was a young Assistant Secretary, Thomas Raffles by name. At the age of twenty-four he was just beginning his career in the East after serving in the Company's London office from the age of fourteen. His appointment at Penang was a part of the scheme for its expansion. Ironically, he was to discover the possibilities of another island which would limit Penang's development.

DATES OF EVENTS

1771   Talks between Francis Light and the Sultan of Kedah.
1772   Monckton's mission to Kedah.
1784–5   Francis Light again in Kedah; further talks.
1786   {Penang occupied by East India Co.
        {Francis Light first Superintendent.
1791   {Sultan of Kedah prepared to invade Penang.
        {Invasion-fleet dispersed by Light.
        Treaty: Kedah Sultan accepts annual payment of 6,000 Spanish dollars.
1794   Death of Francis Light.
1795   Major Macdonald becomes Superintendent.
1799   Sir George Leith becomes Lieutenant-Governor.

1800 {Province Wellesley added to Penang by treaty.
{Sultan's annuity increased to 10,000 dollars.
1804 R. T. Farquhar becomes Lieutenant-Governor.
1805 Penang named a Presidency; P. Dundas becomes first Governor; Raffles an Assistant Secretary.
1812 Plan of naval base at Penang finally abandoned.

Chapter 6

MALACCA (A.D. 1795–1824) AND SINGAPORE (A.D. 1819–1824)

Among the circumstances which led to the East India Company's great hopes for Penang in 1805 must be counted the use of the port for two naval expeditions. In 1797 Penang was the rendezvous for a large expedition sent from Indian ports with the purpose of attacking Spanish shipping at Manila, in the Philippines. Arthur Wellesley (then Colonel Wellesley and later Duke of Wellington), who was with the expedition, sent to India a very favourable report on Penang.

Two years earlier, in 1795, a much smaller naval expedition had sailed from Penang to Malacca in order to take over the port from the Dutch. The background for this move lay in Europe. Revolutionary France was at war with Britain and Holland in 1793, and French armies invaded Holland in the winter of 1794/5. Holland was conquered, and a puppet republic was established under French influence. The Dutch Stadtholder,[1] William V, fled to England, where he presided over a 'Free Dutch' government in exile. The problem of who would control Dutch overseas interests now arose, in the same way that similar situations occurred with regard to both France and Holland in the Second World War. Dutch opinion was itself divided, containing both pro-French and pro-British elements.

William V issued from England instructions known as the 'Kew Letters', whereby the governors of Dutch overseas territories were to admit British troops and offer no resistance to British warships, which should be regarded as the vessels of a friendly power. The aim of the 'Kew Letters' was to prevent Dutch territories from coming under the control of the pro-French

[1] His son was the first to take the title of king.

republican government. At the same time the French were posing as the 'friends of Holland', who had liberated the country from the 'yoke of Orange' and were sharing with the Dutch the benefits of the French Revolution. One writer has neatly summed up the situation: 'For twenty years from 1795 the unfortunate Dutch had the privilege of being regarded as friends and allies both by France and England; the French overran and ruled their country, and the English took their colonies and their trade.'[1]

It was in the spirit of the 'Kew Letters' that in 1795 a British force captured Malacca with virtually no opposition. A British garrison was installed, and a joint Anglo-Dutch administration was established under a British Resident. The Dutch influence was a subordinate one from the first, and it became less and less important as the years passed. This British occupation of Malacca was intended as a wartime measure only, but it lasted for twenty-three years. Apart from a short-lived peace treaty in 1802 (The Peace of Amiens), the European wars continued until 1815, and Malacca was restored to the Dutch in 1818.

The trade of Malacca had dwindled during the eighteenth-century wars between Dutch and Bugis, but it now enjoyed a temporary revival under British control. This led to some jealousy and friction with Penang, and Penang merchants used their influence with the Company to belittle Malacca's importance. It was argued that to build up trade at Malacca was simply to make a present to the Dutch, to whom it would eventually be restored. The heavy costs of the Malacca garrison and administration were also pointed out. When the Company decided to raise the status of Penang to a Presidency in 1805, it also made the decision to divert Malacca's trade to Penang and, eventually, to abandon Malacca altogether. As a preliminary measure, the old Portuguese-Dutch fortifications were to be pulled down and the site completely cleared. The merchants and the native population would then be moved to Penang, to the advantage of all concerned.

William Farquhar, Resident at Malacca, protested against this policy, and used delaying tactics. Even the Penang government remonstrated against these drastic measures, but the orders from

[1] J. S. Furnivall in *Netherlands India*, p. 55.

India were not changed. In 1807 the work of demolition began on the walls and towers. Farquhar, on his own responsibility, ordered the preservation of the Dutch church and Government House (Stadthuys), as well as other public buildings.

At this stage of events, Raffles came to Malacca on sick-leave from Penang.[1] He stayed with Farquhar while recuperating from an illness to which overwork and general conditions in Penang — despite the reputation it already had as a 'health-resort' — had contributed. During this time he took it upon himself to investigate the Malacca situation, and to write a long and detailed report which he submitted to the Governor and Council at Penang. He also despatched a copy of it to the Governor-General at Calcutta, Lord Minto.

This report embodied a mass of evidence and reasoning in favour of the retention of Malacca. Raffles stated that there was a large resident population, many of whom had been settled for generations in Malacca. This was in contrast to the new and shifting population of Penang. The land around Malacca was well cultivated, the people were orderly, and they paid their taxes. They had been promised, and were deserving of, British protection. The site of Malacca on the Straits was too good to be left abandoned for ever; if the Company withdrew, some other 'European enemy' would settle there, and this could make Malacca a threat and a danger to Penang. Not the least interesting or valuable part of Raffles's report was a detailed analysis of the trade of Malacca, especially with the many groups of peoples in island South-East Asia.

Raffles's report had two important effects. It caused the Directors of the East India Company to change their policy and to retain Malacca, and it brought Raffles to the notice of the Governor-General, Lord Minto, who had been impressed by the ability and the detailed knowledge shown in the report. Raffles was now earmarked for promotion. Two years later, in 1810, he was appointed by Lord Minto 'Agent to the Governor-General for the Malay States' for the express purpose of furnishing infor-

[1] According to C. E. Wurtzburg he came for two periods, November 1807–January 1808, and July–October 1808.

mation and advice for a naval expedition against Dutch Java. Raffles had previously taken leave from Penang in order to meet Lord Minto personally at Calcutta, and to present to him a memorandum proposing the annexation of Java.

The idea of an attack on Java was already in the Governor-General's mind. By 1810 the French were attempting to consolidate their hold on Holland and their claims on Dutch possessions overseas. In 1808 Marshal Daendels arrived in Java as the new Governor-General. He had formerly been a rebel against the Dutch House of Orange, and he had entered Holland again with the French armies in 1795. The English Company regarded Daendels as a dangerous enemy.

Napoleon's control of Holland was increased by outright annexation in 1810; for all political purposes, Holland had become France. Meanwhile, from Réunion and Mauritius in the Indian Ocean, French naval vessels had been causing much damage to British shipping. Minto had received instructions from London to attack these bases in the Indian Ocean, and to subdue the Dutch government, with its military installations, in Java.

One of the main drawbacks to an invasion of Java was the lack of detailed knowledge both of political conditions in Java and of sailing routes and suitable landing points. The appointment of Raffles as the Governor-General's Agent was thus a very important one; his information and advice would dictate the broad strategy of the expedition. Raffles had to combine the roles of intelligence officer and diplomat; part of his work was to make contacts with Java and issue proclamations aimed at reducing any resistance from the Javanese population.

Raffles chose Malacca as his headquarters, and it was from there that the English invasion fleet sailed for Java in June, 1811. Both Minto and Raffles sailed with it. What followed must be very briefly stated here. Dutch resistance was overcome, and Raffles was appointed Lieutenant-Governor of Java, an office which he held for five years. During this period, he made bold and liberal reforms, and involved the Company in heavy expenditure. He became even more violently anti-Dutch than before, and he hoped and worked for the retention of Java in British hands. He also wanted to see the permanent extension of British influence to the islands lying eastwards of Java.

Raffles's patron and supporter, Lord Minto, died in 1813, and the new Governor-General, Lord Moira (afterwards the Marquis of Hastings), was less favourably disposed towards him. General Gillespie, who had commanded the troops in Java, made accusations against Raffles's administration, and the Governor-General, whilst leaving these open for further enquiry, decided that Raffles's policies were both expensive and imprudent. Raffles was dismissed shortly before Java was restored to the Dutch, and he returned to England for health reasons before taking up the alternative appointment which was offered to him at Bencoolen.

Raffles was fêted by London society, and knighted in 1817 for his *History of Java*; meanwhile the East India Company were investigating the charges brought against him in Java. He was acquitted of any charges which suggested moral injustice, and his character was cleared, but judgment was reserved on the wisdom of some of his measures. His appointment at Bencoolen was confirmed, and he was to retain the title of Lieutenant-Governor. Raffles arrived in Bencoolen in March 1818.

Much had happened during Raffles's two-years' absence from South-East Asia. Following the terms of the Congress of Vienna (1815), Dutch possessions in the East Indies had been restored to Holland. Java was restored to Dutch rule in August 1816, and the Dutch again became strongly entrenched in the Malay Archipelago. During the last quarter of the eighteenth century there had been in Holland much criticism of, and investigation into, the affairs of the Dutch East India Company. Finally, on the last day of the year 1799, the Company, which was heavily in debt, had been dissolved, and the administration of its property was taken over by the State.

When the Dutch came back to the East Indies in the years following 1815, they came as direct representatives of the home government. A large fleet and army was sent to reoccupy all the settlements of the old Company. The old treaties with local rulers, including those which granted trade monopolies, were again enforced, and new treaties were made with other rulers.

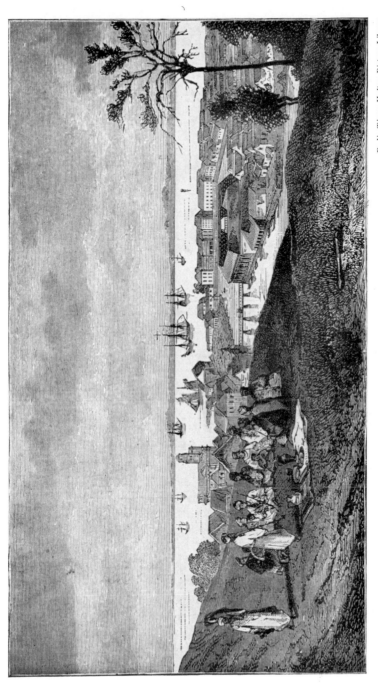

SINGAPORE. THE RIVER AND THE HARBOUR c. A.D. 1845

New posts were established on many islands where the Dutch had not been settled previously.

British ships were forbidden to trade in the Archipelago, except at Batavia, and South-East Asian traders were directed to use Dutch settlements for their markets. Patrols of Dutch ships ensured that this policy was carried out.

By 1818, therefore, despite the long entanglement with France and the temporary British hold on their overseas territories, the Dutch were back in South-East Asia, and stronger there than ever before. Curiously enough, it was British policy which made this possible. The European peace treaties had as one of their main aims the prevention of future danger and aggression from France. British statesmen, especially Castlereagh, wanted Holland to be so strong that a repetition of the French invasion of 1793 would not be possible. At the same time Britain wanted to keep Dutch friendship, and to ensure that there would be no dangerous alliance between Holland and France. It was to further the policy of Britain's interests in Europe that the Dutch were helped to restore their authority in the East Indies. The British retained Ceylon and Cape Colony, which were known to be valuable for British trade, but gave the Dutch a free hand in the East Indies, which most British statesmen thought to be of little importance. From the point of view of Penang or Bencoolen, or even Calcutta, however, this resurgence of Dutch power was very alarming.

The English Company, in the light of events in recent years, now realised that Penang lay too far to the north and west to attract a vast amount of trade from Java and islands to the east of Java. Raffles had asserted as early as 1808 that Malacca, lying 240 miles nearer to the Archipelago, was better situated than Penang for the trade of the islands, and that island-traders would only proceed to Penang for some special advantage in a particular commodity. The Company's trade in Java and the 'eastern islands' during the period 1811–16 had again demonstrated the fact that Penang could never be the centre of the East Indies trade; it lay outside the gate.

There were, therefore, two main reasons for the English East

G

India Company's search for another port somewhere to the south and east of Penang. These were a reluctance to see the old Dutch policy of control and exclusion fully in force again with whatever further restrictions and pressures might follow, and a desire to be more in touch with the trade of the Archipelago than was possible at Penang. The personal initiative in conducting this search came from Raffles.

Raffles was very conscious of his relative isolation at Bencoolen, but even there he was not idle. He devoted his energies in particular to trying to advance British influence in Sumatra at the expense of the Dutch. This brought Dutch complaints, and Raffles was censured by the Company for his conduct.

In October 1818 Raffles sought and gained permission to visit the Governor-General, Hastings, in Bengal. This meeting was arranged in order to discuss future plans for Bencoolen; it ended by Raffles obtaining a cautious approval from Hastings of his plan for a base at Acheh and a new settlement at the southern end of the Malacca Straits. This plan aimed to ensure the free passage of British ships in the Malacca Straits, and also to establish a new port-of-call and trade-centre for the Company in a situation convenient for the Archipelago. In Hastings's written instructions to Raffles, the port of Rhio was mentioned as possessing 'the greatest advantages', but Johore was suggested as a possible alternative if the Dutch had already occupied Rhio.

A small fleet was put at Raffles's disposal, with Penang as the assembly-point and base for the expedition. Acheh was to be visited first, and subsequently Raffles was to proceed southwards in the Malacca Straits towards Rhio. Raffles sailed from Calcutta to Penang in December, 1818. There he found the Governor, Colonel Bannerman, opposed to his schemes and attempting to put obstacles in his way. Bannerman seems to have been motivated by a mixture of personal jealousy and genuine concern for the future of Penang itself. He insisted that Raffles should postpone his visit to Acheh until a reply was received to some points he wished to raise with the Governor-General. This had the effect of hastening Raffles's other — and more important — mission towards Rhio, for he agreed to visit Acheh later, but set sail without delay to seek the new port, whereas Bannerman had hoped to keep him waiting in Penang.

Raffles was joined at Penang by William Farquhar, who, as Resident of Malacca, had recently completed the details of handing over to a Dutch Governor and his staff. He was due to return to England on leave, but he had now been nominated by Hastings to serve as the Resident of the new settlement at Rhio or elsewhere, and he was to take orders from Raffles, who would remain Lieutenant-Governor of Bencoolen.

During his last months at Malacca Farquhar had not been idle in promoting the interests of his Company. He had made treaties allowing Company trade with Malay rulers at Siak in Sumatra, and Rhio and Lingga in the Archipelago; he also had ideas about the possibilities of a British settlement in the Carimon Islands. It had been Raffles's original intention to send Farquhar in charge of the expedition to the southern end of the Malacca Straits, while he himself proceeded to Acheh. Bannerman's tactics resulted in Raffles overtaking Farquhar and sailing in the same company.

While he was at Penang Raffles learned that the Dutch had already installed a Resident and garrison at Rhio; this made him all the more impatient to explore the other possibilities in the Straits, and in Johore, before it was too late. Farquhar's treaty with Rhio had been nullified by the arrival there of the Dutch. Meanwhile Hastings decided he had given Raffles too much freedom of action, and sent instructions against his forming any new settlement. These arrived at Penang too late.

The little fleet sailed along the coast of Siak, explored the Carimon Islands, which were found unsuitable, and finally made for Singapore Island. Raffles's knowledge of the tradition of an early kingdom at Singapore may have had some influence on his decision to consider this island, but Farquhar had also thought of Singapore in the previous August, when he had visited Rhio and Lingga. It seems safe to say that Rhio on Bintang Island would have been their first choice but, as this was under Dutch control, another island in the same region might offer a good alternative.

Raffles and Farquhar landed on the south coast of Singapore Island on January 29th, 1819. The island was inhabited by a

Malay community under the rule of the Temenggong of Johore, a riverside group of 'Orang Laut', and a few Chinese settlers inland. The Temenggong received his visitors in the Malay kampong, and here the first negotiations began. The possibilities of Singapore with its good harbour and wide river had been quickly noted; there remained the important matter of a legal treaty.

Raffles and the Temenggong signed a 'Preliminary Agreement' on January 30th. This allowed the English East India Company to establish a 'factory' on the island. While this factory remained, the Temenggong would not enter into relations with any other power, or allow it to settle within his territory. In return, the Company would protect him and pay him 3,000 dollars a year.

For Raffles, this treaty was a promising beginning, but he knew well enough that the Temenggong was not a sovereign in his own right but was subject, at least in theory, to the Sultan of Johore. There could be no firm legal basis for this new settlement at Singapore unless he could obtain permission for it from the Sultan.

At this time authority in Johore was divided, and titles did not mean what they should have meant. When Sultan Mahmud died in 1812, his eldest son and destined successor, known as Tunku Long, was away in Pahang. Bugis influence secured a doubtful title of succession for Tunku Long's younger half-brother, Abdu'l Rahman. When Tunku Long returned from Pahang to Rhio, he found that Abdu'l Rahman was the nominal Sultan, living on the island of Lingga, and that the Bugis Raja Ja'far, formerly Yam-tuan-Muda, was the real ruler. Ja'far had given himself the title of Raja Muda, which normally meant Crown Prince, or heir to the throne. Unable to gain his rights against the forceful Ja'far, Tunku Long retired to live on the island of Bulang. Here he found himself in the company of another disgruntled prince, Muhammad, who felt that he had a just claim to the title of Raja Muda, and had therefore refused the offer of the office of Temenggong. The Temenggong who made the Preliminary Agreement with Raffles (whose name was also Abdu'l Rahman) was a nephew of this Muhammad.

In other words, the Johore Sultan Abdu'l Rahman was living

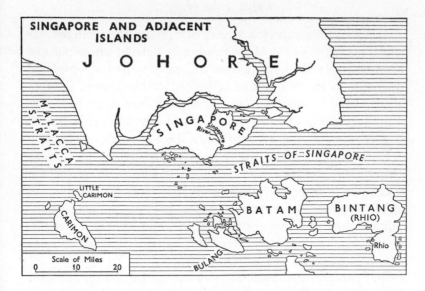

SINGAPORE AND ADJACENT ISLANDS

at Lingga with virtually no executive powers, while the Bugis so-called Raja Muda, Raja Ja'far, was living at Rhio and exercising the functions of government. It was Raja Ja'far who in August, 1818, had concluded an agreement with Farquhar to allow English East India Company trade within his territories. Three months later he had concluded a treaty with the Dutch which allowed a Dutch Resident and garrison at Rhio, and declared only Rhio and Lingga to be free ports. Elsewhere in Johore trade was to be open only to Dutch and local vessels. Meanwhile, in the background, there was Tunku Long at Bulang,[1] whose real claims to be Sultan were known to both Raffles and Farquhar.

From Singapore, two vessels departed. One was an English ship with Farquhar on board, sailing to Rhio; the other a Malay boat with two messengers from the Temenggong, sailing to Bulang. At Rhio, Farquhar was unable to obtain permission for the Singapore settlement from Raja Ja'far on account of his fear of the Dutch; in private, Ja'far is said to have asked for British help to drive out the Dutch, and to have promised to confirm the Singapore situation when this was done.[2]

[1] Most writers have placed Tunku Long at Rhio in 1819, but, on other evidence, he could still have been at Bulang.
[2] C. E. Wurtzburg, *Raffles of the Eastern Isles*, p. 490.

93

Raffles had not expected success from Farquhar's journey. He pinned his hopes on the Malay mission to Bulang, whose purpose was to invite Tunku Long to come to Singapore and be recognised by Raffles as the true Sultan of Johore. Subsequently, the new Sultan would be asked to discuss terms for the trading base. The Temenggong was a supporter of Tunku Long, and the Malays on Singapore could be relied on to follow the Temenggong's lead.

Tunku Long arrived without delay, and agreed to Raffles's scheme. With all the ceremony that could be mustered, he was named and greeted as Sultan Hussein of Johore. All this was highly irregular, of course, but the reigning Sultan, Abdu'l Rahman, had also been installed in an irregular way, no regalia having been handed over to him. Raffles acted on his own initiative in 'proclaiming' this new Sultan of Johore.

On February 6th the second treaty was signed, this time between the Sultan, the Temenggong and Raffles. The Company was given the right to build a 'factory'; the Sultan and the Temenggong agreed to make no treaty with any other European or American power. The Sultan and the Temenggong were to be protected whilst they remained at Singapore, but the Company did not commit itself to interference in the internal affairs of Johore, or to maintaining the Sultan's authority by force of arms. The Sultan was to receive an annual pension of 5,000 dollars, and the Temenggong one of 3,000 dollars. In addition, the Temenggong was to receive half the dues paid by native vessels for the use of the port.

On the day following, Raffles left Singapore for Acheh, where he obtained a treaty of alliance which brought no positive results, and finally he arrived back at Bencoolen. Farquhar was left to develop and, if necessary, protect Singapore.

The future of Raffles's settlement was by no means assured at this stage. Its success or failure under normal conditions would have depended on many factors. The geographical importance of Singapore had still to be proved. Much would depend also on the granting of favourable conditions for traders and settlers, and the effective maintenance of law and order. Conditions at Singapore were, however, not normal, because there was a great deal of opposition to Raffles's *coup*, and there were serious dangers to the survival of the port which he later called his 'political child'.

From Sultan Abdu'l Rahman there was little to fear. He had virtually no authority and apparently no desire for it. He had been forced seven years before by the Bugis Yam-tuan-Muda to take a title to which he did not aspire and for which he was not prepared. His father had destined him for a religious life.

Raja Ja'far was a much more forceful character, but he tended to change sides, so far as the English and the Dutch were concerned, according to expediency. Hussein's protection by the British was, in any case, limited to Singapore, and therefore offered no immediate threat to his position at Rhio. Ja'far did, however, register his protest, and take steps to make Abdu'l Rahman's title more secure.

The main danger came from the Dutch. The name of Raffles was already only too bitterly familiar to them, and this latest escapade of his amounted, in the Dutch view, to an intrusion into an area where they had exclusive treaty rights. From Batavia, and from Malacca, they demanded the complete withdrawal of the Singapore settlement, and, failing this, threatened to use force.

The whole matter depended upon how much support Raffles would receive from his own Company, and here opinion was divided. Bannerman, Governor of Penang, took the Dutch view, and wished to see Singapore abandoned by the Company. The Governor-General in Calcutta and his Council were extremely annoyed with Raffles for having placed them in a very delicate position. Hastings, in particular, had stressed the importance of avoiding conflict with the Dutch. He had also countermanded all his earlier instructions to Raffles, but this message had not reached Raffles in time.

There now developed what has been described as a 'paper-war', and, in an age of slow communications, this took a great deal of time. Messages passed by sailing-ship between Batavia, Malacca, Penang, Bencoolen, Calcutta, London, and The Hague.

Two attitudes were decisive. The Dutch Governor-General at Batavia, Baron van der Capellen, hesitated to use force. Had he sent a military expedition in the early months of 1819, it must surely have been successful, and it is very doubtful whether the English East India Company or the British government would then have risked the possibility of an Anglo-Dutch war in order to secure Singapore.

Van der Capellen relied on a withdrawal by the English Company in the face of Dutch protests. Hastings had rebuked Raffles earlier in Sumatra for anti-Dutch measures taken on his own initiative; it seemed likely that this would happen again. Hastings, however, decided not to give way too much to the Dutch protests this time. He admitted that Raffles had exceeded instructions, but argued that to withdraw unconditionally from Singapore on account of the Dutch would imply that the Dutch had rights there. This, in Hastings's view, was not established. He was prepared to accept a decision reached in discussions by the home authorities in Britain and Holland. To this the Dutch agreed. As a precautionary measure, Hastings ordered the reluctant Bannerman to send troops for the defence of Singapore.

The legal battle between the British and the Dutch for Singapore thus dragged on, and as time passed there was less and less likelihood that Singapore would be abandoned. The new settlement was quickly proving its value, and the Singapore of 1822 or 1823 was very different from that of 1819.

Farquhar, as Singapore's first Resident, had to face problems similar to those which had confronted Light at Penang. There were many difficulties for which his experience at Malacca provided no precedent, but his military career helped him to work with some sense of routine, and to make on-the-spot decisions. Raffles guided general policy from Bencoolen, but this was inevitably a slow and spasmodic procedure against a background of uncertain sailings and the daily pressure of events in a growing pioneer community. Moreover Raffles and Farquhar held different views on many topics related to the planning and government of Singapore.

Within the first two or three years there was a great influx of peoples and trade into Singapore. Various population figures have been given for this period, but they are all rough estimates and tend to exaggerate. A count taken in January 1824 gave a population between ten and eleven thousand, of whom rather less than half were Malays and about a third were Chinese. Many smaller groups, both Asian and European, were also settled there. Free trade, land, British protection, and an increasing variety of employment connected with the port, brought immigrants to Singapore.

East India Company records show the arrivals and departures of shipping and smaller craft in these early years.[1] East Indiamen sailing between Bombay and Canton shared the harbour with Chinese junks, boats from Siam and Trengganu, and even an occasional Dutch ship from Batavia. Smaller boats from the Malay Peninsula and the islands brought their colourful produce to the riverside — tin, spices, pepper, resin, rattans, hand-woven sarongs, rice, shellfish, sea-slugs, birds'-nests, coconuts.

'The history of Singapore', says Winstedt, 'is written mainly in statistics.'[2] By 1820 the revenues of the port were meeting the cost of administration. By 1822 the trade of Singapore exceeded that of Penang, and it continued to do so in increasing proportions. Penang continued to trade with the Sumatran coast, especially northern Sumatra, and with Burma and west Siam, as well as maintaining some direct links with China. Singapore had considerable trade with Siam and the east coast of Malaya, and also with Java and island South-East Asia east of Sumatra. Singapore also had an increasing importance in trade with China, especially through the larger vessels which came to use Singapore in preference to Penang.

During a long visit to Singapore (October 1822–June 1823), Raffles worked out plans for the future of the growing settlement. A provisional code of law was drawn up, based on English law, but with allowances for other customs. Twelve merchants were appointed to act as magistrates for the time being, and a police force was established. A land-registry was planned, with land to be mainly leased out for a fixed period of years. Regulations were made for the management of the port, and a multi-racial committee was employed by Raffles to mark out housing sites for the main

[1] Examples are given in C. D. Cowan, 'Early Penang and the Rise of Singapore 1805–1832', *JRASMB*, Vol. 23, pt. 2, 1950.
[2] *Malaya and its History*, p. 60.

communities which came to settle in the town. Raffles's plans reflected his own personality — a mixture of idealism and realism. He decreed penalties against any kind of slave-traffic, and also — and this was more controversial — against gambling-houses and cockpits. He laid out Singapore's first Botanical Gardens, and established a college to be known as the Singapore Institution, where, among other subjects, the languages of China, Siam, and the Malay Archipelago, were to be taught. The Gardens and the Institution both lacked adequate interest and support after Raffles's final departure from Singapore in July 1823, but something of the spirit behind them was to be revived at a later date.

Finally, there were still some further treaties. In June 1823 Raffles negotiated with Sultan Hussein and the Temenggong for the Company to control all the trade of Singapore in return for further pensions in lieu of loss of income. In August 1824 Crawfurd, who succeeded Farquhar as Resident, obtained from the Sultan and the Temenggong jurisdiction over the island of Singapore for the English East India Company in return for money-sums and increased pensions.[1] This treaty avoided any military or political ties between Britain and Johore.

In the meantime (March 1824) a treaty had been signed in London between the British and Dutch governments. This Anglo-Dutch Treaty, which had great significance in the light of later events, represented a postscript to the work of the Congress of Vienna (1814–15) in so far as British-Dutch relationships were concerned. By 1824 the British Cabinet was not so much worried about possible dangers from France as about the sharp differences of opinion which had arisen among the former wartime allies, Britain, Prussia, Austria, and Russia. From the British point of view, it seemed particularly desirable to keep and strengthen existing friendships, yet there was a danger that the Anglo-Dutch friction caused in the East, for instance, by Raffles's policies, first in Sumatra and then by the founding of Singapore, might cause a rift between Britain and Holland in Europe. The main purpose of the Anglo-Dutch Treaty was to settle existing differences between

---

[1] 33,200 dollars and 1,300 dollars per month for the Sultan, 26,800 dollars and 700 dollars per month for the Temenggong.

representatives of the two countries, and to plan for the future in such a way that there would be little risk of further trouble.

The clauses of the treaty fall into two categories, (1) territorial and (2) commercial.

(1) Holland ceded to Britain all the Dutch 'factories' in India and also 'the town and fort of Malacca and all its dependencies'. At the same time, Holland withdrew the existing objections to British Singapore. Britain, on the other hand, surrendered Bencoolen to the Dutch. In addition to these exchanges of territories held by the rival trading companies, undertakings were given about future commitments. The Dutch undertook to make no further settlements or treaties with rulers in the Malay Peninsula, while the British gave a similar pledge both with regard to Sumatra and to the islands south of the Straits of Singapore, including the Carimon Islands and the Rhio-Lingga Archipelago. None of the trading bases given up under the terms of this treaty (Bencoolen, Malacca, and, presumably, Singapore — as well as those in India) were to be transferred to any other power, and if any were abandoned, rights of occupation passed to the other treaty-country (i.e. Britain or Holland). Neither country was to make any new settlement in the 'Eastern Seas' without previous authority from the home government in Europe.

(2) On the commercial side, vessels of each country were to be admitted to ports of the other at agreed and fixed charges. Neither country was to make treaties with other states which might injure the other's trade. Within the Malay Archipelago the Dutch were not to attempt to monopolise trade, or to discriminate unfairly against British trade. By way of exception, the Dutch would retain a monopoly of the spice trade of the Moluccas, though this no longer held the same importance for the European market as it had done in the seventeenth century. Neither side was to interfere with the other's trade with native ports, and both countries were to combine for the suppression of piracy.

The spirit behind the territorial clauses was one of keeping out of each other's way. By mutual exchanges, separate spheres of interest were created, and this certainly did much to prevent territorial disputes, and remove friction.

Neither Bencoolen nor Malacca were prosperous ports at this time. Bencoolen had never been a success, whilst Malacca was overshadowed by Penang and Singapore at the northern and southern ends of the Malacca Straits. Malacca was also suffering from the silting-up of its river mouth. The significant aspect of the exchange of these two ports was the fact that three British trading settlements were now spaced along the Malayan side of the Malacca Straits, whilst the Dutch were obliged to keep out of the Malay Peninsula. Although it was not consciously planned in this treaty, contact between these three settlements and the Malay States was eventually to bring British political influence to bear in Malaya. On the other hand, the exclusion of Britain from Sumatra, the Moluccas, and islands to the south of Singapore, left a vast island-area open to Dutch trade and influence which was later to become the Netherlands East Indies and, eventually, Indonesia. British relationships with the Sultan of Brunei in the mid-nineteenth century, especially the cession to Britain of Labuan, gave rise to disputed interpretations of the 1824 Treaty. Britain argued that this part of Borneo lay north of the Singapore Straits, while the Dutch claimed that Borneo, lying partly south of Singapore, was covered by the terms of the treaty, and that Britain was also acting in a manner contrary to the spirit of 1824 by provoking clashes in Borneo.

The dependencies of Malacca which were transferred to Britain were not clearly defined. During their tenure at Malacca the Dutch had, from time to time, attempted to exercise some measure of overlordship over Malay states which had once formed part of the Malacca/Johore Empire. These included Johore, Selangor, and some of the Minangkabau States. The Dutch were not concerned about conquests of territory; their main interest had been to secure the tin trade, or to check the power of the Bugis. Their rights of overlordship were vague and, except in the case of disputed payments from the little state of Naning behind Malacca, the English East India Company made no serious attempt to define or exploit these rights.

Johore itself was divided by the terms of the treaty; it would perhaps be more accurate to say that the existing division was confirmed and made permanent. Singapore remained British. Mainland or Peninsular Johore lay within the British sphere. There was a Sultan under Dutch influence in the Rhio-Lingga Archipelago, and both a Sultan and a Temenggong on Singapore Island. The Bendahara followed his own destiny as ruler of Pahang, although some attempts were still to be made to combine Johore and Pahang under one ruler. Mainland Johore (that is, the modern state of Johore) was to be the subject of a long dispute between the family of Sultan Hussein and that of the Temenggong Abdu'l Rahman.

In Notes attached to the Treaty both Britain and Holland expressed the hope that there would be cordial friendship and co-operation between the two powers in the East. This was perhaps too much to expect, for old feelings and attitudes die hard; the British in particular complained that the Dutch hampered their trade in the Archipelago wherever possible, while the Dutch protested equally vigorously that these charges were untrue. The treaty was however undoubtedly responsible for reducing the number of clashes between the two powers, and for limiting the possibilities of another Singapore 'situation'.

The real significance of the treaty lay not in its intentions but in its long-term results. Although it was not consciously foreseen in 1824, the Anglo-Dutch Treaty anticipated the pattern of British and Dutch colonies and protectorates in the nineteenth and early twentieth centuries. It also confirmed the existing political barriers between eastern Sumatra and the west coast of Malaya, and between the Johore mainland and Singapore on the one hand, and the islands of the Rhio-Lingga group on the other.

DATES OF EVENTS

1795   English 'capture' of Malacca from the Dutch.
1805–8   Policy of abandoning Malacca, in the interests of Penang.
1808   Raffles's report on Malacca.
1811   Malacca used as base for invasion of Java.
1818   Malacca restored to the Dutch.
(1811–16   Raffles remains Lieutenant-Governor of Java.)
1818   Raffles becomes Lieutenant-Governor of Bencoolen,

1819　{Founding of Singapore by Raffles.
　　　　{Preliminary Agreement and treaty with Sultan Hussein.
1823　　Raffles's second treaty with Sultan Hussein and the Temenggong.
1824 (March)　　Anglo-Dutch Treaty, or Treaty of London.
1824 (August)　　Crawfurd's treaty with Sultan Hussein and the Temenggong.

Chapter 7

SIAM, THE MALAY STATES, AND THE STRAITS SETTLEMENTS

A.D. 1817–1863

Singapore from its beginnings as a trade settlement had a Resident responsible to the Governor and Council of the East India Company in India. At first the Singapore Resident took orders from Raffles at Bencoolen, but after Raffles's departure for England, in 1824, he was in direct contact with India. Malacca, from the date of its transfer by the Dutch in 1824, was also a Residency linked with India.

The East India Company decided to unite the administration of the three settlements, so in 1826 Malacca and Singapore became dependencies of the Presidency of Penang. The Governor of Penang now had the responsibility for the three settlements, although each, including Penang, had its own Resident Councillor. This arrangement lasted only for four years.

The Presidency of Penang was a heavy financial burden for the Company. The important *entrepôt* and naval station which had been hoped for in 1805, when this Eastern Presidency had been established, had never materialised, and the growth of Singapore brought rumours of economies to Penang. In 1826, when Malacca and Singapore were made dependencies of Penang, only Singapore, of the three, was paying its way. The Governor-General, Lord Bentinck, visited Penang in 1829 and was disturbed by the number of top-ranking officials, with their high salaries. In 1830 Penang was reduced to the status of a Residency. Its administration was reduced and, together with Malacca and Singapore, it now became directly dependent upon India. The three settlements had become three separate Residencies.

For convenience, however, it was decided that one of the three settlements should have a central Chief Resident, or Governor. The claims of Penang were put forward as being the oldest settlement, and those of Malacca because of its central position between the other two. Finally, however, Singapore was chosen because of its sound economic condition and its continued rapid expansion. When this changeover was made, in 1832, Singapore's chief official was given the old Presidency title of Governor, while Penang and Malacca had Resident Councillors. The three settlements still remained only Residencies, taking policy instructions from India, but the Governor of Singapore had a central responsibility for all three. It was from about 1832 that the term 'Straits Settlements' was commonly used and the chief official at Singapore was known as the Governor of the Straits Settlements.

While these administrative changes were taking place, the Malay states of Kedah, Perak, and, to a lesser degree, Selangor, were feeling the pressure of Siam.

The question of Siamese claims to suzerainty over Kedah has been referred to in an earlier chapter.[1] By the early years of the nineteenth century Siam, under the rule of the Chakri dynasty, had become a powerful state with its capital at Bangkok. Although there were wars with Burma from 1785, these had been mostly reduced to raids and skirmishes, with the Burmese held in check. To the east, Siam made successful military and diplomatic moves to gain control of large areas of Cambodia.

This resurgence of Siamese power began to make itself felt southwards into Kedah. It was not just a matter of the regular payment of the 'Bunga Mas'; Siam also demanded armed boats and supplies of rice for military operations against the Burmese along the west coasts of Burma and Siam. The Siamese regarded the Malay states which lay close to their own frontiers as vassals, whose foreign relations were to be handled by Bangkok, and whose rulers had to be confirmed in office by the Siamese Government. The Siamese had possibly not forgiven Kedah for ceding, first Penang and, later, Province Wellesley, without reference to the Siamese Court. They also suspected the reign-

[1] See Chapter 5.

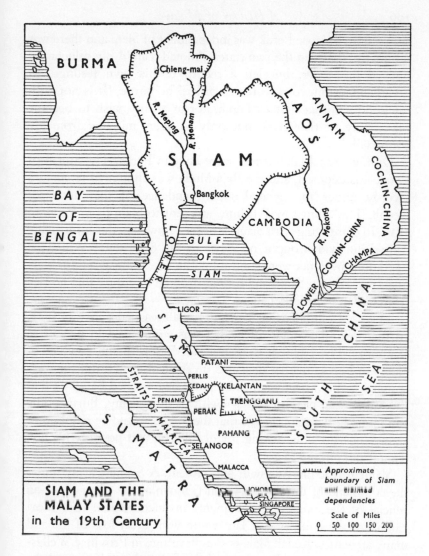

BURMA

Chieng-mai

R. Meping

R. Menam

SIAM

Bangkok

LAOS

ANNAM

COCHIN-CHINA

BAY

OF

BENGAL

CAMBODIA

COCHIN-CHINA

R. Mekong

COCHIN-CHINA

CHAMPA

GULF

OF

SIAM

LOWER

LOWER SIAM

LIGOR

SOUTH

CHINA

SEA

PATANI

PERLIS

KEDAH

KELANTAN

STRAITS OF MALACCA

PENANG

TRENGGANU

PERAK

SUMATRA

PAHANG

SELANGOR

MALACCA

JOHORE

SINGAPORE

SIAM AND THE
MALAY STATES
in the 19th Century

Approximate
boundary of Siam
and claimed
dependencies

Scale of Miles
0   50 100 150 200

ing Sultan of Kedah, Ahmad Taju'd-din (1798–1843), of intriguing with Burma against them.

In order to strengthen the Siamese position in Kedah and, at
the same time, to extend Siamese influence further south in the
Peninsula, Bangkok ordered the Sultan of Kedah in November,
1816, to invade the state of Perak and arrange there for the collection of the 'Bunga Mas' tribute. This represented an act of pure

H   105

aggression, because Perak was independent of Siam and there was no quarrel between the two states. Ahmad Taju'd-din reluctantly obeyed the order, but left a record of his own feelings. 'It greatly afflicts me to execute this order,' he wrote, 'It is not with my good will that I attack Perak, nor at all my wish to become the enemy of that Raja, but only to avert mischief from my country.'[1]

During 1817 Kedah forces were busy in Perak. The Sultan of Perak was deposed, and the Raja Muda was appointed to act as a viceroy under the general superintendence of the Sultan of Kedah. The 'Bunga Mas' tribute was sent to Siam from Perak in 1819. In complying with Siamese orders, however, the unfortunate Taju'd-din had brought no relief to his own state. While the operations in Perak were continuing, he was being asked for war-boats and rice by Siam, and he was ordered to ensure that no rice from Kedah went to Penang.

This cold war between Siam and Kedah reached a crisis in 1821. In that year the Sultan of Kedah was summoned in person to Bangkok. The Siamese were not satisfied with the conduct of affairs in Perak; further demands on Ahmad Taju'd-din for war-supplies had not been met, and reports had reached Bangkok that the Sultan had been in contact with Siam's enemy, Burma. The summons to Bangkok meant that the Sultan would be required to answer charges and, fearing for his liberty, and possibly his life, Taju'd-din refused to go.

Siamese reaction was swift and violent. A Siamese army under the command of the Raja of Ligor (known as the Chau Phya, an official of the Siamese government) invaded Kedah. In a short campaign the country was laid waste with great loss of life and many atrocities. Kedah Malays sought refuge in Province Wellesley and the island of Penang, and the Sultan himself crossed the strait from Prai and asked for the protection of the Penang government. Kedah's military unpreparedness and lack of a defensive alliance with some stronger power had led to the tragedy of this invasion. Ironically, the East India Company,

[1] R. O. Winstedt and R. J. Wilkinson, 'A History of Perak', *JRASMB*, Vol. 12, pt. 1, p. 64.

which had refused such a military pact, now found itself in the role of protector to Ahmad Taju'd-din.

These events caused alarm in Penang. The Siamese had gained control of Kedah, and across the strait from Penang lay the Siamese fleet. The Chau Phya sent a haughty message to the Governor of Penang, demanding that the Kedah Sultan should be surrendered to him, and threatening to break off trade and friendly relations if this were not done. Governor Phillips refused this demand but, at the same time, was not prepared to meet the Sultan's request for military forces to restore him in Kedah.

The Penang government was faced by a dilemma. It sent soldiers to Province Wellesley to check Siamese troops from penetrating there in pursuit of fugitives. The tension between Penang and Kedah, however, still remained. Trade was disrupted; the Siamese could prevent essential foodstuffs from reaching the island, and there was a possibility of further Siamese aggression from Kedah against Province Wellesley, or against Penang itself. Siam now seemed to have an opportunity of nullifying the cession of Penang thirty-five years previously. To add to the worries of the Penang government, Taju'd-din, unable to get help from the Company, was corresponding with Burma and Selangor for a combined invasion of Kedah. The Penang government was even less anxious to have Burmese influence in Kedah than Siamese. Quite apart from the Kedah situation, the Penang government had also been concerned for some time both to increase trade with Siam, and to establish more favourable customs regulations there.

On the question of trade, Penang made representations to Bangkok in 1818 and 1819, and sent an unofficial agent in 1821. Acting on reports and advice from Penang, the Governor-General in India also sent an ambassador to the court of Siam in 1822. The man chosen was John Crawfurd, a scholar, knowledgeable on Malayan affairs and later to become Resident at Singapore. The aim of this Crawfurd mission was principally to establish good relations between the Company and Siam, to obtain Siamese acknowledgment of the Company's right to Penang, and to seek ways and means of fostering a peaceful and expanding trade between the two. A secondary motive was to seek the restoration of the Sultan of Kedah. Further, the mission was to be of a fact-finding nature, for the Company's knowledge of Siamese affairs was very vague.

Crawfurd achieved little success, finding the Siamese hard bargainers, while he himself was not a great diplomat.[1] He came away with the impression that the Siamese had acknowledged the fact of a British Penang, but with no firm agreement either on this issue or on trade. The Siamese, far from agreeing to restore Ahmad Taju'd-din, whose intrigues from Penang had angered them further, pressed for his transfer as their prisoner, and for the payment of the Company's 10,000 dollar pension to a nominee of their own. The most valuable result of Crawfurd's mission, from the Company's point of view, was the general information which he collected. This was published in book form six years later.[2] It had the immediate effect of stressing the difficulties of trading with Siam, and also of belittling the importance of Siam's military power.

While Crawfurd was in Bangkok, the Siamese hold on Kedah and on Perak, where Kedah officials had been replaced by Siamese or by pro-Siamese Malays, was being challenged. In Kedah the Siamese garrisons were faced by guerilla-warfare, while the Bugis Sultan of Selangor was invited to help drive out the Siamese elements from Perak. In 1822 Perak was liberated from Siam, but paid instead a tribute in tin to Sultan Ibrahim of Selangor in return for his services.

During 1823 and 1824 little general change took place in the Kedah-Perak-Penang situation, but a number of significant incidents occurred. Two missions were sent by the Company to the Raja of Ligor to ask for military co-operation with the British in the Anglo-Burmese war which had just begun. Neither mission was a success; it was discovered that, in any case, the Raja of Ligor could take no important measures without the approval of Bangkok. At the same time the Raja of Ligor was preparing to send

---

[1] The Siamese felt no need for trade with the West at this time, and were reluctant to sign treaties in which they saw political dangers. They discouraged European merchants by restrictive trade practices.

[2] *Journal of an Embassy from the Governor-General of India to the Courts of Siam and Cochin-China*, London, 1828.

reinforcements to Kedah, and to invade Perak and restore Siamese supremacy there. In August 1824 a new Governor, Robert Fullerton, arrived at Penang, and he began to take a much bolder and more independent line than his predecessors. In particular, he was in favour of taking up a stronger policy with the Siamese in order to prevent the spread of their influence in the Malay States, with its possible dangers for Penang. He pressed the Governor-General to make further representations to Siam, and this led to the mission of Captain Henry Burney to the Raja of Ligor in 1825.

Burney's instructions were to discover the Siamese attitude to the continuing Anglo-Burmese war, and also to question the Raja of Ligor about Kedah, and about the possibilities of a commercial treaty with Siam. He was also to discuss a possible mission to Bangkok. While these talks were still in progress,[1] Fullerton warned the Raja of Ligor about his threatened invasion of Perak and, by this time, of Selangor also. On his own initiative and authority, Fullerton despatched gun-boats to the Trang river-estuary in May 1825 to check the sailing of a fleet of 300 war-vessels down the west coast of the Peninsula. This was a piece of sheer bluff, but it worked; the sea invasion was called off.

The Raja of Ligor now made plans to control Perak and Selangor by sending armies overland. The Sultan of Perak had earlier been persuaded by Siamese envoys to write to Ligor, asking for assistance against Selangor. It was in this atmosphere of threatened attacks on Perak and Selangor that Burney talked to the Raja of Ligor in July 1825. A Preliminary Treaty was drawn up. Burney was to take this to India, and, if it were accepted by the Governor-General, Burney would return to Ligor and accompany the Raja to Bangkok, where the Preliminary Treaty would be used as a basis of negotiations to settle the questions at issue between the Company and Siam. By the terms of this treaty, the Raja of Ligor promised to send no Siamese forces by land or sea to Perak and Selangor; the Company promised to intervene in Perak and Selangor by diplomacy in order to settle the quarrel between the two states. As for Kedah, the Company made pledges on

[1] Burney made two visits to Ligor; in January and in July–August 1825.

behalf of the Sultan in return for his restoration. He was to send the 'Bunga Mas' every three years to Bangkok, together with 4,000 dollars a year. The Company intended to increase the Sultan's annual pension to help him pay this sum. The Raja of Ligor declared that, if Bangkok agreed to this, he would withdraw his opposition, and not attack Kedah from land or sea. The rest of the treaty dealt with a common policy for suppressing piracy,[1] and the possibilities of a commercial agreement at Bangkok.

Burney took this treaty to India, where its terms were agreed to, and he returned to Ligor as the Company's envoy to the Siamese Court. The Raja of Ligor accompanied him to Bangkok and took part in the subsequent talks. While these events were happening, Fullerton at Penang received news of the Preliminary Treaty, which he described as 'extremely satisfactory', and he sent John Anderson, Secretary to the Penang Government, on a peace-making mission to the Sultans of Perak and Selangor. Anderson was well received in both states. Sultan Ibrahim of Selangor agreed to withdraw the Bugis contingent, which was stationed in Perak under Raja Hassan. He also agreed to regard the River Bernam as the frontier between Selangor and Perak, and to make no further claims to suzerainty or tribute in relation to Perak. Sultan Abdullah of Perak accepted the same river-boundary, and undertook not to interfere in the affairs of Selangor. He still retained some fears of the Siamese, and was willing to send the 'Bunga Mas' in order to avoid the fate of Kedah, if the Penang government advised him to do so.

Perak's fears of Siamese activities were not without cause. Within a few weeks of signing the Preliminary Treaty the Raja of Ligor sent a small force to Perak to assist the Sultan in his government. The object was to establish a dominant pro-Siamese faction around the Sultan, and to gain Siamese control by diplomatic pressure. Evasive answers were given from Ligor when Fullerton protested from Penang at this early violation of the Preliminary Treaty.

Burney's mission to Bangkok lasted from the end of 1825 to

[1] This appeared commonly in such treaties and was little more than a formality.

June 1826. He had instructions both from India and from Penang. The Governor-General stressed the main aims of his mission as the restoration of friendly relationships between the Company and Siam and, in particular, an assurance to the Siamese government that recent British victories in the Anglo-Burmese war did not indicate any plans for the expansion of British power in Siam or the Malay Peninsula. Other issues such as a commercial treaty, the restoration of the Sultan of Kedah, or the independence of Perak and Selangor, were all subsidiary, and were left to Burney's discretion.

Fullerton, who was invited by the Governor-General to express his views, made a very different approach. He instructed Burney to put the question of the Malay States first and foremost, and to take a strong line against Siamese claims and pretensions. In the cases of Kedah and Perak, some concessions might have to be made, but the negotiations should be aimed at improving their status as much as possible. If complete independence could not be gained for Perak, Siamese claims should be limited to the sending of the 'Bunga Mas'. No Siamese claims to interfere in any other Malay states should be allowed.

Burney was faced not only with this problem of conflicting priorities, but he was given no authority to threaten the use of force, and he had little to offer by way of conciliation. His position would have been much stronger had the Company empowered him to offer Siam something from the recent British conquests on the Tenasserim coast of Burma. The Siamese were extremely suspicious of every proposal, and the treaty which was finally arrived at was a masterpiece of vagueness and ambiguity.

This Anglo-Siamese Treaty, or Treaty of Bangkok, was signed in June 1826. Its main terms were as follows:

The Siamese were to remain in control of Kedah. Sultan Ahmad Taju'd-din was not to be allowed to live in Penang, Province Wellesley, Perak, Selangor, or Burma. The English undertook 'not to permit' the 'former governor' (i.e. ex-Sultan) of Kedah or any of his followers to attack Kedah or any other Siamese territory.

The Siamese engaged not to 'go and molest, attack or disturb'

Perak and Selangor, and the English also undertook not to trouble Perak, and to ensure that Selangor did not attack Perak. In the case of Perak, however, certain openings were left to Siam. The Company promised not to interfere if Perak and Siam wished to send each other diplomatic missions of up to forty or fifty men, and also undertook not to prevent the Sultan of Perak from sending the 'Bunga Mas' to Perak, 'as heretofore', if he wished to do so.

Two other Malay states were mentioned — Kelantan and Trengganu. The Siamese intention was to show these two states as tributaries with which Siam would allow some English trade. Burney's idea was to limit Siam's relationships with Kelantan and Trengganu to the customary tribute of the 'Bunga Mas'. In the event of further Siamese interference, as had recently happened in Kedah and Perak, the Company could conclude that commerce had been obstructed or interrupted, and take what action it chose, on the grounds of a broken treaty. This clause about Kelantan and Trengganu was so delicately worded that it could be interpreted in completely opposite ways, with scope for some other shades of opinion between them.

In addition, there was a commercial agreement concerning trade between English and Siamese territories. Its provisions went some way towards reducing taxes, and standardising British trade with Siam, but they tended to be circumvented afterwards.

The treaty was ratified in India, but it was subjected to much criticism in Penang, especially by Governor Fullerton. In the Penang government there was a strong anti-Siamese group, and considerable sympathy for the Malay point of view. Fullerton held that far too much had been conceded to Siam. He, of course, was left with the distasteful task of informing Sultan Ahmad Taju'd-din that the Company could offer him no further support in his attempts to regain Kedah, and that he must remove himself from Penang. Burney, against whom this criticism was directed, defended himself by stressing, first of all, the difficulties which he had encountered in making any treaty at all with the Siamese. The fate of Kedah and its Sultan had been an essential condition for Siamese concessions elsewhere. Taju'd-din had plotted with

Siam's enemies — Burma and Selangor — and the Siamese were insistent that he should live somewhere where he could do them little harm. Selangor's independence had been proclaimed, and Perak's independence, apart from minor concessions, was also clear. As to Kelantan and Trengganu, Burney had worded this clause himself so as to appear to meet Siamese pretensions and yet give the Company a legal basis for taking action, if necessary, against any further Siamese interference in these two states.

For Burney, it may be said that it was a considerable achievement that he had secured a treaty at all. As far back as 1688 Siam had ceased to have diplomatic relationships with Western countries, and only a small beginning to resume such contacts had been made during the reign of Rama II (1809–24). Burney's treaty of 1826 was the first one which Siam had granted to a Western envoy since the seventeenth century. His success was due to the moderateness of his requests, to his patient diplomacy, and to his study and use of the Siamese language. Before he left Bangkok Burney was given the unusual honour of a farewell audience by King Rama III.

Another reason for the treaty lay in the Siamese fear of British intentions at the conclusion of the First Anglo-Burmese War in 1826. In this sense, the treaty was an early indication of a policy of calculated concessions which Siamese rulers were to make to Western countries later in the century. To the Siamese the Burney Treaty was a political necessity. They conceded only what they thought to be essential in order to preserve peace and independence.[1]

Kedah was thus left to its own fate — a curious postscript to the early negotiations for Penang. Selangor's freedom from Siamese claims was safeguarded. Perak had a partial guarantee, but the Siamese expected its Sultan to be willing to send the 'Bunga Mas'. The reference to diplomatic missions to and from Siam seemed to be closely connected with this idea, as well as creating opportunities for a further expansion of Siamese influence in Perak.

What happened in Kelantan and Trengganu would depend

[1] W. Vella, *Siam under Rama III (1824–1851)*, pp. 120–1.

upon their own powers of resistance to Siam, and with what strength the rival interpretations of the 1826 Treaty were supported.

So far as Perak was concerned, Fullerton decided to send assurances of support in case of Siamese aggression. In particular, Fullerton suspected the activities of the Raja of Ligor, whose tactics since the Preliminary Treaty of 1825 had amounted, in the Governor's view, to intimidation of the Perak Sultan. Captain James Low, with forty sepoys and a small warship, was sent as special envoy to Perak. Low's instructions were to give the Sultan verbal promises of British support, to discover what Siamese agents were in Perak and warn them to leave, and to advise the Sultan to put in writing his wish to be independent of Siam.

Captain Low was a strong supporter of the anti-Siamese group in Penang, and finding that Siamese embassies and even troops were normal visitors to Perak, he proceeded with enthusiasm to exceed his instructions. He persuaded the Sultan to remove from office Malay chiefs who had accepted Siamese bribes. He then concluded a treaty with Sultan Abdullah on October 8th, 1826, which caused protests in Siam and India, but which was defended by Fullerton in Penang.

By this treaty the Sultan promised to have no political dealings with Siam, Ligor, Selangor, or any other Malay state. He would not send the 'Bunga Mas' or any other form of tribute to any of these states, and no party from any of these states should enter Perak. He would receive British assistance, as and when necessary, to carry out these promises. The Anderson Treaty of 1825 was confirmed, and it was made clear that traders were not barred from entering Perak; the prohibitions were aimed against political interference. The Sultan offered to Britain a strip of the Dindings coastline, and a number of adjacent islands, including Pangkor.

This treaty ran exactly counter to the normal policy of the East India Company of avoiding political commitments in the Malay States. The Burney Treaty of 1826 and the Anderson Treaties of 1825 had, of course, given the Company some responsibility for the protection against Siam of Perak, Selangor,

Kelantan and Trengganu, but none of these gave such a firm alliance with a Malay ruler as this treaty negotiated by Low. Moreover Low had himself interfered in the affairs of Perak by persuading the Sultan to change his administration. It was a classic example of a bold policy carried out by a man on the spot, which would not be favourably viewed by a distant Governor-General in Council in India.

Low committed a further act of interference under the orders of Fullerton, and with the consent of the Sultan of Perak, when he attacked a pirate-centre on the Kurau River and captured Udin, its chief. Udin was in league with the Raja of Ligor to stir up trouble in Perak, and Low sent him to the Raja for trial as a pirate. The Raja of Ligor claimed that Kurau was in Kedah, and that Udin was a Siamese official, and therefore Low had violated Siamese territorial rights; moreover he denounced the Low Treaty with Perak as a piece of sharp practice.

The Raja of Ligor's views reached India, supported by reports from Burney, who now seemed to have adopted a pro-Siamese policy.[1] A sharp rebuke was administered by the Governor-General to the Penang government, and Low received heavy criticism. Pending further investigation, he was suspended from all political activity.

Fullerton defended Low's actions as well as his own. He proved satisfactorily that Udin was a pirate who had been employed by the Raja of Ligor, and that Kurau was in Perak; the River Krian marked the joint border of Perak and Province Wellesley. Accordingly, the Governor-General reinstated Low and withdrew some of the previous censures. The 1826 Treaty with Perak was, apparently, never confirmed in India, yet on later occasions it was invoked by Sultans of Perak who requested aid, and it was taken as binding by the Company and the British Government.

The Low Treaty successfully reinsured Perak against Siamese attacks or infiltrations. Kedah received no such support. Following the Burney Treaty, the Sultan of Kedah was asked to move to Malacca, but he refused to go until 1831, after his pension had

[1] Burney probably saw his own treaty endangered by Low's actions in Perak.

been temporarily stopped and he had been threatened that he might be removed by force. Taju'd-din had used Penang as a headquarters for rallying Malay support to his cause, and a strong rising against the Siamese in Kedah in 1831 met with success at first. The Siamese were able to reconquer Kedah largely because the Penang government patrolled the coastline to prevent supplies from Penang reaching the Malay rebels. Governor Ibbetson of Penang even ordered attacks on rebel boats. He was reminded from India that the Burney Treaty did not require armed co-operation with Siam.

In 1836 Taju'd-din left Malacca on the pretext of a visit to Deli in Sumatra. Instead he sailed northwards to Bruas in Perak, and began to gather a Malay force for an invasion of Kedah. When he refused advice from Penang to return to Malacca, two ships were sent to scatter his boats and escort him back there.

Another rebellion against the Siamese in Kedah in 1838 was crushed, with Penang once again co-operating in a blockade of the coast, though not this time attacking rebel craft. General opinion in Penang was very much on the side of the Malay rebels, but the government held itself strictly bound by the terms of the Burney Treaty to aid the Siamese against any threatened restoration of the Kedah Sultan.

Finally, in 1841, the Sultan sent his eldest son to Bangkok to ask for pardon and restoration. The prince took with him a letter from the Penang government urging that this request be accepted, and adding that Penang would not assist in the suppression of any further rebellions in Kedah. The Raja of Ligor was now dead and the Siamese were weary of holding down a state which brought them no profit and a great deal of trouble. The Sultan's submission was accepted in 1842. Siamese officials were withdrawn from Kedah, and Ahmad Taju'd-din was restored to a smaller kingdom.[1] One of the areas partitioned from the old Kedah became the new Malay state of Perlis, independent of Kedah though also under Siamese protection. Taju'd-din tried to compensate himself for loss of territory by seizing, in 1843, the Krian district of Perak to

[1] A Siamese method of punishing a rebellious state was to divide it under separate rulers. Patani was divided for the same reason.

the south. There followed a long dispute in which Penang became involved on behalf of Perak. Finally, in 1848, under the pressure of threats from Penang, the Kedah troops were withdrawn from Krian, and the matter ended there.

By the mid-nineteenth century, Siamese influence on the west coast of Malaya had been restricted to Perlis and Kedah, which sent customary tokens of allegiance, but had their own Malay rulers. Perak and Selangor were independent.

Two subjects related to the Company's settlement at Malacca, subsequent to the Anglo-Dutch Treaty of 1824, call for a brief mention. The British administration at Malacca had to deal with a very complicated problem of land-tenure. The Malacca Territory outside the town itself was in the possession of a small group of individuals, mainly Dutch, who claimed rights of ownership. By Malay custom, however, private individuals were only entitled to a revenue from the land, usually a tenth of its productive value. The ownership of the land lay with the government, which claimed to succeed to the rights of the former Malay Sultans. Since these land-'proprietors' did not usually live on — or even visit — the lands which they claimed, but 'farmed-out' the collection of their tenths to the highest bidder, agriculture suffered. Much land which could have been worked remained uncultivated, and the peasant tenants were often seriously oppressed by the middlemen tax-farmers. The problems which faced the Malacca administration included the removal of the 'proprietors' by payment of compensation, the granting of legal titles to land, and the surveying of land. In particular, there was the impossible situation whereby English law was used side by side with a system of customary Malay land-tenure. The Malay tenants were naturally conservative and suspicious of any changes which were attempted, even if these were aimed at the improvement of their own position. There was still a land problem in the state of Malacca at the end of the nineteenth century.

The second subject arose from the investigation of land-tenures in Malacca. It centred on the relationship of the small Minangkabau state of Naning, about ten miles from Malacca town, and the government of Malacca. Naning had been founded by immigration from Sumatra in the sixteenth and seventeenth centuries. In the eighteenth century its chiefs had acknowledged a nominal kind of overlordship to the Dutch at Malacca. In theory Naning was due to pay a tenth of its crops to the Dutch, but in fact this was commuted to a fixed amount of tribute which represented about a thousandth of the padi-harvest. There was little or no interference by the Dutch in the internal affairs of the little Malay state.

Lewis, a zealous Superintendent of Lands at Malacca, and Fullerton, Governor of Penang — at a period when Malacca took instructions from Penang — combined in an enquiry into the Naning-Malacca relationship. They came to the conclusion that the Naning peasant tenants were due to pay to the Malacca administration a tenth of their produce, and they proposed to appoint the Naning chiefs as tax-collectors, or to pay them pensions by way of compensation. The raayat class would not have been worse off by this arrangement, because they already paid more than a tenth to the chiefs as well as being liable for conscript labour and military service. These proposals, however, received no support in Naning, and Abdul Said, the chief, or Penghulu, of Naning, who had a high reputation among his men, opposed the introduction of such radical changes. When Abdul Said refused to pay the tenths, it was feared that the Malacca residents might follow his example. A small force of troops was sent to his capital at Taboh in 1831 to make him submit. This marked the beginning of an eleven-months' war, usually referred to as the Naning War. Forces sent from Malacca suffered from a lack of knowledge of the country, and the complete absence of anything resembling a road. Abdul Said was assisted for a time by Malays from the neighbouring state of Rembau. In the end, the East India Company spent £100,000 and engaged some 1,400 troops to win this war. Naning was incorporated into Malacca, with a Superintendent and village headmen responsible for the collection of the tenths. Abdul Said was given a house in Malacca and a pension. The amount of revenue gained from Naning did not cover the cost of its administration.

Finally, some account must be given of Siamese pressure on the

Malay states which lay on the east coast. The Burney and Low Treaties had checked the expansion of Siamese influence on the western side of the Peninsula, but the positions of both Kelantan and Trengganu were by no means settled. Kelantan, bordering on Siam, suffered most from Siamese demands. In addition to the 'Bunga Mas', the ruler of Kelantan was troubled by irregular demands for money or services. By the 1830s Kelantan, although nominally under its Malay ruler, was for all practical purposes almost a Siamese state. Trengganu put up a stronger resistance and was virtually independent, apart from sending the 'Bunga Mas' every three years.[1]

Both Kelantan and Trengganu were mentioned in the Burney Treaty of 1826, but the clause was open to conflicting interpretations. These east-coast states were of little interest in themselves to Penang. The trade links between the east coast of the Peninsula and Singapore, together with Singapore's political supremacy, from 1832, over the other Straits Settlements, caused the Singapore government, however, to keep a watchful eye on Siamese activities.

The main incidents centred around a civil war in Pahang (1858-63). The Pahang ruler had the title of Bendahara, and he was nominally a viceroy of the Sultan of Johore. Since the great weakening and division of Johore, however, he had been an independent ruler. When Bendahara Sewa Raja Ali died in Pahang in 1857, he was succeeded by his elder son, Tun Mutahir. Another son, Wan Ahmad, claimed that the old Bendahara had intended to make the two brothers joint rulers. He also protested that Mutahir had not appeared at his father's death-bed to receive his last wishes. Both Mutahir and Ahmad found armed supporters, and a long war of raids and skirmishes broke out. The Governor of the Straits Settlements, Colonel Cavenagh, concerned by the disruption of trade with Pahang, offered to mediate between the two brothers. Mutahir would agree only to his brother being pensioned off, a condition which Ahmad rejected.

In 1861 Ahmad was driven out of Pahang and made his way to

---

[1] During the reign of Sultan Omar (1839–76), Trengganu ceased for a time to send the 'Bunga Mas', but the practice was revived later.

Bangkok to seek help. At the Siamese court there was another
political refugee, Mahmud Muzaffar Shah, ex-Sultan of Lingga.
Mahmud was a descendant of Sultan Abdu'l Rahman, and had
been deposed by the Dutch in 1857 for constantly intriguing
against them. Reviving the old Johore claims over Pahang, he
sought to become Sultan of Pahang, but, gaining no support,
he attached himself to Wan Ahmad's side to further his own
ends.

The presence in Bangkok of a claimant to the throne of Johore
and another to the Bendaharaship of Pahang gave the Siamese
government an opportunity for interfering in Pahang. In 1862 a
Siamese warship, accompanied by a fleet of small boats, landed
these two princes in Trengganu as a taking-off place for operations
in Pahang.

Three other Siamese warships arrived at about the same time.
The ruler of Trengganu, who had previously given support to
Ahmad, had managed to keep himself independent of Siam apart
from the customary payment of the 'Bunga Mas', and the idea
that the Siamese Ministers intended to place the ex-Sultan of
Lingga on the throne of Trengganu has not been established. At
this juncture, all that can safely be said is that Siam was helping
both Ahmad and Mahmud, and waiting on events in Pahang.[1]

Governor Cavenagh had enquiries made in Bangkok about the
Siamese moves, but he received disarming replies. He was suspicious of Siamese intentions, and regarded the 1826 Treaty as a
statement of the independence of Kelantan and Trengganu.
Pahang, which was not mentioned in that treaty, was clearly
independent of Siam. Quite apart from his own feelings, Cavenagh
was pressed to take action against Ahmad and Mahmud by interested parties in Singapore. Merchants complained of loss of
trade, and Temenggong Ibrahim, who himself aspired to rule
over Johore and Pahang, had no wish to see the ex-Sultan of
Lingga making any similar claim. Cavenagh obtained authority
from the Governor-General to take what measures seemed to him

[1] Cf. L. A. Mills, 'British Malaya, 1824–1867', p. 165, and N. Tarling,
'British Policy in the Malay Peninsula and Archipelago', *JRASMB*, Vol. 30,
pt. 3, 1957, pp. 70–1.

necessary to protect British interests and maintain peace in the Peninsula.

He first tried to persuade the Siamese to remove the two princes from Trengganu, but when these efforts failed and the north-east monsoon was almost due, in November, 1862, he sent a warship to the Trengganu coast. When his demand that the ex-Sultan of Lingga should be returned immediately to Bangkok was refused, the fort at Trengganu was shelled.

This brought no immediate results, and Cavenagh's action was later condemned in the British House of Commons. In March 1863, however, the Siamese did remove Mahmud to Siam, and he intrigued no more in the Peninsula. Two months later, with the death of Mutahir, the Pahang civil war petered out. Ahmad succeeded to the title of Bendahara. He was clever enough to keep on good terms with both Siam and Singapore, without losing any of his independence. Twenty years later he changed his title from Bendahara to Sultan.

By 1863 any Siamese forward movement in relation to the Malay states of the east coast came to an end. Kelantan still remained closely linked with Siam, but Trengganu, encouraged by Singapore, managed to steer an independent course, apart from the customary offerings. In a later chapter Siam's relations with these Malay states about the end of the nineteenth century, and the transfer of their protection to Britain in 1909, are discussed.[1]

The possibility of some form of Siamese control over the whole of the Malay Peninsula was not a remote one in the nineteenth century. The check to Siamese expansion came partly from the Straits Settlements, when independent action was taken by officials who risked censure from India and London. Another factor was the will to independence shown by the Malay rulers themselves. Persistent though they were, the Siamese tended to withdraw in the face of determined opposition.

DATES OF EVENTS

1817   Perak invaded by Kedah on Siamese orders.
1819   'Bunga Mas' sent by Perak.

[1] See Chapter 13.

I

1821 {Kedah Sultan summoned to Bangkok.
{Kedah invaded by Raja of Ligor.

1822   Crawfurd mission to Bangkok.
        Perak liberated from Siamese with Bugis help.

1824–5   Further moves by Raja of Ligor for invasions of Perak and
          Selangor, checked partly by Governor Fullerton of Penang.

1825   Preliminary Treaty between Burney and Raja of Ligor.
        Anderson Treaties with Perak and Selangor.

1826   Burney mission to Bangkok. Anglo-Siamese Treaty. Low Treaty
        with Perak.

1831–2   Naning War in Malacca.

1842   Kedah Sultan restored: Perlis created.

1858–63   Civil War in Pahang.

1862   Siamese fleet at Trengganu.
        Trengganu fort shelled.

1863   Wan Ahmad becomes Bendahara of Pahang.

Chapter 8

THE MALAY STATES IN THE MID-NINETEENTH CENTURY

Geography determined the pattern of settlement in Malaya, and the typical kingdom was based on settlements along a broad river valley. The capital lay near the river estuary, where the ruler could control the movements of people into and out of the state, organise defence against any enemy, and levy tolls and taxes on imports and exports. The sea and the rivers provided the main, and often the sole, means of communication, and jungle, mountain, or swamp acted as natural barriers between the scattered areas of riverside settlements.

The population of these river-states was small and scattered; in 1850 it may have been about 300,000 in all the states together. The kampong was the unit of social life, and the state-capitals had a kampong-like appearance, with the addition of one or two larger and more imposing buildings such as the Sultan's residence and mosque.

Each state was a world unto itself, and there was no idea of a larger Malay world, or of a union of Malay states. There had, of course, been an earlier tradition of a dominant state in the southern part of the Peninsula which demanded tokens of allegiance and tribute from the other settlement areas. Malacca in the fifteenth century, and, to a lesser extent, Johore in the sixteenth and seventeenth centuries, had exercised some authority over less powerful neighbours. By the mid-nineteenth century, however, this situation was changed.[1] A Malay state sometimes exercised temporary control over its neighbour, as in the case of Kedah and Perak in 1821, or Selangor and Perak in 1822, and some states were subject to a measure of foreign overlordship from Siam. The typical

[1] Old claims were sometimes revived, but not usually with much effect.

relationship, however, of one state to another was that of isolation and self-containment. Broadly speaking, each state went its own way, and though there were plenty of wars and disturbances, these were usually civil wars arising from domestic disputes within the states themselves.

Even among the Malay population the sense of common racial feeling did not extend beyond the state. A Malay from another state might be regarded as a foreigner, although Islam did provide a common bond. Many Malays were descendants of immigrants from Sumatra. The majority of these were Minangkabaus, but there were also Korinchi, Rawa, Mandiling, and Batak groups. In addition, there were Malays from Acheh and Java as well as Malays of old Peninsular stock. There was a small but influential group of Arabs and people of mixed Arab-Malay descent, and there were Bugis, whose forefathers had come from Celebes. Despite a common general culture, the Malay population was very much aware of the differences between these groups as shown in their languages and customs.

Small Chinese groups existed in most states before the nineteenth century; they lived sometimes in separate villages known as 'Kampong China'. From the 1820s onwards a very much larger Chinese immigration movement was taking place in Sungei Ujong, Selangor, and Perak. This was associated with the development of large-scale tin-mining. The bigger Chinese mining-settlements not only changed the balance of population in these areas to something like equal numbers of Malays and Chinese; they also represented a large element living in, but outside the normal political administration of, a Malay state.

The Indian element in the population was small, and was mainly linked with trade at west-coast ports. It was the development of public services and plantation agriculture towards the end of the nineteenth century which brought about large-scale immigration from India and Ceylon.

The government of the Malay States was organised on very personal and autocratic lines.[1] The formal head of the state was

[1] For a detailed discussion, see J. M. Gullick, *Indigenous Political Systems of Western Malaya*, University of London, 1956.

the Sultan, a title used in all states except Negri Sembilan, which had an elected Yang-di-Pertuan Besar, and Pahang, whose ruler still bore the title Bendahara. The Sultan symbolised the unity of the state, and had a duty to preserve it. He made all major appointments and was the source of all authority; he alone, within the state, had powers of life and death. His person was sacred, and his public appearances were surrounded by ritual and ceremony. He was entitled to the greatest respect, and when a new Sultan was installed the chiefs of the state made a formal and humble public act of submission to him.

It is necessary, however, to distinguish between the Sultan's high position of honour as head of the state and the realities of government. The Sultan was responsible for defence and foreign policy, but the government of the state itself was largely in the hands of the appointed chiefs. The chiefs also had a say in determining the succession. A new Sultan would normally be a member of the royal family of the state, but his relationship to the previous Sultan could vary. Any aspirant to the throne needed the support of the chiefs. In practice, the chiefs would be disposed to support a claimant, who, as Sultan, would interfere as little as possible with their own rights and privileges. In Perak there existed a whole framework of offices through which a potential Sultan was expected to pass before he reached the throne. At any point on this promotion-ladder he might be overlooked by the chiefs if, for any reason, they did not wish him eventually to become Sultan.

The state was divided out into districts usually based upon sections of a river and its tributaries, or, as in the case of Selangor, upon the separate river valleys of which the state was composed. Each district was controlled by a chief whose authority came from the Sultan, but who was very much his own master in his own district. The revenue of the district came from taxes on crops and mining land, and from tolls charged on trade-goods which passed along the river in either direction. This revenue was the personal income of the district chief, who was normally liable by the terms of his office to send a proportion of it in money or commodities to the Sultan. In his own region the Sultan received the revenues in the same manner as a district chief.

From his income the chief supported many relatives of his own aristocratic class who assisted him in one capacity or another, and he also met the expenses of a large household. The most important item of expenditure was the upkeep of a small private army of retainers who acted as a personal bodyguard, manned the stockade from which the district was controlled, and accompanied the chief on his journeys.

When Munshi Abdullah, whose life had been spent in Malacca and Singapore, noted the presence of large numbers of armed men in the east coast states, he was probably referring to these bands of armed retainers, who were just standing around, prepared for trouble when it arose.

The chief was responsible for the defence of his own district and also for the maintenance of law and order. Each village had its own headman, or penghulu, who dealt with minor offences, but any serious trouble was brought to the chief's notice. He could either act as judge himself, or delegate a kinsman to act on his behalf. There were no regular law-courts or codes of law. The courtroom was, as likely as not, the house of the chief, and decisions were made according to custom, but with wide powers of discretion in the hands of the chief, who usually kept the proceeds of fines and confiscations which he had ordered. Only the Sultan had the right to order a death-penalty, but even this power was usurped at times by the chiefs.

Malay society was divided into two clearly marked groups, a class of nobles and a class of subjects (raayat). The nobility itself was a hierarchy which was sub-divided into many grades from the Sultan downwards, but it stood apart from the peasantry, and held important privileges and exemptions. This nobility included relatives of the Sultan and members of families who could claim the right to fill certain chieftainships. This royal and non-royal nobility was based almost entirely on the principle of birth and family descent; only in unusual circumstances, or by exceptional ability, could a man born in the lower class rise to an aristocratic position. When this did happen, the man concerned might often be an immigrant whose own family background was unknown. For their fighting ability or for their wealth as traders, some groups of immigrants were by this time accepted as having equal social status with the Malay ruling class. These included some Achinese and Javanese, Arabs and Bugis.

At the other end of the social scale was the subject class, or raayat. This was made up of the mass of ordinary villagers, engaged in farming and fishing and living their lives, subject to the force of village opinion, to the authority of the penghulu, and to the requirements of the district chief. For many of these people the Sultan was a remote figure whom they might never see. The villages varied in size from a handful of houses to a hundred or more, arranged in clusters along the river bank. The district chief himself would live in a large village, and even the state-capital was not very different in character from this village setting. Most of the farming was of a subsistence nature, and the work was done by family groups. The frequent incidence of civil war, and the demands made by the chiefs for labour and supplies, discouraged the raayat from farming on a bigger scale or saving money. There was a little sale of surplus foodstuffs and cash-crops, and to this could be added sometimes a small income from the collection and sale of jungle produce for export. The raayat had little chance to give their labour in return for wages.

Two customs affecting the lives of the raayat were widespread. The 'kerah' was a system by which the chiefs could call for compulsory labour for any purpose, at any time, and for any length of time. This labour might be required for the building of a stockade, the clearing of a river, the manning of boats for a journey, or the erection of a hall or mosque. There was no payment for this forced labour, which was recruited through the village headmen, but normally food would be provided for the workers. The nature and purpose of the work, and the number of workers required, were matters entirely at the discretion or whim of the chief.

The other custom was debt-slavery, or, more accurately, debt-bondage. When a subject was in need of money or goods, he went to his chief and a loan was arranged with a fixed date for repayment. If the debtor was unable to repay the loan after a further period of grace, he became one of the chief's bondsmen, and had to carry out any orders which he was given until the debt was repaid.

In the case of a married man, the status of bondage would also include his wife and family and their descendants. In some cases the debtor would be taken into the chief's household and provided with food and clothing. His services for the chief would not count towards the repayment of the debt, and if he was given money, it added to the original debt. In this way, it was often quite impossible for a bondsman to be able to save and pay off his original debt, and if he married, or his children married, this only served to increase the number of debt-bondsmen. This system provided the chiefs with a large supply of unpaid labour for all purposes, including the domestic work of the household; it also added to the ranks of his private army and increased his own prestige. When a chief wished to raise money, or was tired of his bondsmen, he could sometimes transfer them to another chief to whom they were strangers, and they might suffer by the transfer.

In much smaller numbers, there existed a class of slaves doing the same work as the bondsmen, but with no prospect of redeeming their status except by an act of grace on the part of the chief who owned them. These slaves were non-Muslims — Africans, aborigines, and Bataks.

Malay society in the mid-nineteenth century was thus composed of two extremes, a class of rulers and a class of subjects. The ruling class had wide powers in administering the law and in demanding services. As individuals, they had a large retinue at their beck and call, some of whom were fighting-men whose services were paid for, while others were debt-bondsmen and bondswomen. The social classes were clearly apart, and there was little or no chance of a subject entering the ranks of the rulers. The question arises — to what extent was the subject-class oppressed, and what means, if any, had this class of defending its own interests?

In practice there were a number of checks on the powers of the chiefs. One who oppressed his people might find them drifting away to other districts. During times of civil war whole village communities moved out of danger areas to set up new homes; it was a possible solution in times of general hardship. Again, an individual, goaded too far, might 'run amok', leaving a trail of murdered people of either class whose deaths could be indirectly ascribed to the chief. When making use of the 'kerah' system, the chief had to provide sufficient food, or his workers melted away. Even with his bondsmen he must remember that good treatment would bring the best response. The chief could obviously commit individual acts of oppression with impunity, but to resort to a general oppression of his people would be to work against his own interests. Their labour provided his income and maintained his position; in time of danger they were his defence.

The power of the chiefs depended upon the strength of their following, and this in turn depended upon the amount of their income. In states where there was little or no mining, the Sultan, who was in the best situation to profit from the normal varieties of river-trade, was wealthier than his chiefs, and correspondingly stronger. The development, in some states, of large-scale tin-mining gave advantages to those chiefs on whose land tin was found. They could obtain a royalty for the tin taken from their land, a tax from the river-borne tin on its way to the coast, and taxes on the commodities imported by river for the mining communities.

The development of large-scale tin-mining in the Malay States arose on the one hand from the existence of merchant capital in the Straits Settlements, and on the other from the enterprise of Malay chiefs, who invited Straits merchants to organise the opening-up of new tin-fields in their territories. If the mining community was comparatively small, the Malay chief might take a share in the management of the mine, and in its profits. In the case of a larger community, the chief would participate and profit only as a landlord and tax-gatherer.

By 1850 the tin industry was very largely Chinese. It was financed by Chinese merchants from Penang, Malacca, or Singapore. For several reasons, Malay labour was not easily available. Most Malays of the raayat class were either not free to make a change of occupation, or were already sufficiently occupied in subsistence-farming. Malays had taken part in small-scale tin-mining as a part-time employment; generally they had no desire to make it a full-time and sole occupation. Furthermore, the new mining areas of the 1840s and 1850s were in desolate, swampy, places where there was little or no Malay settlement. The life of the Malay was bound up in his village community on the riverside; for him there was no attraction in the pioneer conditions of an isolated mining camp.

In any case the financiers of the mining enterprises were Chinese, and they naturally appointed Chinese managers and headmen, and Chinese agents to recruit labour.[1] Chinese labour was obtained first from the Straits Settlements. When these could no longer meet the demand, there developed a recruitment drive for immigrants from the provinces of south China. The large Chinese mining camps in Perak and Selangor in the mid-nineteenth century lay outside the normal political life of the Malay state. Under its own 'Capitan China', the Chinese community, which was almost entirely male, lived its own life and settled its own disputes. Its contact with the Malay authorities was fundamentally an economic one, and consisted in the payment of royalties or rents for the land, and taxes on the tin produced and on the commodities imported. A political situation could — and did — arise when there were quarrels about land or taxes between the Malay chief and the Chinese miners. The Malay chiefs also had cause for worry when disputes arose between rival groups of Chinese miners within the same state. What was virtually a form of Chinese civil war could take place within the confines of a Malay state, and there was no Malay authority strong enough to suppress it. A third possibility lay in the event of a long drawn-out civil war between Malay chiefs and their supporters. Either side, seeking to gain victory, might enlist support from the Chinese mining communities by the offer of rewards.

The Chinese peasants who arrived to seek a new living in Malaya came to make money for themselves and their families, and not to make wars. A combination of circumstances could, however, transform a peaceful mining group into an armed and dangerous fighting force. The rough conditions of pioneer settlements, the break with a traditional way of life and the

[1] The Chinese had also developed their own mining techniques. See Chapter 11.

influence of the family, and the temptation to spend the money earned in mining tin on spirits and gambling, all contributed to an element of lawlessness. The early mining camps included among their inhabitants a proportion of criminals and adventurers whose aim was to gain a fortune quickly by their wits, or by methods of intimidation. Finally, the Chinese miners settling in Malaya either were, or became, members of one Secret Society or another. The organisation of these Secret Societies ran right through the Chinese mining industry from mine-owner to the humblest worker.

The Secret Society had its benevolent side, and it offered much to the raw immigrant in need of security. It guaranteed him protection of his person and his interests. It gave him physical protection if he needed it, and if he died it looked after his funeral and sent money to his dependents. It created a strong bond of fellowship between a man and those with whom he was working; they were all members of the same brotherhood. All this was very acceptable to the immigrant miner. On the other hand, there was a high price to be paid. The Society demanded the utmost secrecy about its affairs. To discuss these matters with non-members was a serious crime which normally carried the death penalty. Allegiance to the society and to its leaders had to be absolute, and unquestioning obedience was expected. A member had to be ready to take up arms at his leader's bidding, and to attack any group or individual whom the Society had denounced as an enemy. The Society held trials and passed judgment on its own members and, at times, ordered and carried out sentences of death. The political authority to which the Chinese mining communities in the Malay States were subject in the mid-nineteenth century was the leadership of their own Secret Societies.

The Malay States of the mid-nineteenth century contained many elements of potential disorder. The power of the Sultan within his own state was often weak; many chiefs were strong, and a law unto themselves. Disputed successions were the most frequent causes of civil wars, and the keeping of armed retainers and debt-bondsmen provided the chief with a private army. The development of large Chinese mining settlements created new problems of law and order, for which the existing political and judicial structure of the Malay state had no ready answer.

It is not possible to trace evenly the course of events in every Malay state. Earlier in this book emphasis was placed on the Malay kingdom of Malacca, and its successor-state in Johore. Later, those states which had some connection with Portuguese or Dutch Malacca, or with the Bugis came under our scrutiny. More recently, those states associated with Siamese claims or influence from the Straits Settlements held our attention. By the end of the nineteenth century all the Malay States were under some measure of Siamese or British influence or control; it therefore seems convenient here to attempt a brief survey of the States as they were by the 1850s or 1860s.

All except one of the names of the states which comprise Federal Malaya today were in use in the mid-nineteenth century. The exception was the little group of states lying between Malacca, Selangor, Pahang, and Johore, now known as Negri Sembilan. The nucleus of the present nine states was there at this time, consisting mainly of inland states which had been settled by Malays from the Minangkabau area of Sumatra, from the fifteenth century onwards. This immigration had taken place over a long period and in small numbers, and the earliest immigrants had come to terms with a small number of Malacca chiefs who were already established in the same area. The Minangkabaus were, for the most part, people skilled in agriculture, and these states were essentially inland settlements. They had access to the Malacca Straits along the Linggi and Muar rivers. A loose form of political confederation had existed from 1773, when the tradition of a leader elected from one of four states began. This federal Head of State, or Yang-di-Pertuan, was probably intended at first as a war-leader for the purpose of a common defence against the Bugis. Each state, however, still had its own ruler, jealous of his own powers.

The two most prominent Minangkabau states at the time of our survey were Sungei Ujong and Rembau, and the Linggi formed part of the boundary between them. The Linggi valley was one of the western areas of the Malay Peninsula where tin deposits had been found, and Chinese tin-miners were at work up-river in Sungei Ujong. The mining and export of this tin brought profit to Chinese towkays in the Straits Settlements, and represented an important source of income to the Malay chiefs in whose territory lay the mines or the river along which the tin passed by boat to the coast. The Malay chiefs received an income from the Chinese mine-owner for the use of the mining-land, and they also levied tolls on the river-trade in both directions. A particular source of grievance to all concerned arose, in this instance, from the fact that, for part of the course of the Linggi river, Sungei Ujong lay on the north bank and Rembau on the south bank. Tin which was mined and taxed in Sungei Ujong was again taxed by Rembau chiefs before it was allowed to reach the coast. This caused disputes between Sungei Ujong and Rembau, between Chinese merchants and Malay chiefs, and, indirectly, between Malacca (where much of this sector of the tin-trade was organised) and these two Minangkabau states. To complicate matters even more, Sungei Ujong was itself divided into two parts, ruled by rival chiefs.

The rest of the Malay states consisted of river-settlements, usually near the coast, but sometimes, as in Perak, along the valley of a long main river. All took their name from the main river which passed through the area, and this river basin was usually the chief settlement zone. In Selangor, by way of exception, five river valleys lying in an east-west direction subdivided the state into five areas of settlement and political control. Even on these rivers, in 1850, nearly all the population lived near to the coast.

For Kedah the first half of the nineteenth century had certainly been a time of troubles. There had been, first, the heavy demands of Siam, including the order, in 1816, to invade Perak. Then followed the Siamese invasion in 1821, and a Siamese government, backed by armed forces, for the next twenty-one years. Guerrilla warfare and rebellions on behalf of the exiled Sultan marked this period, with its further tale of human miseries. The restoration of the Sultan in 1842 was accompanied by a Siamese reduction of the size of Kedah, and the creation of a small northern neighbour in Perlis. As though Kedah had not suffered enough warfare and tension, the restored Sultan tried to take by force the Krian district of Perak, and provoked a frontier situation which was only ended by intervention from Penang.

Neither Kedah nor Perlis were strong or wealthy states in 1850. Perlis was a new and small state; Kedah was impoverished and depopulated. Both were obliged to send tokens of tribute to Bangkok.

On the opposite coast, Kelantan and Trengganu were claimed by Siam as dependencies. Kelantan, like Kedah, was subject to demands and orders from Siam. In 1831 the Raja of Patani took refuge in Kelantan after being defeated by the Siamese. The Sultan of Kelantan was then compelled to surrender the fugitive, and to send a large indemnity to Bangkok. The anti-Siamese group in Penang regarded these activities as a violation of the Burney Treaty of 1826, and urged the establishment of an English 'factory' in Kelantan. A contemporary writer[1] claimed that the Sultan of Kelantan had requested such a 'factory', and that it would bring 'very considerable advantages'. Nothing came of this suggestion. Kelantan was rather remote; there was no desire for an open clash with Siam on the part of either the Penang or Singapore governments at this time. Penang, in fact, was helping the Siamese to put down rebellions in Kedah.

Weakness in external relations was combined in Kelantan, as in several other Malay states, with periods of divided authority and civil war. The death of Sultan Muhammad in 1835, without an heir, led to a struggle for power and a civil war.

Trengganu managed to avoid some of the heavier demands of Siam, but only with risks, and by granting occasional concessions in addition to the 'Bunga Mas'. A particularly capable ruler, Sultan Omar (1839–76), did much to centralise authority in the state, and to avoid dangers which too much interference in outside affairs might have brought. He refused, for instance, to help his nephew, Mahmud, the deposed Sultan of Lingga, in a scheme for reviving

[1] T. Newbold, *Political and Statistical Account of the British Settlements in the Straits of Malacca*, 2 vols., Murray, 1839.

the Johore-Pahang Sultanate under Mahmud's leadership. On the other hand, he gave assistance to Wan Ahmad in the Pahang civil war (1858–63), possibly to meet his nephew's wishes. He tried unsuccessfully to dissuade Mahmud from going to Siam, an act which brought Siamese ships to the Trengganu coast in aid of the ex-Sultan. It is likely that Siam would have preferred a weaker and more subservient ruler on the throne of Trengganu, but there is no evidence of any actual plan to depose Omar in 1862. Two years later Omar crushed the efforts of a rebel prince of his own state who had recruited fighting men from Kelantan.

The capital of Trengganu in 1836 was a haphazard patchwork of houses and shophouses, set in narrow and crooked lanes. The Sultan's palace was made of stone. There was a large Chinese quarter under a Capitan China, and the richest man was a Chinese Muslim. Fish and vegetables were plentiful, and exports included gold, tin, coffee, pepper, betel-nut, silk cloth, and fine sarongs interwoven with gold and silver thread. Opium, thread, and European cloth were imported. Conspicuous in the harbour was a fleet of beautifully painted fishing-boats.[1]

Pahang was a large but sparsely populated state, once part of the Johore Empire. With the weakening and division of this Empire in the eighteenth and early nineteenth centuries, the ruler of Pahang was independent, though still using the title Bendahara, and not that of Sultan. Pahang was torn by a civil war for five years (1858–63) after the death of Sultan Ali. It was a typical Malay war of the period, fought between the supporters of two brothers, one of whom sought help from Trengganu and Siam. There wore ambushes and raids, with more protracted fighting around stockaded positions. In the end Ahmad emerged victorious and strong because he had shown himself to be a forceful leader and had weakened his opponents among the chiefs.

Munshi Abdullah, who visited Pahang in 1838, was not very favourably impressed with what he saw. The country appeared to be fertile, but there was a lack of shops, markets, and roads, and the houses were poorly built. Men went about armed with numerous weapons. Fruit and vegetables were expensive, and

[1] Munshi Abdullah's account in *Pelayaran Abdullah*, Singapore, 1949.

people lived by keeping buffaloes, cattle, goats, and fowl. Gold and tin, and some jungle produce, were exported, and a little silk-weaving was done. In the vicinity of the capital at Pekan there was a Chinese and an Arab community. There were settlements along the Pahang river as far inland as Jelai, where gold was mined.

Johore traditionally consisted of both mainland and island elements. By the mid-nineteenth century the islands, apart from Singapore, were under the theoretical rule of the Sultan of Lingga, but he was under Dutch influence; Singapore was under the juris-diction of the English East India Company. Mainland Johore was in dispute between the son of Sultan Hussein and the son of Temenggong Abdu'l Rahman. Increasingly settlement was taking place on the mainland, the settlers including Chinese who developed flourishing pepper plantations.

Ali, son of Sultan Hussein, who died in 1835, had the misfor-tune of being both younger and less capable than Ibrahim, the son of the Temenggong, who had died ten years earlier. The East India Company was very dilatory about recognising Ali as Sultan, and Ibrahim, for his part, was unwilling to lose the start he had gained in controlling mainland Johore. An agreement was reached in 1854 by which Ali's title of Sultan was confirmed, together with a pension from the revenues of Johore, and he was given land in the district of Muar. Ibrahim and his successors, however, were recognised as having rights of sovereignty in Johore. Ibrahim died in 1862 and was succeeded by his son Abu Bakar. The final break in the claims of the descendants of Sultan Hussein came with the death of Ali in 1877. The land at Muar came under the control of Abu Bakar, and Ali's son was known only as Tunku and not as Sultan, although in the agreement of 1854 both the land and the title should have passed to Ali's heirs. By way of compensation Abu Bakar, who had the support of the Governor of the Straits Settlements, paid an increased pension to Ali's son. During the long reign of Abu Bakar (1862–95) the modern state of Johore took shape, with its capital at Johore Bahru.[1]

[1] See Chapter 13.

The wealth of the Malay States in the mid-nineteenth century lay mainly in the deposits of alluvial tin which were being increasingly worked by large mining communities. There was little known tin in the east coast states or in Johore; the main tin-fields lay on the western side of the Peninsula, in the river valleys between the mountains and the coast. There had always been tin-working in Kedah, and there were recent developments in Sungei Ujong, but the greatest expansion took place in Perak and Selangor, and we must now consider these states in a little more detail.

Around 1840 large-scale tin-mining developed in the Larut district of Perak, near modern Taiping. Long Ja'afar, the Malay chief who collected taxes in the Larut district of Perak, discovered large tin deposits in what was then a swampy and isolated part of the state. He invited Chinese business enterprise from Penang to exploit them. The Larut river was the highway for Chinese workers and the supplies they needed, as well as for the tin sent back to Penang. The population of these mining groups ran into many thousands,[1] and was divided into two rival camps. The division was on a Secret Society basis. All Secret Societies among the Chinese in the Malay Peninsula were offshoots of the Triad Society, otherwise known as the Three in One, or the Heaven, Earth, and Man Society. This was a particularly strong and widespread movement in south China during the eighteenth and nineteenth centuries, and its main political creed was opposition to Manchu rule and a restoration of the old Ming dynasty. Within the larger movement rival groups emerged, and two such groups lived and worked in adjacent territory in the Taiping-Kamunting area. These were the Ghee Hin and the Hai San, otherwise known from their districts of origin in China as the 'Si Kwans' (Four Districts), and the 'Go Kwans' (Five Districts).

The divisions between the Ghee Hin and Hai San in terms of language and place of origin were not absolutely clear, but in general the Ghee Hin were Cantonese-speaking, while the Hai San spoke Hakka or Hokkien. The Ghee Hin became centred on

[1] Various estimates have been made, none very reliable. The most quoted figure is 40,000 by 1870. Warfare caused great fluctuations.

K

Kamunting and the Hai San on the site of modern Taiping, beginning, curiously enough, near the site of the later Taiping gaol. Rivalries between these two groups existed in China and in Penang; in the environment of the early Larut mining camps these rivalries led to violence. The two groups were too close together for comfort, and the extension of mining operations led to boundary disputes and quarrels over the diversion of river water, while clashes were caused by personal incidents and provocations.

Long Ja'afar, the district chief, died in 1857, and was succeeded in office by his son, Ngah Ibrahim. Both chiefs, father and son, became wealthy on the revenues from the tin-mining, but they had no means of exercising effective control over the miners themselves. In 1862, following the massacre of a party of Ghee Hin who had unwisely entered the Taiping area and were attacked in a gambling-saloon, serious fighting broke out. The Ghee Hin were driven from their mines and fled back to Penang. Ibrahim, unable to control events, made known his support of the victors, the Hai San. Many of the Ghee Hin were Straits-born British subjects, and they appealed to the Governor of the Straits Settlements for redress. The Governor was Colonel Cavenagh, a man of action, and he demanded from the Malay government of Perak payment of compensation to the Ghee Hin. Cavenagh followed his demand by sending a warship to patrol the coast near the Larut estuary, to block the tin trade.

The Sultan of Perak passed this demand to Ibrahim, who, after some delay, agreed to come to terms. As a reward for this the Sultan conferred wider powers over Larut and Krian on Ibrahim, making him, in practice, an independent ruler there. He was also given the title of 'Mantri', one of the four main titles of the Perak nobility.

The struggle between Ghee Hin and Hai San did not end here. The Ghee Hin returned, the old rivalries resumed, and by 1872 a full-scale Chinese war was once again in progress in Larut.

Meanwhile the Malay chiefs of Perak had problems of their own. When Sultan Ahmadin died in 1806 the sons of each of his three wives were recognised as having sufficiently high status to found royal lineages. The Sultan was to be taken in turn from each of the three lines; if possible, the choice would fall on the eldest legitimate son of a previous Sultan of the same line. An aspirant to the throne normally passed through the offices of Raja-di-Hilir, Raja Bendahara, and Raja Muda, before he became Sultan. In theory this provided that the Sultan would be a man experienced in office-holding, and known by the chiefs. In practice the Sultan tended to be advanced in years by the time of his installation, and to have a short reign.[1] Also the chiefs could, and did, overlook a candidate for office whom they did not like, or who was likely to become a strong Sultan. Politics in Perak were also affected by the tendency of the chiefs to group themselves regionally, one group in Upper Perak, the other in Lower Perak. There was a danger that each of these groups might support a claimant of its own choice.

When Sultan Ali died in 1871 the order of succession to the throne differed at every point from the normal conventions. Raja Abdullah, son of Sultan Ja'afar, was heir-apparent, or Raja Muda, but he had been promoted directly to this office on his father's death, while other candidates had been by-passed. Raja Ismail was Bendahara, but he was not a descendant of the royal house on the male side. In the background was a Raja Yusuf, son of Sultan Abdullah, who had no support among the chiefs and whose claims to office they had consistently overlooked. Yusuf was unpopular, partly on the grounds of a moody personality, and partly because, during his father's lifetime, he had tried to limit the chiefs' powers. Ibrahim, the Mantri, was not directly involved in this succession question, but as the wealthiest chief in Perak his support — wherever he gave it — was extremely valuable.

The succession dispute which arose in Perak in 1871, and the renewed outbreak of fighting between the Ghee Hin and Hai San in the following year, had a direct bearing on the question of British intervention in Perak in 1874, and the whole situation is discussed more fully in the following Chapter.

In Selangor there was a counterpart to the situation in Perak. There was a Chinese mining settlement at Lukut as early as 1824,

[1] Cf. Sultan Abdullah, 1851–7; Sultan Ja'afar, 1857–65; Sultan Ali 1865–71.

and this was followed by others at Kanching in the Selangor
valley (1840), and Ampang in the Klang valley (1857). Malacca
merchants played an initial part in these mining enterprises, and
Malacca served as an outlet port for the tin, though its importance
became overshadowed later by Singapore. Each of the five main
Selangor rivers was under the authority of a district chief related
to the Sultan and, as in Larut, Chinese mining was made possible
by the enterprise of Malay chiefs wishing to raise the revenues of
their own districts.

The mining communities were organised into the same Secret
Societies as those of Perak. The Ampang miners, whose settlement marked the beginning of Kuala Lumpur, were Hai San, and
those at Kanching and Lukut were Ghee Hin. Lukut lay well south
of the other two groups, and mining there was in decline before
1860. The main rivalries lay between Kanching and Kuala Lumpur.
These two settlements were near enough to each other for occasional forays and raids to take place, and the arrival of refugees
from the Larut wars added extra bitterness to the proceedings.
Only after a Malay war had broken out in Selangor, however, did
the two Chinese centres take to large-scale fighting.

Succession to the Selangor throne was not linked with any
promotion-ladder, but it was subject, as in Perak, to pressures and
influences from the chiefs. Two Sultans' reigns spanned the period
between 1826 and 1898.[1] The ruling class of Selangor were of
Bugis or mixed-Bugis descent, and the leading chiefs and the
Sultan between them controlled five separate river valleys. The
Sultan normally lived on the Klang River, near its estuary. This
dispersal of wealth and authority weakened the Sultan's position
at the expense of the chiefs.

When Sultan Mohamed died in 1857 his eight-year-old royal
son, Raja Mahmud, was recognised as Raja Muda, but a son-in-
law, Abdul Samad, who was a grandson of Sultan Ibrahim,
claimed the throne, and was acknowledged as Sultan by the other
chiefs after an interval of some years. It was an uneasy situation.
The late Sultan had had two non-royal sons, Raja Sulaiman, who
had died in 1853, and Raja Laut. He also had three daughters, all

[1] Sultan Mohamed, 1826–57; Sultan Abdul Samad, 1857–98.

of whom were married. It was the chiefs married to these three daughters who now gained political office. One son-in-law, Abdul Samad, became Sultan, a second son-in-law, Raja Juma'at, became the chief at Lukut, and the third son-in-law, Raja Abdullah, became the chief at Klang. Abdul Samad chose to live near the estuary of the Langat rather than at Klang. Abdul Samad's own son, Raja Musa, was given charge of the Selangor River. This meant that those who had married into the former Sultan's family had profited at the expense of his own sons. One of these sons had already died, another lacked status on account of not having had a royal mother, and a third — who had had a royal mother — was only eight years old. This boy, Mahmud, was some forty-four years younger than Abdul Samad, and it might well have seemed likely that Abdul Samad would reign until the boy grew up. As it happened, Abdul Samad outlived most of his contemporaries and reigned for forty-one years!

These arrangements, made mostly at the time of Sultan

Mohamed's death, had the effect of dividing the Selangor chiefs into two factions. It was a case of the 'haves' against the 'have-nots'.[1] The discontented princes were Raja Laut, the Raja Muda, Mahmud (when he was old enough to appreciate the position), and Raja Mahdi, son of the deceased Raja Sulaiman who had been chief at Klang until his death in 1853. It was only a matter of time before one of these felt strong enough to challenge the established order. In 1866 Raja Mahdi attacked Klang and drove out Raja Abdullah; the Selangor civil war had started. Legally, Mahdi had no right to Klang, because the appointment of a chief by the Sultan was for life only, and, at Mahdi's father's death, Sultan Mohamed had given the post to Raja Abdullah. As a grandson of Mohamed Mahdi felt that he had a real grievance when a son-in-law was preferred to him. Another point was that, thanks to the business enterprise of Raja Abdullah and Raja Juma'at, tin-mining on a big scale had begun in the Klang valley near modern Kuala Lumpur, and by 1866 the post at Klang was a very profitable one.

When Mahdi refused to evacuate Klang, the chiefs took sides, while the Sultan, at Langat, managed to keep on good terms with them all, granting them help impartially when they came to see him. That the reality of power in the state was in the hands of the chiefs could not have been more clearly demonstrated. In 1867 the Sultan brought in an outside prince to act as viceroy and arbitrator. This was Tunku Zia'u'd-din, better known as Kudin, younger brother of Sultan Ahmad of Kedah. Kudin was already married to Abdul Samad's daughter, and he was an able and resourceful leader. This act only increased the opposition of the rebel chiefs, and the war spread further into the valleys. The Chinese tin-mining communities were now in the war zone, and needed little encouragement to take up arms on opposite sides; they were already on fighting terms with each other. Kudin secured a powerful ally in Yap Ah Loy, the Capitan China at Kuala Lumpur, while the Ghee Hin at Kanching joined forces with Mahdi, Mahmud, and Sayid Mashhor, a warrior of Arab stock who was in the service of the rebels. From 1870 to 1873 these alliances waged a fierce war against each other, often crossing

[1] J. M. Gullick, *Indigenous Political Systems of Western Malaya*, p. 72.

and recrossing the same territory. Early Kuala Lumpur had its full share of the accompanying destruction.

Thus, by 1871–2 the two main tin-bearing states, Perak and Selangor, were in a troubled condition. The Chinese had renewed their fighting in Larut, and there was a succession question to be solved for the throne of Perak. In Selangor the jealousies and rivalries of the Malay chiefs had become interwoven with the hostilities of the Ghee Hin at Kanching and the Hai San at Kuala Lumpur, in what can perhaps be described as a general showdown. The tin trade came, at times, to a standstill, and the coasts of these states became unsafe for honest shipping.

TIME CHART: A.D. 1824–1873

Perak		Selangor	
c. 1840	Long Ja'afar invited Chinese to mine tin in Larut district.	1824	Tin Mining at Lukut.
		c. 1840	Tin Mining at Kanching.
1857	Death of Sultan Abdullah. Death of Long Ja'afar.	1857	Tin Mining at Ampang. (Kuala Lumpur).
1862	Outbreak of 'Larut wars', between Ghee Hin and Hai San.	1857	Death of Sultan Mohamed.
		c. 1860	Recognition of Sultan Abdul Samad.
	Ibrahim paid compensation to Penang.	1866	Raja Mahdi's attack on Klang.
1863	Ibrahim appointed Mantri.		Beginning of civil war (1866–73).
1865	Death of Sultan Ja'afar.		
1871	Death of Sultan Ali.	1867	Kudin appointed viceroy.
1872	Renewed outbreak of 'Larut wars'.	1870–3	Extension of civil war to include Chinese at Kanching and Kuala Lumpur.
1871–3	Disputed succession to the throne.		

(A) FAMILY OF SULTAN MOHAMED OF SELANGOR

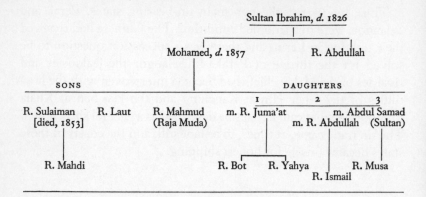

Sultan Ibrahim, *d.* 1826

Mohamed, *d.* 1857   R. Abdullah

SONS   DAUGHTERS

                                              1   2   3

R. Sulaiman   R. Laut   R. Mahmud   m. R. Juma'at   m. Abdul Samad
[died, 1853]   (Raja Muda)   m. R. Abdullah   (Sultan)

R. Mahdi   R. Bot   R. Yahya   R. Musa
                                                        R. Ismail

(B) SUCCESSION IN PERAK

(i) *The normal 'ladder'*
   Sultan
   Raja Muda
   Raja Bendahara
   Raja di Hilir

(ii) *The position in 1871*
   Sultan Ali—deceased
   Raja Muda—Abdullah
   Raja Bendahara—Ismail
   No office—Yusuf

   (*a*) Abdullah had moved up too quickly
   (*b*) Ismail's claims rested on marriage
   (*c*) Yusuf was senior to Abdullah, and should by this time have been Raja Muda, but he had been consistently overlooked by the chiefs

Chapter 9

BRITISH INTERVENTION IN THE MALAY STATES

A.D. 1874

The year 1874 marked the introduction of British administrators into three Malay states, and British advice and protection was extended later to other states. The traditional policy of the English East India Company, ever since the first negotiations for Penang, had been opposed to any active interference either in, or on behalf of, a Malay state. In practice, however, a fair amount of such intervention had taken place. The Crawfurd and Burney missions to Bangkok in 1822 and 1825–6 had the subject of Kedah on their agenda, even though it was well down the list. The Anderson Treaties with Perak and Selangor, and Fullerton's gun-boats at Trang, were aimed at preventing the Siamese from intervening in states south of Kedah. The Low Treaty of 1826 gave, under certain conditions, the protection of the Company to the Sultan of Perak.[1] In 1843 Penang intervened in a dispute between Kedah and Perak over the boundary between them. In 1862 the Governor of the Straits Settlements blockaded the Larut estuary in order to enforce the payment of compensation from Perak for the forced flight to Penang of Ghee Hin, who claimed British citizenship. In the same year the same Governor sent a warship which shelled Trengganu fort, because Trengganu was harbouring a Malay prince who was receiving Siamese support.

Long before 1874, therefore, there was no lack of incidents in which the Straits Settlements had taken some action which

[1] Meanwhile, in 1831, and again in 1838, Penang supported Siam against Malay risings in Kedah, in accordance with the Anglo-Siamese Treaty of 1826.

implied intervention in affairs of the Malay States. Even Malacca had conducted a war (1831–2) in the Minangkabau territory of Naning over the payment of taxes. There were undoubtedly contradictions in the policy of the East India Company in relation to the Malay Peninsula, yet there still remained an underlying reluctance to be involved in the affairs of the Malay States. The Straits Settlements were regarded from the viewpoint of India, and they were, of course, until 1867, subject to policy direction from India. They were seen as three bases neatly placed along a main shipping route, the Malacca Straits, and were of importance as collecting-centres and ports-of-call. The Company certainly did not regard them as jumping-off grounds for any kind of penetration into other parts of the Peninsula. The Malay States were seen as a troubled zone where alliances and commitments would entail military forces in unknown territory for uncertain results. The Naning War was a classic lesson on these lines.

Why, then, did the Company take action at all in relation to matters concerning the Malay States? Much of this action was aimed primarily at preserving the Company's existing interests. The missions to Bangkok were mainly intended to improve relationships between the Company and Siam, and to parry any Siamese threat to Penang. They were concerned, in part, with the removal of irksome Siamese restrictions on trade with the Company and the possibilities of expanding such trade in the future. The safeguarding of the independence of Malay states on the west coast was very much more a Penang attitude than a Calcutta one. Similarly, it was the Singapore government which was concerned about the possible extension of Siamese influence in the east-coast states.

To some extent, therefore, the East India Company's actions on matters relating to the Malay States can be seen as arising from self-interest, because of existing or possible trade disruption, risk to food-supplies, or political threats from the power of Siam. It should be noted also that action taken by men like Fullerton and James Low from Penang, and Cavenagh from Singapore, often represented individual initiative rather than official Company policy. The 'man on the spot' was much more willing to commit the Company in matters affecting the Malay States than seemed desirable from the distance of India. Fullerton, as early as 1825, anticipated that, sooner or later, the Company would protect those states which remained independent of Siam.[1]

Other interests also pressed the Straits governments to inter-vene in Peninsular affairs. As the years passed the population of the Straits Settlements began to include an increasing number of people who were born there, and therefore entitled to the rights of British subjects. The majority of these were Chinese of all classes, including merchants and miners associated with the tin enterprises in Perak, Selangor, and the Minangkabau States. When trouble arose, in Larut or Kuala Lumpur or Sungei Ujong, appeals for assistance, protection, or compensation, were made to Penang, Malacca, or Singapore. In particular, the merchant groups in Penang and Singapore were frequently petitioning for some form of intervention to settle the disorders on the west coast of Malaya.

The Secret Society rivalries and wars also had their counter-parts in the Straits Settlements. In Penang, for example, there were leaders and headquarters of both Ghee Hin and Hai San factions and fighting in Larut could mean problems of law and order in Penang itself. A house in Penang owned by Ibrahim of Larut was blown up by angry Ghee Hin, because he had shown himself on the side of the Hai San. In 1867 there was street-fighting of a serious nature in Georgetown, between the two rival groups. The elements of Secret Society warfare were present, in any case, in the Straits Settlements,[2] but trouble in the mining camps made things worse for the Straits authorities.

Piracy was another great source of anxiety to the Governor of the Straits Settlements. It was an old occupation in the Malacca Straits, but it was always worse when conditions were disturbed in the coastal states. The first half of the nineteenth century was a particularly bad time for Chinese junks plying between China and the Straits, and for small craft from the Malay Archipelago.

[1] L. A. Mills, 'British Malaya, 1824–1867', p. 145.
[2] Cf. Victor Purcell, *The Chinese in South-East Asia*, pp. 301–3.

During the wars in Perak and Selangor in the 1860s piracy was engaged in by one side or another as a means of gaining necessary supplies.

There was also smuggling in the form of gun-running, especially from Penang to Perak. This was done often under the noses of the Penang authorities, and patrolling ships found it as difficult to suppress as piracy itself.

As seen from the Straits Settlements, there was much cause for concern about conditions along the west coast of Malaya around 1870. There were Chinese rivalries, soon to break out again in open warfare in Larut; in Selangor there was full-scale warfare, with Chinese and Malay groups on either side; in Sungei Ujong there was civil war between two Malay groups. Piracy was perhaps not so prevalent as ten years earlier, but it was still a menace. Complaints and petitions from individuals and groups[1] were almost an everyday occurrence.

In 1871 a new political situation arose in Perak with the death of Sultan Ali at Sayong. This was entirely a Malay problem concerned with the loyalties and divisions of the Malay chiefs. Abdullah, who, as Raja Muda, had the best claim by title to succeed to the throne, could rely upon support in Lower Perak, where he lived. Yusuf at Senggang was, strictly speaking, senior to Abdullah, and had been overlooked for office previously because of his unpopularity with the other chiefs. In 1869 he had written to the Straits government claiming his right to the throne when Ali died, and he now indicated his readiness to fight in support of his claim. Neither Abdullah nor Yusuf was particularly acceptable to the chiefs of Upper Perak.

Yusuf, a man with a grievance, and liable to take a strong line if he had the chance, had offended the chiefs in his father's lifetime, and they had no reason to think he had changed. In 1870 Abdullah had granted concessions of land in the Krian district of Perak[2] to a Penang trader and adventurer named Bacon. This was not only against Sultan Ali's wishes; it also offended Ibrahim, the

[1] E.g., The Singapore Chamber of Commerce.
[2] This had formerly been part of the Sultan's own domain; it was granted to Ibrahim in 1863.

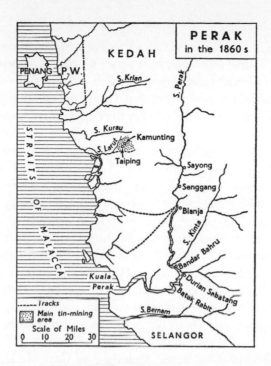

PERAK
in the 1860 s

KEDAH

PENANG P.W.

S. Krian

S. Perak

STRAITS

S. Kurau

S. Larut   Kamunting

Taiping

Sayong

Senggang

Blanja

OF

S. Kinta

MALACCA

Bandar Bahru

Kuala
Perak

Durian Sabatang

Batak Rabit

- - - - Tracks

Main tin-mining area

Scale of Miles
0   10   20   30

S. Bernam

SELANGOR

Mantri, who claimed Krian as his own district by gift of the Sultan, in addition to Larut. Shortly before Sultan Ali died Abdullah's case was further damaged by the story that his wife, Raja Tipah, had left him to elope with a Selangor prince. The news that Abdullah did nothing to revenge himself except declare his wife divorced was bad enough in Malay opinion; it was made worse by the fact that Raja Tipah was a daughter of Sultan Ali. Rumour had it that Sultan Ali, who was dying, had asked Abdullah to bring Raja Tipah to see him. Fearing a trap, Abdullah was unwilling to go. Raja Tipah then announced that she would go with any man brave enough to take her to her father. The offer was accepted by Raja Daud of Selangor who, on pretext of taking her to Sayong in Upper Perak, carried her off to Selangor instead. Whether true or false, this story did Abdullah a lot of harm.

Two other important chiefs were possible claimants to the throne. The Bendahara, Ismail, had a strong following in Upper Perak. He was not a direct descendant of the royal house, being connected to it only by marriage. He had been Bendahara to two

Sultans without being advanced to Raja Muda, because, in the ordinary course of events, he was not on the 'promotion-ladder'. The Upper Perak chiefs knew him well, however. By comparison with Abdullah he was a traditional and conservative Malay, and an elderly man,[1] the kind of man they apparently wanted as their Sultan.

Finally, in the background, stood Ibrahim of Larut, Mantri of Perak. He was the wealthiest of all the chiefs, and he gave his support to Ismail. This may have been partly because of his feud with Abdullah concerning the Krian district, and partly because he judged Ismail to be the better-supported candidate. In any case Ibrahim was obviously more closely linked with Upper Perak than with Lower Perak, though he was related to both Ismail and, by marriage, to the Laksamana, who was a leader of the Lower Perak group. It has been suggested that Ismail had long-term ambitions for himself. Normal practice would be broken if Ismail became Sultan, and could be broken again for Ibrahim to succeed Ismail.

After Sultan Ali's death Abdullah, as Raja Muda, was summoned to meet the chiefs at Sayong in order to attend the funeral, and take part in the election of the new Sultan afterwards. He did not answer this summons. According to his opponents, he was afraid to pass through the riverside village of Senggang, which was on his way, for fear of Yusuf, who was brooding there. He was also afraid to show himself at Sayong because of the accusations he would have to face from the relatives of Sultan Ali and Raja Tipah. Abdullah's defence was that the invitation had not come from the Bendahara, as was usual, and it had not been accompanied by the token of royalty, the yellow umbrella. He had also been advised to come only as far as Kampong Gajah, where the chiefs could meet him after the funeral ceremony.

In Abdullah's absence from Sayong, the chiefs decided to instal Bendahara Ismail as the new Sultan. He, in turn, appointed the eldest son of the late Sultan as Bendahara, thus restoring the traditional line of succession. The main leaders who were not

[1] Although he did not die until 1889.

present to support Ismail's installation were Abdullah himself, Yusuf, the Laksamana, and the Shahbandar. Of these, the last two were said to have indicated their agreement later, though subsequent events did not bear this out.

Abdullah did not lack courage in his own territory. When Ismail appointed a customs official to replace the Laksamana's son at Kuala Perak, Abdullah and the Shahbandar removed him and restored the estuary trade to their own control. This was open rebellion, but Ismail did nothing about it immediately. By April 1872 Abdullah was calling himself Sultan and interfering in affairs in Krian and Larut. He also made peace with Yusuf and appointed him Raja Muda! Between them, they plotted to make an alliance with the Mantri's enemies in Larut, the Ghee Hin, in order to drive him out. Abdullah promised to pay half the expenses of the Ghee Hin, and to lease the Larut mines to them when they were successful.

These moves coincided with a renewed outbreak of fighting between the two Chinese factions in Larut. The Mantri had no military or police force with which he could control this fighting, and early in 1873 his own position was so dangerous that he withdrew to the lower reaches of the River Krian, which gave him easy access, if necessary, to Province Wellesley. In the previous April Abdullah had arrived in Larut, where he met the Auditor-General of the Straits government, C. J. Irving, and handed him a letter setting out his claims to be Sultan. To add to the confusion, Straits officials were being approached by Penang residents who held land concessions or tax-farms from Abdullah to secure acknowledgment of his claims to be Sultan. The financier, Bacon, was most active in this sphere.

For a short time Abdullah and the Mantri became reconciled. Abdullah recognised the Mantri as holding 'the government of Larut and its dependencies' while the Mantri recognised Abdullah as Sultan. At the most this was a marriage of convenience, and it soon broke apart. In June 1873 they quarrelled, and the Mantri went to live in Penang, where, in September, Governor Ord recognised him as the rightful ruler of Larut.

Meanwhile the Chinese wars continued and spread to the coast, with the accompaniment of blockades and piracy. Malay groups had now been formed to support both sides. A 'White Flag' society aided the Ghee Hin, and a 'Red Flag' society the Hai San. Trade and tin-mining in the area were at a standstill, and there was grave danger of an extension of the fighting in Penang. The Ghee Hin had been victorious at first, but the Hai San returned in force from Penang to regain their positions. A contemporary writer described the situation in these words:

'In the autumn of 1872, the Go Kwans (Hai San) who had been expelled, and had spent their time in warlike preparations, made an effort to regain their position. Arms and ammunition were sent up the Laroot River, and at last a desperate attack was made upon the faction in possession of the mines.'[1]

The Mantri tried to change sides with the fortunes of war and, not surprisingly, he ended by earning the hostility and contempt of both sides. For this reason, and because his own life was in danger, he withdrew first to Krian and then to Penang. He engaged the services of a strange, adventurous Englishman, Captain Speedy, who was then Superintendent of Police at Penang, to act as a Chief of Police for him, and to recruit a small police force from India.

Several officials of the Straits government had views on what they thought should be done about this state of affairs in Perak, as well as about the civil wars and piracies in Selangor and the Minangkabau States. As early as 1869, when Raja Yusuf put his claim to succeed to the throne of Perak to the Straits government, the Colonial Secretary, Colonel Macpherson, expressed his regret to the Governor that it was not possible to support this claim, as a means of placing a British nominee in the State and thus provide an indirect form of British rule. In 1871 a committee proposed that Residents should be sent to the Malay States. In 1872 the Lieutenant-Governor of Penang, Sir George Campbell, wrote

'I speak with diffidence, being so new to this portion of the East, but I think it worth consideration whether the appoint-

[1] F. McNair, *Perak and the Malays*, London, 1878, p. 353.

ment under a British Government of a British Resident or Political Agent for certain of the Malay States would not, as in India, have a markedly beneficial effect. . . .'[1]

Yet, in the same year, the Straits government was replying to complaints of losses in Selangor made by Malacca merchants by pointing out that if they chose to adventure in 'these countries' under existing circumstances, they must not expect help or protection from the Straits authorities. This attitude of limiting intervention to attempts to suppress piracy, or to demanding redress for aggression on British peoples and territories when it was deemed necessary, was approved by the Colonial Office in London in December 1872, and again in July 1873. From very shortly after this latter date, however, the Colonial Office moved towards a policy of positive, though cautious, intervention.

In August 1873 Lieutenant-Governor Anson of Penang arranged a meeting between Ghee Hin and Hai San leaders in an attempt to bring the Larut Wars to an end. The meeting was also attended by Abdullah, Yusuf, and the Mantri, as well as by Kudin, the Kedah prince who was Regent or Viceroy in Selangor. The Chinese leaders agreed to an armistice pending arbitration from Penang, but, in fact, the fighting continued. Abdullah issued a proclamation to the Chinese headmen in Larut which was completely ignored.

Two events followed within a few weeks of this unsuccessful meeting at Penang. Abdullah visited Singapore to seek support from the Straits government; he was advised by a Singapore merchant, and member of Council, W. H. Reade, to wait until after the arrival of the new Governor, Sir Andrew Clarke. In November 1873 the new Governor arrived at Singapore; Abdullah was in due course taken to meet him, and, at the end of December, Abdullah wrote a letter to the Governor asking him for British protection for Perak, and for the appointment of a Resident to 'show us a good system of government'.[2]

[1] As quoted in R. O. Winstedt and R. J. Wilkinson, 'A History of Perak', p. 97.
[2] C. D. Cowan (editor), 'Swettenham's Perak Journals, 1874–1876,' *JRASMB*, Vol. 24, pt. 4, p. 21.

L

Before Clarke left England he was given new instructions by the Colonial Office. These were contained in a cautious message, clothed in the long, flowing prose of the period. The use of British influence with the native princes was recommended with a view to rescuing, if possible, 'these fertile and productive countries from the ruin which must befall them if the present disorders continue unchecked.' Further, the Governor was ordered to enquire into the conditions in the Malay States, and to report whether, in his opinion, any steps could be taken to restore peace and order there and to secure the protection of trade. In particular, consideration was to be given to the advisability of appointing a British officer to reside in any of the states, with the full consent of the native government and with the expenses of such an appointment defrayed by the Straits Settlements.

These orders were hardly revolutionary in tone. They were hedged by conditions, and they suggested investigations and reports before the taking of any action. Clarke, however, regarded them as a passport for action. With this measure of support, and with the letter from Abdullah, he begun to negotiate, first for a settlement of the Chinese disputes in Perak, and then for the recognition of a Malay Sultan of Perak who would accept the services of a British Resident.

Before discussing these negotiations, this might be a suitable point at which to consider the general reasons which lay behind the policy of guarded intervention outlined in Lord Kimberley's despatch from the Colonial Office on September 20th, 1873. It is necessary to go back a little.

In 1858 the territories of the East India Company passed to the control of the India Office, and in 1867 the Straits Settlements were transferred from the India Office to the authority of the Colonial Office. This second move occurred partly in answer to expressions of Singapore opinion. The changeover in 1858 had left the Straits Settlements still linked to India. Their importance, as seen from Calcutta, was minimised, and their interests neglected. From India, the Settlements were regarded as expensive, especially on account of the cost of military garrisons, which was only partly met by the revenues. For its own administrative and financial reasons, the Indian government tried to force the use of Indian currency in the Straits and to interfere with free trade. Singapore's prosperity was, of course, based on free trade, and its authorities and merchants alike bitterly resented any attempt to change this policy. In Singapore there were also grievances that the Settlements were used in the interests of India — for example, as a dumping-ground for convicts. Last, but not least, the commercial classes in Singapore were, for various reasons, looking towards Malaya as a field for economic enterprise. So long as the Singapore government remained tied to India, there seemed little chance of a change of policy which would do something to improve the prospects of trade in the Malay States.

So far as the relations between the Straits Settlements and the Malay States were concerned, the change to the Colonial Office in 1867 had two effects. The Straits Settlements could now be viewed from London in a broader perspective. They were colonies on a map of the world, and not, as formerly, appendages only to the sub-continent of India. This broader viewpoint meant that policy for the Straits could be worked out in relation to events in other parts of the world. It could, for instance be related to the activities of other European colonial powers in the Far East.

Secondly, the Singapore trading community, especially the Chamber of Commerce, could press harder than before for the achievement of settled conditions for business enterprise in the Malay States. The first Colonial Governor of Singapore, Sir Harry Ord (1867–73), was made very much aware of these views.

By the late 1860s, Singapore merchants had a number of reasons for feeling insecure, and the Colonial Office, too, had some cause to be concerned about the situation of the Straits Settlements.

The Dutch were increasing their control in the Netherlands East Indies. Ships flying the British flag (and this included Chinese who were Straits traders) were barred from the coastal trade in Dutch-controlled territories, and discriminatory duties were placed on British goods. The area of Dutch political influence had increased in several islands since the Anglo-Dutch Treaty of 1824, and by 1865 Dutch control in Sumatra had reached the southern border of Acheh. By 1871 it was apparent that the whole of the island would eventually come under Dutch rule.

From the late 1850s the French were embarked on a policy of expansion in Indo-China and, after the humiliating defeat of France at the hands of Prussia in 1870–1, some French leaders at least saw further expansion in Asia as the best means of reviving French prestige.

The opening of the Suez Canal in 1869 increased European commercial interest in the East and the number of steamships in eastern waters and Singapore merchants feared that this would lead to direct trade between Europe and the South-East Asian markets. If this happened, Singapore would lose its position as chief *entrepôt* of the region. The laying of a submarine cable from London to Singapore put London business houses in quick contact with the state of the markets there, and seemed to threaten the position of the resident distributors. Chinese merchants complained of the appearance of large numbers of European firms who seemed to be squeezing them out of one trading area after another. European firms complained of the pressure of competition in Singapore itself, while one member of the Singapore Council pointed out the great increase in the number of German merchants in the port.[1]

To some extent the European firms represented a search for new market areas for manufactured goods from Western Europe. They also sought new sources of raw materials and primary products. It seems likely that during the ten years before the introduction of British Residents in the main tin-bearing Malay States, there was an increased demand for tin in the West. This was reflected in the export-figures of Malayan tin from Singapore to Britain and North America.

The disorders of the Malay States must be regarded as a contributory cause of British intervention, but when the mild instruction was given from the Colonial Office in September 1873, other forces were working towards the same objective. The fear of intervention in the Malay Peninsula by some other European

[1] C. D. Cowan (editor), 'Swettenham's Perak Journals, 1874–1876', p. 9, and cf. C. N. Parkinson, *British Intervention in Malaya, 1867–1877*, p. 36.

power, and the quickening of British interest in eastern trade, were both part of the spirit of the times in the early 1870s. The merchant class of Sinagpore clamoured for orderly conditions in the Malay States as a necessary condition for trade, investment, and the development of natural resources.

Now to return to Sir Andrew Clarke. He first sent his officer in charge of Chinese affairs, Mr. W. A. Pickering, to meet rival Chinese leaders in Penang to discover whether they would be prepared to reach an agreement and accept the arbitration of the Straits Governor. When Pickering reported a successful result from his talks, Clarke proceeded to invite the leading Malay chiefs in Perak to meet him at the island of Pangkor near the estuary of the Perak River for a general settlement of the troubles of Perak.

The Pangkor meeting took place in mid-January 1874. It ended by the signing of two documents, the Chinese Engagement and the Pangkor Engagement. Under the first heading the Ghee Hin and Hai San leaders undertook to keep the peace under penalty of a fine of 50,000 dollars. A small disarmament commission was appointed, including the Chinese leaders themselves and British officials from the Straits Settlements. This was to supervise the handing-in of weapons, destruction of stockades, and exchange of prisoners. This work was done, on the whole, competently and quickly. The Chinese themselves were heartily weary of wars, and given a reasonable settlement were prepared to resume normal tin-mining. The mining lands were divided again between the two groups, with a marked boundary ditch. It was not the end of the Secret Society rivalries, but it did mark the beginning of a period of comparative peace and prosperity. The population of the Larut district had dropped almost as low as 4,000 by the time of the Pangkor meeting; by the end of 1874 it had risen to 27,000. For some years Ghee Hin and Hai San competed healthily in the production of tin.

Ibrahim, the Mantri, was confirmed at Pangkor in his position of ruler at Larut, but he was not acknowledged as having independent sovereignty there. Clarke had no written evidence of Ord's recognition of the Mantri as an independent ruler in

September 1873, because the papers concerning this were in Penang, where Ord had dealt with the matter. The Mantri was considered to have special rights and privileges in Larut, but to be holding these by appointment from the Sultan.[1]

The Mantri's Chief of Police, Captain Speedy, was to stay in Larut, but in a new capacity. He was appointed Assistant Resident in Perak, a salaried official of the Straits government.

The question of the Perak succession was much more delicate and controversial. None of the Upper Perak chiefs, except the Mantri, attended the meeting. Ismail was invited, but did not come; Yusuf was not even invited, but this was probably due to the Straits government's ignorance of his claims. From Ismail's point of view there was no purpose in attending a meeting to discuss the rightful succession to the Perak throne. He had been properly installed, and the matter was settled. The same view would have been taken by the up-river chiefs who had supported him. The Mantri came to Pangkor largely to assert his own rights or defend his own interests; in particular, he must have hoped to gain confirmation of Ord's recognition of him as an independent ruler.

Clarke presided over the meeting, and claimed afterwards that decisions taken at Pangkor were not his decisions but those of the interested parties who had met under his chairmanship. The decision taken about the Sultan could, in view of the partisan grouping of the chiefs present, hardly have been otherwise. Apart from the Mantri and the Temenggong, all the chiefs were from Lower Perak, and supporters of Abdullah, who was also present. They agreed to recognise Abdullah as Sultan, the Mantri doing so after some hesitation. Afterwards it was clear that they had felt this to be the decision which Clarke wanted, and no doubt they were right. Ismail was a remote figure with whom no Straits official had yet held discussion. Abdullah, on the other hand, was frequently in evidence in Penang or Singapore, and his home territory was not far from Kuala Perak and convenient to coastal

---

[1] C. N. Parkinson (*British Intervention in Malaya, 1867–1877*, p. 132) holds that Clarke may have known about Ord's decision, and that he intended to reverse it.

traffic. Moreover Abdullah had offered to take a British Resident to help him provide good government. As Clarke saw it, Abdullah seemed the candidate to the throne best able to establish his position and, at the same time, most likely to take British advice.

Ismail, who was not present, was pensioned-off with the courtesy title of Sultan Muda and an income and land adequate to his position. He was to be told of these terms, and to be asked to hand over the regalia to Abdullah. Yusuf was not mentioned.

Sultan Abdullah was to receive a British Resident whose advice must be asked and acted upon on all questions other than those touching Malay religion and custom. The collection and control of all revenues, and the general administration of the country, was to be regulated under the advice of the Resident.

With the signing of this agreement[1] Perak had a British-acknowledged Sultan supported by the chiefs in Lower Perak, and by the very doubtful support of the Mantri, who probably only agreed in order that his own position would not suffer in any way. In Upper Perak, Ismail continued as Sultan with no desire for a pension or a courtesy-title. Pangkor had no meaning for Ismail and his up-river chiefs. A greater novelty lay in the two British appointments to the government of Perak. The Assistant Resident was already on the spot. The Resident was not appointed until some months later. What the position of this Resident would be in practice remained to be seen. If Clarke was, in a sense, using Abdullah as a means for introducing a British administrator to his state, was not Abdullah perhaps merely using this Resident idea as a means of obtaining British recognition? As for Malay opinion in Upper Perak, this was inevitably opposed to decisions reached at Pangkor, and not least to the intrusion of a foreign official into Malay politics. News of the new boundary revisions also served to increase Malay mistrust of British intentions.

Clarke next turned his attention to Selangor. At the time of his arrival in Singapore, in November 1873, the civil war in Selangor was drawing towards an end. Kudin was extremely resourceful

---

[1] The Engagement also contained new boundary definitions for the Dindings and Province Wellesley, both of which were open to different interpretations.

in recruiting military forces. At one stage, in the late months of 1871, he had in his service two European officers (one a Dutchman, the other an Italian), twenty European and Eurasian non-commissioned officers, and nearly two hundred Indian Sepoys. In addition, he recruited Malays where he could, including some from his own state, Kedah. Yet until March 1873 Kudin and his supporters were very much on the defensive. Mahdi's forces were in control of the whole of the interior of Selangor, with an outlet to the sea at Kuala Selangor, and friendly contacts with the chiefs of Sungei Ujong and Ulu Bernam. It was the advance of a large force from Pahang which turned the tide of victory for Kudin. He had sent an envoy to the Bendahara of Pahang in December, 1871, and he made a personal visit, for the same purpose of enlisting military support, a few months later. Wan Ahmad was willing to help because of the captivity of a kinsman in the hands of the Selangor 'rebels', and because of the incursions made into his own territory by Rawas, who used Selangor as a base. The Straits government was favourably impressed by Kudin, but Wan Ahmad made sure there would be no objections from Singapore before he sent an expedition to Selangor.

The main Pahang army came over the passes from Raub and Bentong, while a smaller force reached Kuala Selangor by sea. Together they gained command of the central Selangor area. In March 1873 they co-operated with Capitan China Yap Ah Loy in a successful battle for the recapture of Kuala Lumpur, which had been held for seven months by Mahdi's forces. This victory was the turning-point of the war, and it marked the ascendancy of Kudin; but in the late months of 1873 Mahdi and Mahmud were still free men and by no means reconciled to defeat.

As in Perak, the Selangor war had been accompanied by acts of coastal piracy. In 1871 a Chinese junk was plundered and its crew and passengers killed by pirates who were alleged to be operating from Kuala Selangor. In Malacca and Singapore there arose the usual cry for action against piracy and the safeguarding of the lives of British citizens and peaceful traders. A naval ship, H.M.S. *Rinaldo*, and the Colonial steamer, *Pluto*, were sent to Kuala Selangor to arrest the pirates. This expedition found an armed stockade held by Sayid Mashhor which resented their demands, and firing broke out. The stockade was shelled and its garrison driven into the jungle. This action had the effect of gaining Kuala Selangor for Kudin.

In November 1873, at the time of Clarke's arrival in Singapore, another incident of piracy occurred, this time off the estuary of the Langat, where Sultan Abdul Samad lived. A Malacca vessel was plundered and eight of its nine crew and passengers murdered. A similar attack on a Malacca boat was made in the following month, but with no loss of life, as the crew swam to safety.

A party of Selangor Malays, thought to be the pirates of the November incident, was arrested in Malacca, and Clarke decided to take up the question of their trial with Sultan Abdul Samad. These negotiations took place at Langat in February 1874, just a month after the Pangkor meeting. The Sultan, possibly overawed by the nearness of a British naval squadron deliberately anchored off the Selangor coast, agreed to the trial of the alleged pirates by a court under the presidency of the Viceroy, Kudin. The trial was held, and the men were convicted and executed, with the Sultan's approval.[1] Compensation was paid for the loss of life and property of British subjects, in this case Malays and Chinese.

This meeting of the Sultan, the Viceroy, and Sir Andrew Clarke, prepared the way for further diplomatic relationships, though Clarke was hesitant about pressing for the introduction of a British Resident in Selangor until the effects of his experiment in Perak could be seen. He aimed at cultivating the friendly relationship now begun with the Sultan, the Viceroy, and his supporting chiefs, so that British intervention could come as 'the result of the free and unanimous choice of all the chiefs themselves'. By September 1874 he had left at Langat the young Frank Swettenham to give the Sultan informal advice. Swettenham made a good impression, and Clarke sought Colonial Office approval for a more formal appointment. The appointment of a Resident in Perak had been approved by Lord Carnavon, successor to Lord Kimberley, in March 1874 and confirmed, with more enthusiasm,

---

[1] According to Swettenham, these men were not guilty of this particular crime, but this was known only to Malays at the time.

in the following May, after a debate in the House of Lords.

As Resident in Selangor, Clarke chose Mr. J. G. Davidson, a friend and adviser of Kudin and an experienced colonial official. Swettenham was left where he was with the Sultan at Langat, as Assistant Resident. These appointments were made in November 1874, when the practical experiment of a British Resident in Perak was just beginning.

Meanwhile Clarke had made approaches to Sungei Ujong. Here he acted on the grounds of long-standing grievances and complaints in relation to the river-tolls on trade to and from Malacca. The political situation was complicated by the rivalries of Sungei Ujong and Rembau, and by the uncertainties of rule in Sungei Ujong itself, where two chiefs, the Dato Klana and the Dato Bandar, led rival groups. In April 1874 Clarke obtained a treaty from the Dato Klana, who promised to govern with justice and to protect the lives and property of traders, as well as to give no assistance to the enemies of the British government or of states allied to, or at peace with, Britain. In addition, the district of Sempang was given to the 'control, order and direction of' the British government. Sempang lay on the Linggi, in the boundary-zone between Sungei Ujong and Rembau. Four months later the Date Klana was asking for a British Resident, and in November Captain Tatham was appointed 'Assistant Resident' in Sungei Ujong. The Dato Bandar was very much opposed to this intervention from the Straits government, and he refused to meet either the Klana or the Governor. He was only brought to submission by the use of a small British force in support of the Dato Klana's troops.

By the end of 1874 British officials were operating in Larut, Lower Perak, Klang, Langat, and Sungei Ujong. Their terms of reference could be related to those of the Pangkor Engagement, which were themselves not lacking in ambiguity and contradiction. Backed by the new directions from the Colonial Office, Clarke had succeeded in introducing an uncertain form of British indirect rule into three Malay states during his first year of office at Singapore. In the next Chapter, an account is given of how this experiment worked out in practice.

Chapter 10

THE BRITISH RESIDENT SYSTEM

A.D. 1874–1895

The early British Residents in the Malay States had no system to follow and no clear rules to guide them.[1] This experiment of British 'advice' depended partly on how much the advice was wanted by the Malay authorities, and partly on how strongly the Resident was likely to be supported by the Straits government. Under the terms of the Pangkor Engagement the Resident was entitled, strictly speaking, to advise on very little. Questions touching Malay religion and custom were not included among those on which his advice was to be sought and acted upon. There was some possibility of separating purely religious matters from Malay politics, but custom ran through everything. How were the revenues and the general administration of the state to be regulated under the advice of the Resident without touching matters of custom? The revenues were, by custom, the personal incomes of the Sultan and his chiefs; there were also all kinds of customary claims, through family descent, to the offices of state.

Even in the case of a Sultan willing to take advice, there remained the practical difficulty of how to carry out any changes. The governments of the Malay States at this time were not centralised, and there was no civil service. The early Resident, on taking up his appointment stood very much on his own; if his advice was to be put into practice, he was the one who had to do it. The Resident, it would seem, had the choice of either doing nothing much, or of giving advice and acting upon it himself. In

---

[1] 'Nothing', says Swettenham, 'with any pretensions to a system had ever been formulated,' *British Malaya*, p. 217.

the latter case, he inevitably became a government executive, and not just an adviser.

In Malay opinion the Resident, if he actively undertook to change the administration and the revenue system, was a foreigner, ignorant of Malay ways, and possibly seeking to make a fortune. The Malay state was a collection of private estates and private privileges and interests, and anyone who ventured to interfere with these was bound to meet opposition of one kind or another. The conception of a modern and impersonal state, existing as a public institution, had no place in the minds of the Malay Sultans or their chiefs in 1874. Even the appointment of a Malay prince from another state to act as the representative of the Sultan helped to fan the flames of civil war in Selangor. It is not difficult to see the reasons for hostility towards a British Resident who, in 1875, obtained similar powers in Perak, and was using them in a very revolutionary manner.

The position of the early British Resident would have been delicate and difficult enough even if the Malay States had been in a stable condition when he took up his appointment, but this, of course, was far from being the case. It was the civil wars among Malays and Chinese, and between elements of both, together with the subsidiary piracy operations in the Straits, which had provided the opportunity for British intervention, and many problems of law and order were still outstanding in the three states to which British Residents were first sent. The Resident had no strong military force with which he could handle a violent situation. Captain Speedy, Assistant Resident in Perak, was better off than most in this respect, because he already had a police force which he had trained while in the service of the Mantri before his appointment as Resident by the Straits government. He was also in the worst trouble-spot so far as the Chinese rivalries were concerned. Yet his forces were not large. He had a 'Residency Guard' of twenty-five Sepoys, and a police force of about one hundred and sixty, mainly Indian, but including a small group of Chinese. At Bandar Bahru, in Lower Perak, the first British Resident had a small garrison numbering between fifty and sixty, nearly all Indians. Not only were these garrisons small, but they have also been described as unreliable.[1] Recruits from India were of mixed quality, and at first it was impossible to recruit reliable Malays.

The Resident's opinions could therefore not be backed up by an impressive show of force, unless this was forthcoming from the Straits Settlements. In a matter of serious dispute between the Sultan and the Resident, it was possible for a Straits Governor to use pressure, and even a threat to withdraw British acknowledgment of that Sultan in favour of another prince, but a Governor would be unlikely to send armed forces unless he felt that he could clearly justify his action to his home government. On the other hand, from the Malay point of view, the British government might seem to be standing squarely behind the Residents. Malays told Swettenham that he and other Residents were thrown out as bait by the British government. 'If the Malay chiefs swallowed the bait, they would find themselves on the British hook; of course, no one would worry about the bait.'[2] The general directions from the Colonial Office in the 1870s were much more cautious, however, than the moves made both by Clarke and by Sir William Jervois, his successor at Singapore.

British military forces were used in two instances. On a small scale they were used in support of the Dato Klana of Sungei Ujong against his rival, the Dato Bandar. On a much bigger scale they were employed to hunt down the leaders of the movement which had caused the murder of the first British Resident in Perak. The campaign in Perak had the effect of removing from the scene all the main opposition leaders, and, at the same time, of serving as a warning against militant opposition in the future.

Much, of course, depended upon the personal relationship between the Resident and the Sultan and his chiefs. The Viceroy of Selangor had had friendly contacts with Singapore before 1874, and he was pleased to have British recognition of his status. The Resident appointed to advise him, late in 1874, was J. G. Davidson, who had already been his personal adviser and financial supporter

---

[1] E.g., by J. M. Gullick in 'Captain Speedy of Larut', *JRASMB*, Vol. 26, pt. 3, pp. 45–6.
[2] F. Swettenham, *British Malaya*, p. 219.

during the civil war. Kudin and Davidson were, in Swettenham's words, 'old friends'. As a newcomer to Selangor, and
victorious over those chiefs who had resisted his authority,
Kudin was both less conservative about the Selangor administration and better able to enforce the introduction of any
changes. Davidson, by all accounts, was a quiet and patient man
tactful about Malay affairs, and sound on financial matters. He and
Kudin made a modest start with a government treasury and police
force at Klang. For six years the mainly Chinese settlement at
Kuala Lumpur continued under the rule of Capitan China, Yap
Ah Loy. Even after the transfer of the British Residency from
Klang to Kuala Lumpur in 1880, Ah Loy was still a power to be
reckoned with, and he found ways and means of politely obstruct-
ing the Resident's plans when these did not suit him. Generally,
however, he was on friendly terms with the British Resident,
especially while Swettenham held that office, from 1882 until Ah
Loy's death in 1885. Previously Swettenham himself had been on
good terms with the old Sultan, Abdul Samad, at Langat.

Yet all was not peaceful in Selangor. In November, 1875, Raja
Mahdi, from exile in Johore, was planning a renewed revolt
against Kudin (and, indirectly, against British intervention), with
the aid of Sumatran Malays at Cheras and Kajang in the Langat
valley. Davidson had a police force under the command of a very
able young officer, Syers, who had trained as military police a
detachment of Malay and Indian mercenaries who had fought for
Kudin. With these police, and further Malay recruits, Syers and
Davidson reached Kuala Lumpur, where Ah Loy added a Chinese
contingent. Cheras and Kajang were then easily taken, and the
revolt was over.

In Sungei Ujong, the Dato Klana's position was bolstered by a
British military garrison. He was attacked by the Yang-di-Pertuan
under the influence of other Minangkabau states which did not
approve of the Klana's dealings with the British. Although the
Yang-di-Pertuan, Tunku Antah, was defeated and went into
temporary exile, official British influence in the Minangkabau
states remained limited to Sungei Ujong until 1883. By the time of
Tunku Antah's defeat in 1878, the Colonial Office, bearing in

mind the recent Perak War, recommended that no further extension of the Resident system should be attempted in this region
until the experiment had proved itself successful elsewhere.

It was with Perak that the first negotiations for a British Resident had taken place during the meeting at Pangkor in January
1874. Perak also provided the scene for the dramatic murder of the
first British Resident, and, later, for the work of the most successful exponent of the early Resident system.

In Larut Captain Speedy, as Assistant Resident, had a fairly
free hand between January and November 1874. No Resident
was appointed to Perak until November, and the Mantri, dis-
satisfied by the proceedings at Pangkor, took practically no part
in the government. He even contemplated sending his Penang
lawyer to England in an attempt to have his claim to status as an
independent ruler recognised again.

Speedy was fortunate in having the minimum of Malay
opposition. Apart from the Mantri, there was no other chief of
importance in Larut. Although the Mantri became drawn into the
plot for the overthrow of the British Resident in Perak, he was not
an active opponent of Speedy. Many of Speedy's early problems
were concerned with the Chinese tin-mining groups. 'Fighting
men', who had been imported from China during the Larut wars,
stayed on, and their leaders demanded a share in the profits of the
mines which had been promised to them. Friction occurred
between the headmen of the miners and the leaders — or
'Panglimas' as they were known — of the fighting men. Speedy
took a firm line, and banished some of the leading trouble-makers.

Speedy next attempted to ban the Secret Societies altogether,
making them illegal in Larut. This proved to be a task beyond his
powers, for the two Societies continued to function, really in
secret, whilst their leaders made an appearance of co-operation by
betraying the existence of any new Society which was starting up.
Speedy did, however, use the Chinese headmen, who were
Secret Society leaders, as liaison officers with the Chinese
community, and he recognised their position by the title 'Capitan
China'.

With the aid of his police force Speedy put down a certain

amount of lawlessness, and he established a Court of Law in Larut, where the Penal Code of the Straits Settlements was applied. It seemed as though a satisfactory condition of law and order had been achieved, yet it is doubtful how far Speedy's policies were acceptable. When, in November 1875, conspiracy against British rule in Perak was reaching a climax further south, the Malays of Kuala Kurau were preparing to rebel against Speedy; the Chinese headmen in Larut had been informed of the plans of the Malay chiefs, and were keeping quiet.

The export duty on tin was made a direct government levy, and Speedy had two British officials to supervise this work, Marples as Treasurer, and Peterson as Harbour-Master and Customs Officer at the Larut estuary. There were import duties on opium and spirits, which were paid at first by the Chinese headmen, who imported these commodities for resale to the mine-labourers. In 1875 the Resident of Perak decided to farm out the revenue from these sources, as was the usual practice in the Straits Settlements. The choice of the first tax-farmer was unfortunate. He was Cheng Tee, a Ghee Hin, who was in partnership with a Singapore financier, Kim Cheng, to whom Sultan Abdullah was indebted. This tax-farm roused great resentment in the Chinese headmen, who now lost an important source of profit themselves. Those who belonged to the Hai San group naturally had a second reason for hostility, since the farm was in the hands of a Ghee Hin. The miners themselves felt they would be worse off under the new arrangement, and as many as 3,000 to 5,000 of them were said to have left Larut for other areas, including Klang, where the opium duty would be less.

The maintenance of law and order and the establishment of a revenue system were among the most important of the Resident's duties. Other tasks included the planning and developing of townships, and the improvement of communications. In Larut Speedy laid out a site for a new town in each of the two main mining areas. The town in the Hai San area he named 'Thaipeng' ('Everlasting Peace'); the Ghee Hin town took the local Malay place-name, Kamunting. Swettenham described these towns in very favourable terms in the Journal of his visit to Perak in the months of April and early May 1874. He noted that the houses at Thaipeng (which he identified as Tai Kong) had been built in a 'marvellously short time, and very nice looking houses they are too, all alike, going up on both sides of what will be very shortly a good street'.[1] There were at least 250 houses in all. Similarly, Kamunting with its 200 or 300 houses had all the appearances of a peaceful and flourishing new township.

The only roads in Larut at the time of Speedy's appointment were those built by the Mantri, consisting of one road seven miles long from the mouth of the river Larut towards the mines, with another branch extending to Kota and Bukit Gantang. Logs sunk in the mud provided the road surface, and this was in very bad condition. Ox-carts and buffalo-carts provided the usual means of transport when the road could be used; elephants could follow a track of some sort in the most difficult of conditions.

Speedy repaired this road system as well as he could by using stone from the tin-workings, and he even extended the roads inland. His biggest difficulty was that of preparing a good road surface for the coastal stretch of the road, which lay on very swampy land several miles from the nearest supply of stone. Public buildings, including a Courthouse, a Residency building, and the renovation of the Mantri's gaol, were also part of Speedy's work, entailing further expenditure and also technical problems for which no experts were available.

The Mantri received a fixed income of between 8 per cent and 9 per cent of the Larut revenue each year, and Speedy governed largely without consulting him. Speedy published his own Report for 1874, including a statement of revenue, from which it was quite obvious that the administration was directly in his hands. The Mantri's feelings on the matter must have been bitter. Although he enjoyed greater personal security, his income was much smaller than previously, and he had heavy war-debts in Penang. He saw the Larut district governed by a man whom he had originally employed and paid as his own Chief of Police. He could only forestall awkward questions from Malays by spreading the idea that Speedy was working under his orders. It is not

[1] C. D. Cowan (editor), 'Swettenham's Perak Journals, 1874–1876', p. 44.

M

surprising that the Mantri was willing to join a Malay resistance movement against the new order.

From November 1874 Speedy was subject to supervision from the newly-appointed Resident of Perak, James Birch. Birch had been in the colonial service for nearly thirty years, mainly in Ceylon. Since 1870 he had been Colonial Secretary to the Straits Settlements. After Pangkor, he applied for the new post of Resident in Perak, and in April-May 1874, he was sent on a visit to the west-coast states, accompanied by Swettenham, to observe conditions and report back to Sir Andrew Clarke. Swettenham was his interpreter and assistant. Birch met Yusuf at Senggang, and Ismail at Blanja, and he reported that they were both opposed to the Pangkor Engagement. A month later Swettenham was sent to try to persuade both Yusuf and Ismail to come to Penang to meet Clarke. This was an extremely delicate mission, and only great perseverance on Swettenham's part made any progress possible at all. Yusuf was persuaded to go to Penang, but Ismail declined and remained at Blanja. Yusuf met Clarke and became willing to accept British policy, seeing in it, perhaps, the possibility of his own advancement.

In the months between the Pangkor Engagement and the appointment of Birch, Abdullah carried on government in his own fashion in Lower Perak. According to Swettenham, he was 'weak, inordinately vain and hopelessly extravagant'. Abdullah farmed out the taxes of Kuala Perak to his Singapore friend and financial supporter, Cheng Tee, for 26,000 dollars, receiving half the payment in advance. He also sold land concessions without any reference to the Governor with whom he had concluded the treaty.

Thus, when Birch arrived in November 1874, the estuary tolls were in the hands of a Chinese tax-farmer who had paid good money to Abdullah. Abdullah had granted land in the Krian district, where the Mantri had claims, to a Rawa chief Che'Karim, for the purpose of opening up tin-mines. Yusuf at Senggang was reconciled, for the time being, to British policy, but Ismail at Blanja, and the Upper Perak chiefs, wanted no dealings with the British Resident.

From the first there was a wide gulf between Abdullah and Birch, and, as time went on, this became wider. Abdullah had taken a British Resident mainly as a means of obtaining acknowledgment of his claim to be Sultan. He probably thought of a Resident as a junior official who would take orders from him, and whose advice, if listened to at all, could either be taken or ignored. Certainly he envisaged no revolutionary changes in the administration of the state, and no diminution of his own existing authority. A sensitive and pleasure-loving man, Abdullah had to be approached with the greatest diplomacy before he would be likely to agree to any changes.

Birch came to his new post with a keen sense of purpose and tremendous energy, but with little sensitivity of the delicateness of his situation. He wished to modernise the administration of Perak along the lines of his experience in Ceylon and the Straits Settlements. Revenue and expenditure would be in the hands of government officials; law would be administered as a function of a centralised government, and a public police force would maintain order. Existing customs which barred the way to these plans would have to go.

Birch was an idealist in a hurry. He had little knowledge, and no appreciation, of Malay traditions. In his zeal for reform he probably failed to grasp just how revolutionary his ideas appeared to the Sultan and his chiefs. Opposition would not, in any case, have deterred him from doing what he considered to be his duty. He realised at times that his life was in danger, but he noted that if one Mr. Birch died, another would take his place. Although his intentions were honest and well-meaning, his actions were high-handed, and they inevitably aroused feelings of slight and injury in Malay leaders sensitive of their own traditional dignities and powers. Birch also suffered from the disadvantage of speaking through a Malay interpreter. A good knowledge of Malay was a primary requirement for a British official in a Malay state, and the advantage which this gave, for instance, to Swettenham and Hugh Low can hardly be overestimated. Personal relationships were all-important in states where government was such a personal affair, and these were not assisted by talks and conferences which had to pass through an interpreter. A Malay interpreter had the worst of both worlds. With habitual politeness he would try to cushion the sharpness of the views exchanged between Birch and the Malay leaders, and, in so doing, he did not help the cause of either side.

Firmness and speed were the essential features of Birch's tactics. He explained that there was to be only one joint farm for opium, spirits, and gambling in the state, and that taxes on all rivers would be collected by government officers backed by a police force. There would be one high court judge for the whole state, who would sentence unlawful tax-gatherers. Birch instituted new customs duties on tin and other commodities, and attempted to regularise both the places and the procedure of tax-collection.

> 'I would tell the chiefs of Perak that . . . we would not allow any of them to levy taxes in their own names, but must have the revenue all collected at proper and stated places, and by a fixed method, and in the name of the Sultan only; and if they chose to attempt to take taxes, or rather levy blackmail on their own account, the result would be that we should stop it by force. . . .'[1]

Birch followed up these instructions by taking action against 'illegal' toll-stations which he came across on his river journeys. These measures were bitterly resented by the chiefs concerned, and by their relatives in other posts of authority.

While Birch was offending the chiefs in this matter of tax-collection, he was also annoying them by his attitude to slavery and debt-bondage. Every chief had bondsmen and bondswomen, and the custom of bondage had deep roots. Some chiefs also had slaves of non-Muslim stock. Birch soon made it clear that these were customs of which he strongly disapproved, and his Residency at Bandar Bahru became a refuge for fugitives of one status or the other who were attempting to escape from their masters. Speedy in Larut met exactly the same problem. The numbers of people concerned were small, but an important principle was at stake. Should the Resident give protection to the refugees, or should he see that they were returned to the chief from whom they had fled?

[1] Quoted from R. O. Winstedt and R. J. Wilkinson, 'A History of Perak', p. 104.

If he protected them, this might well increase the number of such cases, and it would certainly anger the chiefs. If he returned them, he might feel that he was condemning the runaways to unknown punishments, and was condoning a system with which he was not in agreement. Speedy respected Malay custom and returned the slaves or bondsmen; Birch was inclined to give them asylum and support their efforts to escape.

Whilst Birch's relations with the Malay leaders were steadily getting worse, there still remained the task of persuading the up-river chiefs, including the elected Sultan, Ismail, to recognise Abdullah's authority, and to hand over to him the State regalia. In early January 1875 Birch arranged a meeting of the Malay chiefs at Blanja, in the hope that Ismail would on this occasion hand over the regalia and accept Abdullah as Sultan. It was a tribute to Birch's persistence that the meeting took place at all, but it did not work out the way he had hoped. The Mantri came to Blanja, but did not attend the conference. The Maharaja Lela, a down-river chief, stayed away. Abdullah would not talk to Yusuf or Ismail. Ismail was, apparently, polite, but nobody said anything that mattered, and after three hours everybody, including Birch, had had enough. Unknown to Birch, Abdullah had sent a message to Ismail which sabotaged whatever slight hopes there might have been of an agreement. Abdullah told Ismail that he was not coming of his own free will, and asked Ismail not to agree to hand over the regalia, or to the installation of himself as Sultan. Otherwise, added Abdullah, 'Perak will be given over to the English, for my words have caused me to be much indebted to them.'

Abdullah and Birch were, in fact, working at cross-purposes. As Birch went off to Penang to let the opium and spirits farm, Abdullah resumed his normal practices of farming out the taxes for ready money. Birch returned to deliver another of his addresses on the subject of taxation, and to try, without success, to persuade first Abdullah, then Ismail, to visit the Governor of the Straits Settlements. A more reliable indication of the course of events was the building of a strong stockade round his village at Pasir Salak by Maharaja Lela.

A Malay deputation did call on the Governor at Singapore in

May 1875. This was led by the Laksamana and Raja Dris (who was later to become Sultan). It arrived at Singapore at a time when Sir Andrew Clarke was handing over to his successor, Sir William Jervois. The inopportune timing, and the fact that this was a secret mission so far as Birch was concerned, prevented the Malay group from having their grievances seriously heard.

Meanwhile Birch was energetically touring the river valleys of Perak and trying, whenever he saw Abdullah, to have the royal seal affixed to notices for the new taxes. Abdullah could always find reasons for a postponement of the new system. In July Abdullah managed to call together a representative conference of Malay chiefs at Durian Sabatang, a little north of his own head-quarters, Batak Rabit. By this move Abdullah became the leader of a Malay movement for the removal of Birch and all that he stood for. Ismail did not attend, but he sent a letter agreeing to any plan for the removal of Birch. The meeting decided to invite the co-operation of Ismail and the up-river chiefs in driving the British out of Perak, and the Maharaja Lela offered to stab the Resident.

The relationships between Abdullah and Birch became worse as incidents, humiliating to the Sultan or infuriating to the Resident, increased. There were further disputes about taxation and refugee-slaves. Under pressure, Abdullah signed proclamations giving control of all taxes, and the right to appoint and dismiss headmen, to the Resident and the Shahbandar. At the same time the Resident and Raja Dris were appointed Judges. Abdullah followed this by ordering arms from Penang, and by attending a spirit séance at which Birch's death was symbolically forecast by the use of Malay magic.

In September Perak received a visit from Governor Jervois. The new Governor realised that little real progress had been made in Perak either towards the general acceptance of Abdullah as Sultan, or towards the establishment of a public revenue system. He wanted powers of control for the British Resident, not merely the right to advise. The Malay chiefs would be given pensions, and the actual government would be in the hands of British officials appointed by the Crown. Jervois had put these views in a letter to the Secretary of State for the Colonies in July, and his visit to Perak was aimed at seeing what could be done to further them in a series of personal interviews with the Malay leaders.

Ismail would have nothing to do with Jervois's proposals. Yusuf and Dris signed letters asking the British government to take over the government of Perak. Abdullah temporised, but finally, at the end of September, signed a letter accepting the Governor's proposals. Yusuf, Dris, and Abdullah all received written promises of pensions. A further letter from the Governor suggested that Abdullah would remain Sultan, and that British officers would administer the state in his name. Alternatively, in the event of a refusal by Abdullah, the same terms were to be offered to Yusuf.

Abdullah was now pressed by Birch to sign proclamations which gave the new policy in practical terms. British officers in Perak were to have the power of judges and the right to appoint magistrates. They were to be the Sultan's representatives for the collection and administration of revenue, and for the appointment of all chiefs and headmen, together with the general administration of the country. Abdullah only signed these proclamations under threat that they would otherwise be offered to Yusuf.

When these proclamations and Abdullah's earlier letter of acceptance were received in Singapore, Jervois worked out the details of the new form of government, which was to be in the name of the Sultan through Commissioners and Assistant Commissioners of the Queen. Jervois now reported his policy for the first time to the Colonial Office and, almost simultaneously, he received a reply to his earlier letter, written in July. Lord Carnarvon, in this reply, would not agree to any immediate extension of British control in Perak, and stated that the Resident system must be given a further period of trial. The Governor was now, however, too deeply committed to withdraw.

The situation in Perak was approaching a crisis. Despite promises to the contrary, Birch continued to give aid to female slaves or bondswomen who sought refuge at the Residency. Abdullah made contact with Ismail in a common front to oppose the British control to which he had just given his assent. He also sent his approval of the Maharaja Lela's plan to kill Birch when he came to his village at Pasir Salak. Ismail and his chiefs agreed to support the Maharaja, and to follow-up Birch's death with an attack on the Residency.

In late October Swettenham brought from Singapore printed copies of the proclamations and the new instructions, and he went up-river to distribute some of these, and to explain the new system in the inland villages, while Birch was carrying out the same work in Lower Perak. Abdullah and Ismail now both sent supplies and arms to Maharaja Lela, and Abdullah finally sent a kris.

When Birch arrived at the Maharaja's village, Pasir Salak, on November 1st, he was confronted with a scene of armed hostility which he either underestimated or simply ignored. The posting of the proclamations next morning on the wooden walls of a Chinese shop-house served as a signal for the attack on Birch. The proclamations were torn down, and Birch was speared to death through the palm-leaf walls of the riverside bath-house near which his boat lay moored. Swettenham, in Upper Perak, was in a very dangerous situation. As the news of Birch's death moved up-river, Swettenham decided his best chance of escape was to make downstream, even though this meant passing through Pasir Salak. He was accompanied on his journey by Raja Mahmud of Selangor, who had been extremely loyal to him since the ending of the Selangor War. They passed through Pasir Salak unrecognised, at one o'clock in the morning, and reached Bandar Bahru to find that the Residency had not yet been attacked.

There was no well-planned and determined Malay rising. The attack on the Residency by Maharaja Lela's men was called off, possibly by Abdullah,[1] who now posed as having had no part in the attack on Birch. Birch's boat, a 'Sampan Naga', had been sent up-river to Ismail as proof of the assassination, but Ismail sent it downstream again, having no wish to explain its presence in his district. In other words, having agreed on Birch's death, the Malay leaders took precautions, arming their men and sending their wives and families to greater safety, but waited on developments.

[1] R. O. Winstedt and R. J. Wilkinson, 'A History of Perak', p. 115.

The Residency was reinforced from Penang. Jervois came in person with troops from Singapore, and, by the end of November, other British naval and military forces had arrived from India and Hong Kong. This military expedition made its way up-river, with a second column entering via Larut. Little serious resistance was encountered. Only Pasir Salak would appear to have been strongly prepared for defence. By the middle of 1876 all those implicated in the assassination had been arrested. The Maharaja Lela and his followers were tried under two Malay judges and two British assessors at Matang; Lela and two others were convicted and executed.[1] Ismail fled to Kedah and later agreed to live in exile in Johore. Abdullah, the Mantri, and the Shahbandar, for their complicity in the plot were brought to Singapore and sent to live with their families in the Seychelles. Of the leading Malay chiefs only Yusuf was exonerated from blame, and he now became recognised by the British, first as 'Regent', and in 1886 as Sultan of Perak.

Birch, after only one year in office, had fallen a victim partly to his own temperament and actions, and partly to the policy of British control which he and Jervois saw as the only means of bringing modern government to Perak. The attack on Birch was not merely a personal one. It was an attempt by Malay leaders to drive out political and economic innovations which would place them under foreign rule, and which would rob them of their customary sources of wealth, prestige, and authority.

After this 'Perak War', there was much heart-searching on both sides. Malay opposition to British influence now lacked leadership, and became centred in certain villages from which, however, trouble could still be expected. On the British side, Jervois was rebuked by the Colonial Office for his unofficial policy of rule by Commissioners in the name of the Sultan, which was thought to be the reason for the hostile outbreak. The Resident system was continued, with the Resident once again confined to the giving of advice. Co-operation on these lines was still going to be very difficult for many years. There were, however, some

[1] Another Pasir Salak man had previously been tried, under Raja Dris, and executed at Bandar Bahru.

advantages in the situation of 1876. No one was left to dispute Yusuf's title, and all the other prominent Malay figures who had played leading parts in recent years were now absent from the scene. Although resentment still smouldered in some Malay villages, it was not so likely to break out into open rebellion after witnessing the passage along the river of a large British force in 1875–6. Even at the time of Birch's death, no general Malay rising was imminent. On the other hand Yusuf, the new ruler, was moody and unpopular, perhaps increasingly unpopular among the remaining chiefs because of his acceptance of British policy. A new Resident not only had the task of making himself acceptable to the Malays; he also had to use his influence to make Yusuf acceptable to his own subjects.

The new Acting-Resident was J. G. Davidson, the friend of Kudin, who was transferred from Selangor to Perak in 1876. He worked under great difficulties. To begin with, the military commanders were virtually in charge, and when the troops were withdrawn, he had to raise and pay for a large police force of Sikhs and Malays under European officers as a precaution against further troubles. There was insufficient revenue to meet this urgent need, and there was also a heavy war-debt. Within a year Davidson had resigned from his unhappy position. His interests lay mainly in Selangor, and his appointment in Perak had, in any case, been a provisional one.

The appointment of Davidson's successor, Hugh Low, who was to be Resident in Perak for the next twelve years (1877–89), marked the beginning of a happier and more peaceful and prosperous era. Low's success in Perak served as a model for Residents in other states, and, in so far as there was any 'system' at all about the work of the British Residents in the early years of this experiment, it was Low who created it.

Yet at the beginning of Low's term of office in Perak his achievement could hardly have been foreseen. He succeeded an able man who had surrendered the job. There was no reserve of money; there were problems of law and order; Malay co-operation was very doubtful, and there was the difficulty of working with Yusuf. The old issues of taxation and debt-bondage had still to be faced, and there were embarrassing visits from the needy relatives and kinsmen of those leaders who had been sent into exile.

Low was a newcomer to Malaya, aged a little over fifty, with a striking white beard. He was originally — and to some extent he always remained — a botanist. He had spent most of the previous thirty years in Borneo, where he started in the service of Raja Brooke of Sarawak, and he came to Perak from Labuan, where he had been Colonial Secretary.

Low had the advantage of speaking Malay, and he was also familiar with Malay customs, including that of debt-bondage. Just as Birch had lived at Bandar Bahru in Lower Perak so as to be near Abdullah, so Low took up his station at Kuala Kangsar to be near Yusuf. Larut was brought within the direct sphere of the Resident, and the Assistant Resident was moved, at a reduced salary, to Durian Sabatang, in Lower Perak. Captain Speedy, who was not in good favour with Governor Jervois, had to make this unwelcome change of situation, but he resigned late in 1877. His successors in this office need not concern us here. The wife of one of them, a Mrs. Innes, wrote a book with the title *The Chersonese with the Gilding Off*, published in 1885. She gives an unflattering picture of Durian Sabatang. This centre was soon shown to be too far upstream for river steamers to come there with safety, and its place was taken later by Telok Melintang, renamed Telok Anson.

Low judiciously blended great tact and patience with an occasional show of firmness. He worked on the principle that when dealing with members of another race, one should be at least as considerate as to members of one's own race, and infinitely more patient. He made himself accessible to all who wished to see him, and he showed an understanding attitude to the customs and problems of the Malays. He made no attempt, for instance, to interfere in any way with the practice of debt-bondage until such time as it should be abolished by the law of the state. He aimed, above all, at gaining the confidence of those whom he met. In Winstedt's words, 'his personality appealed to the Malay', while the Chinese responded to the more settled conditions and were even given representation in the State government.

Compensation or employment as State officers was offered to the chiefs who would lose their old rights under a system of public revenue. A civil list of pensions and annuities was drawn up, but many chiefs became government tax-collectors, entitled to a fixed salary out of their receipts. The police force was reduced by giving police duties to village headmen. Appointments to offices were made by Low in the name of the Sultan, but Malay opinion was consulted first. A land-tax was substituted for the old personal rights of the chiefs to forced labour. Rivers were placed under State control. Courts of Justice were introduced, presided over by European, often assisted by Malay, magistrates; Raja Dris sat as a Judge for many years in the Kuala Kangsar Court. The state was divided into districts under European and Malay district officers.

Slavery and debt bondage gradually began to lose their importance, and even, in some cases, their function. The new administration outdated, for instance, the role of the armed retainer in the service of his chief, while improvements in communications increased trade both internally and externally and emphasised the importance of a money-economy instead of a system of feudal obligations. On January 1st, 1884, slavery and bondage in Perak came to an end by law, with compensatory sums of money payable to the former masters.

Behind all this was the Resident, but the authority through which he worked was the State Council, which Low, with his flair for co-operation, brought into existence.[1] The Sultan was its President, and the other members included the leading Malay chiefs, and Chinese leaders. The Resident was a member of this Council, but his ideas could only be put into practice with the agreement of the other members. A tactful and respected Resident could often carry the Council with him. Once decisions were taken, they were no longer his proposals, they were the orders of the Council. When his ideas were not accepted, he could drop the subject tactfully and, if necessary, bring it up again on a later and

[1] The idea may have come from the Colonial Office, and, perhaps, originally from Jervois. (Cf. Letter from Carnavon to Jervois dated June 1st, 1876, in C. N. Parkinson, *British Intervention in Malaya, 1867–1877*, pp. 313–17.)

more opportune occasion. All important acts of State stemmed from this Council. It dealt with the annual estimates of revenue and expenditure; the appointments and salaries and pensions of all Malay chiefs and headmen; the confirmation or modification of death sentences passed in the Courts. At the Council meetings, business was conducted in Malay and the Resident discussed all important matters which came within his sphere. The Perak State Council was so successful that its pattern was copied by other States.

Low was careful about money. He practised strict economy in expenditure, and transformed a heavy State-debt into a credit balance within six years. He left Perak, when he retired in 1889, with an annual revenue of over two million dollars, and a credit balance of one and half million dollars. 'It would be difficult', says Swettenham, 'to overstate the value of his twelve years' work.'[1]

The work of the Resident increased in scope with the passage of time and the greater availability of money, either in the form of surplus revenue or in loans negotiated with the Straits Settlements. One field of enterprise was the improvement of communications. This was itself a stimulus to increased production and trade; indirectly, it aided the centralisation of the State government. Rivers were cleared and road-making was begun in the form of six-foot-wide earth bridle roads, which were later widened and metalled. These roads were built in the tin-mining districts, linking the mines with the growing townships; they played only a minor part at first in connecting the mines to the coast. In Selangor, for example, a road was built up by the joint efforts of Ah Loy and the British Resident from Kuala Lumpur to Damansara, fifteen miles down river. From Damansara, it was still necessary to proceed to Klang by boat. By 1885 Selangor had a useful cart-road running from the northern to the southern border.

More spectacular, and more effective so far as the tin trade was concerned, was the introduction of railways. In an age of high faith in railways in Britain, British Residents saw railways as the answer to the problem of tin-transport. By 1885 Low had a

[1] *British Malaya*, p. 252.

railway line operating from Taiping to Sa-petang (later Port Weld) on the Larut River. Before this line was completed, Swettenham had started work on a longer east-west railway to Klang, with half the necessary capital borrowed from the Straits government, the other half to be provided from revenue as the work proceeded. Skilled labour for railway construction in both Perak and Selangor was introduced from India and Ceylon. Before the end of 1886 the Kuala Lumpur line ran to Bukit Kuda on the north bank of the river, opposite Klang. This line was later taken by bridge to Klang, and eventually to Port Swettenham. Before 1895 two other lines were opened, one by government, from Tapah Road to Telok Anson in Perak, the other, by the Sungei Ujong Company, from Seremban to Port Dickson. These railway lines not only speeded up the two-way traffic between the mining areas and the Straits; they also brought additional revenue to the state by stimulating a greater output of tin, and by running at a profit themselves.

All kinds of amenities were required by the growing townships. These included the planning of sites, building regulations, drainage, water-supply, street lighting, and the provision of some kind of public medical service. All these matters formed part of the work of the early Residents, though the development of Town Sanitary Boards about 1890 relieved the Resident of much direct contact with the local details. The Resident felt a particular responsibility for dealing with epidemics such as smallpox and cholera, and it was extremely difficult for him to gain co-operation in the drastic measures which he often had to take to check the spread of infectious disease.

To make the State more prosperous Residents encouraged new settlements and the development of plantation agriculture. Settled political conditions and better communications also, of course, contributed to this end. Plantations of the 1880s and early 1890s included pepper, sugar, gambier, and tobacco, all, except sugar, worked on a small scale by Malays, Chinese, and Javanese, together with a new series of European plantations in Perak, Selangor, and Negri Sembilan, which were mainly concerned with the growing of Liberian coffee. When the coffee-boom gave place to a rubber-boom, it is interesting to note, some experimental work on the Brazilian rubber-tree had already been done by Hugh Low in the Residency gardens at Kuala Kangsar.

The early Resident was not just an office man. A great deal of his time was spent in travelling about the State, meeting people and studying local problems and conditions at first hand. He kept a daily Journal, which was a mixture of official reports and personal diary, and this was sent from time to time to Singapore. In addition, the Resident sent to the Governor of the Straits Settlements for his approval an annual estimate of revenue and expenditure, and an Annual Report. The Residents were nominated by the Governor and approved by the Secretary of State for the Colonies, but, apart from the annual returns, the Governor could only exercise any effective control over a Resident by visiting the State concerned. According to Swettenham, apart from a short period (1876–82) when there was at Singapore a Secretary for Malay Affairs (Swettenham himself), there was no one in Singapore until 1896 who 'had knowledge enough to criticise successfully the actions of the Residents'.[1] This may have left the Residents with wide powers in practice, but they did receive general instructions from Singapore not to exceed their function, which was to advise. They did, of course, very much more than offer advice, but by co-operation, and the machinery of the State Council, the Resident appeared to be more a business partner than a managing director. The Sultan retained prestige and had an important political role as President of the State Council. As the State prospered, both he and the leading Malay chiefs were aware that the new régime was not without advantages for them.

Emphasis has been given to the Resident system in Perak, where it began, where it met its greatest crisis, and where it achieved a success which was copied elsewhere. Reference has also been made to Selangor, where the Residency was first at Klang and later at Kuala Lumpur. It now remains briefly to mention the extension of the Resident system to other Minangkabau States after Sungei Ujong, and, finally, to Pahang.

[1] *British Malaya*, p. 247.

In Sungei Ujong, the Dato Klana was only too willing to accept British advice. The Assistant Resident there introduced a treasury and the collection of revenue in the name of the State, as well as a magistrate's court, a police force, and a prison. In 1877 disputes between the states of Jelebu and Rembau were brought to the Maharaja (formerly Temenggong) of Johore, Abu Bakar, for his arbitration. Abu Bakar was not reluctant to take this opportunity of renewing, to some extent, the former Johore influence in this region, but the Minangkabau leaders themselves were divided on this point, for the tribal headmen had not been consulted by their chiefs. The tribal headmen secured a reversal of this policy, and Rembau and Jelebu asked the Straits government to become arbiter in place of the Maharaja. In 1886 and 1887 respectively Jelebu and Rembau accepted British administrative officers and British protection; in 1889 the rest of the small states also placed themselves under British protection, and the confederation of Nine States began to take shape. British influence, notably the work of an ex-coffee-planter Resident, Martin Lister, served as a unifying factor, and by 1898 Negri Sembilan was a federal state with a Yang-di-Pertuan and one British Resident.

A number of only partially-related circumstances led to British intervention in Pahang. In 1882, with the approval of the Maharaja of Johore, Ahmad, victor of the civil war twenty years previously, took the title of Sultan. During the following year a boundary dispute arose between Pahang and Jelebu, just at the time when the headmen of Jelebu were beginning to seek British protection. The Straits Governor, Sir Cecil Smith, tried to mediate in this dispute. He also tried to re-establish friendly relations between Ahmad and his brother, Mansur, with whom he had quarrelled. Mansur was causing trouble by attempting to use Selangor as a base for attacks on Pahang. In 1885 Swettenham was sent from Perak, where he was Acting-Resident, to visit the Sultan at Pekan to try to settle the boundary question, to seek a reconciliation between Ahmad and Mansur, and to propose the idea of a treaty between Singapore and Pahang. Nothing really came of this meeting, but on his return Swettenham recommended to the Governor the appointment of an Agent at Pekan to watch the interests of British subjects. The Sultan was at this time granting concessions of land to European companies who associated themselves with Malays or Arabs. In tin- and gold-mining areas, these concessions caused trouble because they sometimes overlooked the existing rights of Malay and Chinese miners.

In 1887 the Straits Governor finally obtained a treaty from the Sultan through a diplomatic visit by Hugh Clifford, a young officer who, not long before, had worked at the Residency of Hugh Low in Kuala Kangsar. The main significance of this was the appointment of a British Agent at Pekan, and Clifford was himself placed in this new post. His functions were defined as similar to those of a Consular officer, but he set out to influence the Sultan in favour of a reformed legal and administrative system. Although the Sultan established a Court of Justice on Clifford's advice, cases were heard in a very arbitrary way, and the Sultan's officers sometimes interfered with decisions.

The murder of a British Chinese shopkeeper in the vicinity of the Sultan's palace in February 1888 gave Clifford and the Governor occasion to press Sultan Ahmad further for the protection of British subjects. The Governor visited Pekan, and Ahmad subsequently consulted his chiefs. Opinion was by no means generally in favour of British protection through the Resident system. The ruler of Johore advised Ahmad to accept a British Resident, and the more moderate chiefs agreed. In August 1888 the Sultan wrote to Governor Cecil Smith and asked for the appointment of a British Resident.

Mr. J. P. Rodger was the first Resident, with Clifford as Superintendent of Ulu Pahang. Rodger had previously served in various capacities in Selangor, sometimes as deputy Resident or Acting Resident under Swettenham. He faced real problems in Pahang, of the kind which Birch had met originally in Perak. There were quarrels about revenue collection, pension lists, and land-rents. Bahman, the Orang Kaya of Semantan, a warlike and rebellious chief by nature, led an armed resistance to British officials in 1891, but his support was limited mainly to three hundred of his own men, and the Sultan declared against him. The rebels eventually withdrew to Trengganu and Kelantan.

N

By 1895 the Resident system was firmly established in Perak, Selangor, Negri Sembilan, and Pahang. It had 'evolved' through a kind of trial-and-error experience to a position of British indirect authority in these four central Malay states. From an administrator's point of view, advantages might accrue from some kind of union between these four States, which were all governed on similar principles. Swettenham, whose experience by this time was very considerable, began to make his suggestions for federation. This issue is discussed in a later chapter.[1]

[1] Chapter 13.

Chapter 11

A SURVEY OF SOCIAL AND ECONOMIC DEVELOPMENTS

c. A.D. 1850–1950 (I)

The introduction of British advisers into four Malay states during the period 1874 to 1888 marked the beginnings of a political revolution which eventually created modern Malaya. This was neither a sudden nor a violent movement, but it was a revolution in the sense that it produced a fundamental change in the government and in the very function of the state. From about the middle of the nineteenth century, fundamental changes also began to occur in the economic life of the Malay States. These produced in due course not only new social classes but also large revenues which governments could apply to the provision of what are usually called Social Services — notably, Health, Education, Welfare, and Housing. Some of the Malay States passed through a phase of development similar in many respects to that of the Industrial Revolution in western countries a little earlier. The tin-mining and tin-smelting industries grew tremendously in size, organisation, and output, all of this accompanied by large capital investment and the use of improved technical processes.

Linked with the expansion of tin-mining was a pattern of communications both within the mining areas themselves, and between the mines and the coast, en route to collecting-centres for the export trade. This pattern included, by the turn of the twentieth century, cart-roads, railways, railway-ports, and coastal steamship services. It was the counterpart of turnpike-roads, canals, railways, and docks in Britain during the period 1760–1840.

It was not only Malayan industry which was changing. At least equally striking were the changes in agriculture. In part, these were stimulated by the greater demand for food for an increasing population, including a large proportion of an urban or semi-urban character. The more spectacular aspect, however, was the vast increase of plantation agriculture, which included crops new to Malayan soil, and which was mainly destined, like tin, to supply distant, and sometimes varying, markets.

Employment of labour at all levels accompanied these developments in industry, communications, and agriculture, and the Malay States in which they took place became lands of promise for many people. At one end of the economic scale was the European or Chinese merchant-house or joint-stock company with its capital and executive personnel; at the other end was the Chinese, Tamil, or Cingalese labourer, and the Indonesian villager from Sumatra or Java. Several other occupational groupings occurred amongst the immigrant population. These included traders, shopkeepers, teachers, clerks, and skilled workers, watchmen, and police.

A land of promise was not necessarily a land of settlement and there was emigration as well as immigration. The balance was normally on the immigrant side, thus increasing the overall population. The striking rise in the population of the Malay States from an estimated figure of well below half a million in 1850 to some four millions about eighty years later (1931 census) is only partly accounted for by immigration. Improved health conditions and a consequently lower death-rate played a part which it is difficult to overestimate.

The increasing population was not evenly spread over the nine Malay States. The east-coast states, where relatively little economic change took place, remained thinly populated. Most affected were western Johore, Negri Sembilan, Selangor, and Perak. On a north-south line, a chain of towns developed in these states in the western plain between mountains and sea, and in the river valleys which intersect the higher land. All these towns were products of the economic development of their surrounding areas, though in some cases their growth was also partly due to their choice as centres of government. Growing towns of the 1880s and 1890s, like Taiping, Ipoh, and Kuala Lumpur, had to face all the usual problems of urbanised life — water-supply, street-cleansing, paving, lighting, housing and health regulations, and so on. They were pioneers in municipal government in the Malay States.

Surplus revenues were soon applied on the one hand to improving communications and, in some cases, assisting the passages of immigrants; on the other hand, to the provision of public services in health and education. Both types of expenditure represented an investment in the future. The health measures consisted partly of a campaign against tropical diseases, including preventative and research work, and partly in the provision of public hospitals. Money for education was spent mainly, in the first instance, in subsidising schools established by voluntary organisations, and this practice continued later, side by side with the establishment and maintenance of government schools.

Thus, as the Malay States developed a modern look in the political sense, they also developed economic and social features which are commonly found in modern states to-day. This economic and social revolution affected the west coast states very much more than those of the east coast, and some attempts to remedy this are being made at the present time.

The economic and social history of Malaya has not received the attention from historians which it deserves, although some striking contributions on individual topics have been made. Within the scope of this present work, it is only possible to summarise the main features over the last hundred years or so. It must, of course, be remembered that each topic is not exclusive; there is a great deal of overlapping and inter-connection.

I. MINING

Gold has been worked in Pahang from at least the sixteenth century, and it may have been worked near Malacca in neolithic times. The quantities were not large, and extraction of the gold was a slow and laborious process. Gold-mining and tin-mining were carried on in adjacent areas in the Kuala Lipis region. Tin-mining here as elsewhere was a Chinese industry, but Malays seem to have taken a major part both in the control and the actual working of the gold mines. District chiefs were more subject in Pahang than in the west coast states to the payment of taxes and royalties to the ruler of the state, although they were still inclined to be rebellious if their privileges were infringed upon.

In the 1880s the Sultan of Pahang granted several concessions to western companies for mining purposes. These occurred at a time when it seemed likely that British protection would be extended to Pahang, and they stemmed mainly from business interests in Singapore. There were rumours that Pahang was not only rich in tin, but also rich in deposits of gold. Many of these enterprises never got beyond the prospecting stage; some did not even venture so far. Others involved considerable capital expense, but failed after a few years, usually because of poor management, difficult working conditions, or disturbances following the appointment of a British Resident in Pahang. The one really successful 'Western' venture was the Australian gold-mining company established at Raub in 1889 (Raub Australian Gold-Mining, Ltd.). This has survived as the main gold-mining concern in the Malay States, and the current output from the underground mines at Raub in a normal year amounts to three-quarters or more of Malaya's gold production.

Old alluvial gold-workings also occur in Kelantan, and in the early years of the present century a British company, the Duff Syndicate, undertook, among other activities, dredging and mining for gold, with only very moderate success.

At the end of the nineteenth century there seemed to be some possibilities of a 'gold-rush' in the east-coast states of Malaya, but this did not materialise. Western business enterprise was prepared to follow, or even, in some cases, to precede, British political influence. Many efforts ended in failure, and even the Raub company almost came to an early end when its first manager gloomily inspected the neglected and water-filled hole of the old Malay workings.[1]

During the present century coal-mining began at Batu Arang in Selangor through Western enterprise and the foundation of a company known as Malayan Collieries Ltd. (1913). The technical

[1] A. Wright and T. H. Reid, *The Malay Peninsula*, p. 264.

and clerical staff included both Asians and Europeans, and the labour force consisted mainly of Chinese and Indians as well as a smaller number of Malays. The coal mined here has not been an export commodity, and its main uses have been for railways, power-stations, and dredges. For various reasons, notably the increasing competition of fuel-oil, coal production has gone down, and at the current time the coal industry in Malaya is dying.

Iron-ore has been worked by Japanese enterprise in Johore, Trengganu, and Kelantan, since shortly after the First World War, for export to Japan, where it is smelted. By 1938 the shipments represented about half of Japan's ore imports. Kedah, Perak, and Pahang have also become ore-producing states in recent years, and the industry is expanding. It is again very largely linked with Japan for the Japanese steel industry, and no iron-smelting is done in Malaya.

A number of other mining operations had their origins well in the present century. Of these, the mining of bauxite (aluminium) has had the largest output, and it was, like iron-ore, originally in Japanese hands. The mines are in Johore, and nearly all production, which is still rising, is for the Japanese market.

Something like ninety per cent of mining in Malaya to-day concerns the mining of tin, and the growth of large-scale tin-mining has been a very significant development since about the middle of the nineteenth century; the main tin-producing areas have been in Perak and Selangor. This topic has already been touched upon in so far as it concerned politics and order in Perak, Selangor, and Sungei Ujong. Some attention must now be given to the growth of the tin industry in its own context.

Tin-mining in a simple form had been carried on in Malaya from at least the early centuries of the Christian era. Tin gained from alluvial streams may have been used as a component of bronze-work and as an early form of money. By the ninth century A.D., Arab traders were attracted to Kedah for tin, among other things, and the export trade in tin continued to play an important part in the history of the west coast states during the time of the Malacca Sultanate, and subsequently. Tin in blocks and in coins was an important medium of exchange in fifteenth century Malacca, and tin-bearing states also paid tribute in this valuable metal to the Malacca Sultans. The Portuguese, Achinese, Dutch, Bugis, and the English East India Company, all in turn took a very active interest in the collection of tin from the west-coast states.

Until about the middle of the nineteenth century, however, tin production in the Malay States, important as it was, could only be said to be on a fairly small scale. It was the influx of Chinese capital from the Straits Settlements, and the introduction of Chinese mining techniques, which marked the change in scope of the old industry. Chinese merchants in Penang, Malacca, and Singapore, were often interested in tin as a trading commodity. Through trade they were able to acquire capital which could be employed in other enterprises, and in several areas Malay chiefs, to increase their own income from rents, royalties, and river-tolls, were willing to grant mining concessions. Sometimes the local Malay ruler went into active partnership with the Chinese towkay; sometimes Chinese miners worked in small groups subject to the Malay chief. In the larger mining concerns, however, the Chinese community, although present with the original approval of the Malay ruler, became virtually a separate entity linked with the Malay authorities only through the economic ties of payments for the right to mine and ship tin.

The main Malay method was 'lampan' mining. This consisted of diverting a stream through a prepared channel, and then pulling soil with mattocks down into the running water. The water washed away the earth, and the tin-ore was recovered from the bed of the channel. This technique was suited to extracting tin as a part-time occupation with the minimum of preparation.

The Chinese introduced the open-cast 'lombong' method. A large hole was dug in the ground after a site had been chosen with the aid of a Malay Pawang and the added precaution of trial-boring. The tin-bearing soil was carried to the surface in baskets, with the use of tree-trunk ladders as the mine grew deeper. At the surface the soil ('karang') was washed in a trough of running water (a 'lanchut') to separate the ore from the earth. As this stream continued, the tailings were sometimes washed a second time by women and children, using wooden pans ('dulangs'). The tin-ore was either transported for smelting elsewhere, or smelted in a brazier on the mining site. The brazier was heated by the use of mangrove-wood and charcoal as fuel in alternate layers, and the molten tin was drained off from a pipe which led from the furnace.

Two main technical problems had to be overcome. One was to prevent flooding and subsidence in the mining hole, the other was to provide a controlled water-supply. A variety of devices, some of them adapted with ingenuity from rice-field techniques of South China, were introduced to meet these problems. Streams were dammed and artificial water-courses planned; chain-pumps driven by a water-wheel were used for pumping operations; in some cases bamboo water-pipes were employed. The Chinese miners were also quick to adopt Western devices. About 1879, Hugh Low, Resident of Perak, had a British steam-engine and centrifugal pump on show to interest Chinese miners as an improved method of flood-prevention. This brought a quick response. Yap Ah Loy, for instance, imported a steam-engine two years later for use in his largest mine at Ampang. The gradual, replacement, in Chinese mines, of the chain-pump and water wheel by the steam-engine and centrifugal pump made open-cast mining both safer and possible at much greater depths.

Similarly, the Chinese adopted from early Western enterprises the practices of hydraulic sluicing and gravel-pumping which had been developed in Australia.

It is obvious that this Chinese mining with its large, but not necessarily deep, open-cast hole, and its planning, equipment, labour force, and housing needed considerable capital outlay and organisation, and required a continuous labour supply under fixed conditions. The two main executives in a typical Chinese mining organisation of the nineteenth century would be the financier who supplied the capital and the Headman of the mine who had charge of the mining operations and the miners. The miners worked on various terms. Indenture-labour was common for workers recruited in South China, whose passages in emigrant junks were provided, and who were fed and clothed and perhaps paid a very small sum of money in return for 360 days' labour. As the demand for labour increased, this system became both un-popular and unsatisfactory, and various co-operative systems took its place. These gave the workers a fixed proportion of the profits of the mine — whatever they might be — at the end of each six-months' accounting. At the same time the workers were com-mitted to purchase their personal requirements from the mine owner at rates above the current market price. Sometimes fixed wages were offered as an alternative to the profit-sharing. Since not every mining venture was a success, there was an element of risk on both sides. The mine-owner either gained most or lost most, but he had a second source of income in the trading side of his enterprise.

In the 1880s and 1890s European companies, mainly British and French, began to obtain mining concessions in the Malay States. European investment was stimulated by a number of factors. More settled and favourable political conditions following the introduction of British Residents in the main tin-bearing states seemed to offer greater security. The development of communications, especially railways, was beginning to solve some of the transport problems from the mining valleys to the coast. There was an increased demand for tin in the West, especially in the form of tin-plate for canning and packaging purposes. Western technology in the form first of the steam-engine, centrifugal pump, and winding gear, and, later, of hydraulic methods and, finally, of the tin-dredge, could be used to improve mining methods and output. Steamship services were both quicker, via the Suez Canal from 1870 onwards, and more frequent, and the establish-ment of smelting centres at Pulau Brani near Singapore (1887) and at Penang (1897) assisted the collection of smelted ore, improved its quality, and saved shipping space.

Yet there was no great influx of European mining companies before the end of the nineteenth century, and some of the early enterprises ended in failure. In Selangor there was a short 'boom' of European enterprise in the years 1882 to 1884. Mining land was taken on lease by European concerns, and negotiations were made for the purchase of Chinese mines. Yap Ah Loy sold his Ampang mine to a Singapore firm, but retained shares equivalent to about one-sixth of the purchase price. The boom was short-lived. Within a few years the European companies sold out to the Chinese not only their mining concessions but also the expensive equipment with which they had furnished them. Ah Loy bought his own mine back again, better equipped, at a much smaller price than he had been paid for it.

The reasons for these European business failures lay partly in expensive over-staffing at top levels, and partly in the insufficient attention given to trial-boring. The European firms were also inclined to place too much faith in the economics of expensive apparatus before it had been carefully tried and tested in local conditions.[1]

Until the end of the nineteenth century tin-mining in the Malay States was still very largely a Chinese enterprise, and, even as late as 1912, 80 per cent of Malaya's tin production was under Chinese management. The labour force was — and still continues to be — predominantly Chinese. It was the introduction of the large and expensive tin-dredge, first used in Malaya in 1912, which increased 'Western' interests in Malayan tin, and finally gave European managements a lead over Chinese in the production figures. Dredges for mining were first used in New Zealand; later they were adopted in Australia. Australians first brought the tin-dredge to Malaya. By the early 1920s tin-dredges were being prefabricated in Britain for assembly on Malayan sites, and European mining companies rushed to instal them. The dredge could work in swampy land, and could be employed on land too poor in tin-content to be profitably mined in any other way. The dredges were exclusively used by Western firms on account of the large capital required both for the dredges themselves and for the leasing of wide areas of mining land to make the venture worthwhile. Malayan-Chinese tin concerns could not meet such heavy demands on their resources.

In 1904 Malaya was producing about 50,000 tons of tin annually, more than half the world's output. What has happened since then is that overall production has not increased tremen-

[1] J. M. Gullick, 'Kuala Lumpur, 1880–1895', *JRASMB*, Vol. 28, pt. 4, pp. 55–6.

dously,[1] due partly to competition from other parts of the world, including Bolivia and Nigeria, and partly to international restriction schemes which fix quotas in relation to markets and prices. Malaya still produces about one-third of the world's tin and is easily the main exporter. About half of the present production is by the dredger method, and about 60 per cent of Malayan tin is European-managed, but the technical and administrative personnel of the companies has been increasingly Malayanised. A most striking change is in the actual number of people employed in tin-mining. According to an International Bank Report, published in 1955, there were 200,000 tin-workers in 1913, and they were producing less tin than the 40,000 tin-workers in 1954.

The effects of the revolution in tin-mining cover a wide field of activities. It was responsible for a very substantial proportion of Chinese immigration. It led to improvements in communications. It was the main reason for the growth of towns which served the many needs of the mining areas. Last, but certainly not least, the production of tin became a very important source of government revenue, as it had formerly been the main income of Malay chiefs in the tin districts. Revenue was derived from licences for prospecting and rents for land, but, above all, from an export duty on the saleable tin. This export duty was always a heavy tax, based on the volume or value of the tin. In Larut under Captain Speedy in 1874–5 it was 25 per cent or more of the value of the tin, and this was presumably similar to former practices.[2] The revenue from tin provided the main fund from which early British Residents could meet existing obligations such as pensions, annuities, and the costs of administration, as well as embark on new developments in the form of communications and public welfare services.

In more recent years the tin export duty has fluctuated between 10 per cent and 15 per cent of the value, in accordance with the rise and fall of prices. An income-tax of 30 per cent on net profits of the mining companies raises the question of whether tin-mining has not now reached the limits of effective taxation.

[1] About 60,000 tons annually is the present figure.
[2] Based on information in J. M. Gullick, 'Captain Speedy of Larut', pp. 49–50.

2. COMMUNICATIONS

Brief reference to the construction of roads and railways has already been made in discussing the work of the early British Residents. The work of road-making was slow, difficult, and expensive, and developments were gradual. As Swettenham puts it:

'It is not an easy task to construct really good well-graded roads through an unexplored country, covered with virgin forest and the dense undergrowth of a moist, tropical climate with hill and swamp alternating, and a rainfall of from 80 to 160 inches annually.'[1]

In Perak, and in Selangor, a small Public Works Department was started soon after the appointment of British Residents, while Pahang and Negri Sembilan each had a Clerk or Superintendent of Works. The 'Public Works' included public buildings of all kinds — Residency buildings, courts of law, hospitals, police-stations, prisons — as well as installations such as reservoirs for water. The main item of expenditure in the annual reports, however, seems to have been 'roads, streets, and bridges'. Before the coming of the motor-car, the roads were classified as metalled cart-roads, unmetalled cart-roads, bridle-roads, other paths and 'gravelled'.

Roads were built as revenue became available, and where they seemed most needed for economic development. Most expenditure obviously occurred at first in those states which had most revenue — that is, in Perak and Selangor (both states which had had British Residents since 1874) rather than in Negri Sembilan and Pahang. The Public Works Departments of these four states were amalgamated in 1901, by which time the chief official in each state was known as the State Engineer. By the 1901 arrangement the four State Engineers served under a federal Director of Public Works, and in the years immediately following Pahang and Negri Sembilan received a little more attention; but they still lagged a long way behind the other two, Pahang having easily the least

[1] *British Malaya*, p. 237.

mileage of cart-roads or bridle-roads. By 1906 the Federated
Malay States had a total of approximately 1600 miles of metalled
cart-roads and 270 miles of unmetalled cart-roads.[1] In the years
which followed the end of the First World War this road system
— and that which existed in the other states — was adapted, by
widening and strengthening, for the use of motor-traffic. Emphasis
was given to trunk roads, especially a western road from Johore
Bahru through Kuala Lumpur to Kedah and the Thai border. An
east-coast trunk road, less well surfaced, runs from the principal
trunk road, north of Johore Bahru, to Kota Bharu and Tumpat.
Nearly all the roads which link with these north-south routes are
in the west-coast states, apart from two main east-west linking
roads, one in Johore, the other between Port Swettenham, Kuala
Lumpur, and Kuantan.

In modern Malaya there are many areas with no main road, and
the total road mileage (about 6,000 miles) is not high, but the
pattern of roads constructed since the 1880s compares very
favourably with the road systems of other South-East Asian
countries. A modern scholar asserts that, during the present
century, 'Malaya created a road system that was unique in the Far
East.'[2]

The pattern of railways was similar to that of the roads; in fact,
the western north-south main line preceded the largely adjacent
trunk road. The early railway lines were fairly short ones running
east-west from tin areas to the west coast. They ran from Taiping
to Port Weld (1885); Kuala Lumpur to Bukit Kuda (1886), then
to Klang via Connaught Bridge (1890), and later to Port Swettenham (1899): Seremban to Port Dickson (1891); Tapah Road to
Telok Anson (1893). There were also short lines from Kuala
Lumpur to other mining areas at Rawang and Kuala Kubu to the
north and at Sungei Besi to the south; these lines were constructed
in the period 1888 to 1895.

All except the Seremban — Port Dickson line were govern-

[1] A. Wright and H. A. Cartwright (eds.), *Twentieth Century Impressions of
British Malaya*, p. 316.
[2] G. C. Allen and A. G. Donnithorne, *Western Enterprise in Indonesia and
Malaya*, p. 228.

ment railways from the first. Money came from revenues, aided sometimes by loans from the Straits Settlements. British engineers were recruited from the Ceylon Public Works Department for the work of planning and constructions, and skilled labour was introduced from Ceylon and Bengal. Local Chinese and Malays provided the rest of the labour force.

After the federation of the four central states, the western lines were linked together in the Federated Malay States Railway by a a north-south line which joined up the existing railheads and ran northwards to Prai, opposite Penang, and southwards as far as the borders of Johore at Gemas. This work, planned in co-operation with the Straits Settlements for the Province Wellesley sector, was completed by 1908. In the meanwhile, in 1903, a new branch line ran from the north-south line, between Seremban and Gemas, to Malacca. The Seremban — Port Dickson line was taken over by the F. M. S. Railway from the Sungei Ujong company in 1908.

The next stage was to extend the line southwards from Gemas and northwards from Prai. This was done in co-operation with the State governments of Johore and Kedah. Johore Bahru was reached in 1909, and a ferry service linked with Singapore's island railway, which had been built in 1903. In 1926 a railway was opened across the causeway between Johore and Singapore Island to complete this connection.

Meanwhile the west-coast line was taken north to the Thai border and linked with the Siamese railway in 1918, and a start was made on what was called an east coast railway to join Gemas to Tumpat through Pahang and Kelantan. This was a very slow-moving project which suffered at different times from apathy, lack of money, and difficulties of terrain. In 1921 the northern end was joined to the Siamese railway, but the whole line was not open until ten years later.

Such, in brief outline, was the nature of road and railway developments. There were many significant consequences. Villages and areas of cultivation followed along the track of the roads, new settlement areas followed and land in many districts began to have some value for the first time. Telegraph and postal services developed in conjunction with roads and railways. In the early years of the present century mail carts pulled by 'trotting bullocks' conveyed mails to estates and mines, while motor-car mail services were being introduced into some main centres. Telegraph lines mostly followed the route of the railway, and where there were no post-office lines railway stations accepted telegrams for transmission through their own service.

Trade and industry benefited most. Tin-ore and plantation-rubber could be moved quickly by rail, and later by road, to the ports. Essential supplies travelled in the opposite direction. A number of new ports were created at the coastal railheads — Port Weld, Telok Anson, Port Swettenham and Port Dickson, all named after British officials. These were all railway ports, equipped with wharves and jetties, with Port Swettenham easily the most important. It was built in the first decade of the present century on land reclaimed from swamp, and it provided anchorage for ocean-going steamers and easy access to and from the mining and rubber areas of Selangor. Meanwhile, Penang's position was enhanced by the ferry-link to the railhead at Prai.

Roads and railways absorbed immigrant labour, especially, in the construction and running of railways, from India and Ceylon. They also contributed to the growth of towns. Gemas and Port Swettenham were creations of the railway; Kuala Lumpur owed some part of its growth to its function as a railway-centre with railway workshops. Roads and railways also helped, of course, to increase communication between different states, though not with any direct consequences as regards political unification.

The railway ports were used by local as well as distant shipping, and the Straits Steamship Company was very prominent in this coastal trade. It was founded in Singapore in 1890 with a mixture of British and Malayan Chinese investment. Its capital and shipping-fleet expanded rapidly. By the mid-1920s it had a fleet of forty-eight vessels, many of them specially constructed to suit local conditions, and it was serving fifty-three ports in South-East Asia.[1]

The pattern of roads and railways served both as a cause and an effect of economic development, and also helped to determine its

[1] G. C. Allen and A. G. Donnithorne, *op. cit.*, p. 217.

Malayan Information Services

A CHINESE TIN-MINE IN MALAYA

character. When land was taken for large-scale rubber planting, the sites mainly chosen were ones which lay near existing means of communication, especially railways.

3. AGRICULTURE

The increase in the size and organisation of the tin industry was paralleled by changes in agriculture. It would be too much of an over-simplification to describe the changes as a move from subsistence agriculture to the growth of cash crops, for there had been cash-crops in the Malay States before the nineteenth century, and subsistence agriculture has continued in some parts into the present century. What has happened since the mid-nineteenth century is that the amount of agriculture devoted to saleable crops has increased beyond recognition. The industrial revolution in tin-mining had its counterpart in an agricultural revolution marked by the cultivation of larger food-growing areas for the local population and plantations for the export market.

The population increase through immigration, better health, and more stable political conditions, necessitated either more food production or more imported food in areas where the main increase had taken place. The growth of tin-mining and of towns created an industrial and urban population which depended on others for its food-supply. The new townships became fringed by land under cultivation for rice, fruit, and vegetables, usually through a combination of Malay smallholdings and Chinese market gardens. Kuala Lumpur in the 1880s can be taken as a good example of this concentrated food production for a town market. Padi areas included the whole Ampang valley, as well as Batu and Setapak on the outskirts of the town itself. There were orchards of fruit trees and market gardens along Ampang Road and Batu Road, and there was a ring of Chinese market gardens within a three-mile radius of the town. Yet among the produce sold in the Kuala Lumpur market that of the Malay smallholdings was much in evidence.[1]

Early examples in Malaya of plantation agriculture for export

[1] J. M. Gullick, 'Kuala Lumpur, 1880–95', p. 59.

o

would include pepper in Kedah in the seventeenth century, spices in Penang in the late eighteenth and first half of the nineteenth century, and spices also in early Singapore. Chinese agriculturists introduced pepper plantations into Johore after 1840. In the nineteenth century, the main impetus for plantation crops came from Europeans and Chinese. Pepper was the most important Malayan export crop until about 1850, and nutmeg and cloves had some importance until the advent of plant diseases after 1860.

In the 1830s a few European merchants planted sugar-cane in Penang, Province Wellesley, and Malacca. It was in Malacca that most cultivation took place. A Malacca Sugar Company was formed in the 1840s with land on the River Linggi, while a private planter with experience of the sugar industry in the West Indies began work on a 5,000-acre tract. The work of clearing, planting, and harvesting, was usually done by Chinese, but it was often difficult to obtain sufficient labour, and Tamil workers were brought in, under indentures, by some planters in the 1880s. After indentured labour was abolished in the Federated Malay States in 1910, the Malayan sugar industry declined, and the last factory closed in 1913. For about fifty years, however, sugar had been an important product.

In the 1880s coffee planters arrived from Ceylon, where their crops had failed through the outbreak of a plant disease. These were specialist planters and not, as had often previously been the case with Europeans, merchants venturing into planting. They planted estates with Liberian coffee in Perak, Selangor, and Negri Sembilan, and for a time they prospered. At the end of the century, coffee prices dropped very sharply owing to an increased output of Arabian coffee from Brazil, and a few years later the estates in Malaya were seriously damaged by pests. Coffee-planters either returned to Europe, found other types of occupation, or turned to the planting of rubber. Before coffee gave way to rubber it had been taken up as a smallholder crop by Malays, who also followed the tide of fortune and changed later to rubber.

The introduction of rubber to Malaya has had such important

consequences that the story of the early seedlings has often been told. The first phase was a botanical experiment with a view to possible economic results. The initiative came from the head of the geographical section of the India Office, Sir Clements Markham, and the Director of the Botanical Gardens at Kew, Sir Joseph Hooker. Two expeditions were sent to the Amazon from the India Office. The second of these expeditions, led by Mr. H. A. (later Sir Henry) Wickham in 1876, obtained a collection of 70,000 seeds, and these were despatched to Kew Gardens for germination in the artificial heat of the conservatories. From Kew about 3,000 seedlings were sent to British colonies in tropical regions, most of them to Ceylon. From Ceylon twenty-two plants reached Singapore in 1877; some of these were planted in the Botanical Gardens in Singapore, others were taken by the Curator to Perak and planted in Hugh Low's Residency Garden at Kuala Kangsar. Thus, as a botanist, Low was linked with the experiment, and in Singapore and Kuala Kangsar the Malayan rubber industry was born.

For many years cultivated rubber remained at the experimental stage. Few people had any knowledge of the 'hevea brasiliensis', as this type of rubber-tree was technically known, a yield of liquid rubber (latex) could only be expected after five or six years' growth, and efficient methods of 'tapping' the tree for latex were unknown. Moreover, while the rubber-trees were still in the Botanical Gardens, coffee-planting had been established with success in the western Malay states which were under British protection, and neither government nor planting interests had any enthusiasm for rubber.

A number of factors coincided to produce a rubber boom in the Malay States. The misfortunes of the coffee-planters in the 1890s and early 1900s, when a drop in prices was followed in a few years by plant diseases, made some of them willing to try an alternative crop on land which was already in use for coffee. Some planters, while continuing with coffee, placed rubber-trees between the coffee-plants to give shade, and waited to see what the yield of rubber would be.

The appointment of Henry Ridley as Director of the Gardens

at Singapore in 1888 brought a remarkably able and energetic man to the experimental side of rubber in Malaya. As a scientific investigator he studied every aspect of rubber-growing; he held shows in Singapore at which rubber samples were displayed, and he sent samples to London. He tried to convince the coffee-planters that there was a promising future in rubber, and he distributed seeds, packing them with damp charcoal powder in closed tins. A Chinese writer has described his activities in this way:

'It was his practice to stuff seeds in the pockets of planters and others begging them to make a trial: and among planters he earned the soubriquet of "mad Ridley" or "rubber Ridley".'[1]

Neither the planters nor government officials surrendered easily to Ridley's enthusiasm, but a few were persuaded to put his experiments to a practical test. A Malacca Chinese, Tan Chay Yan, planted forty acres of rubber among tapioca in 1896. A British coffee-estate partnership in Selangor planted five acres as a separate rubber crop in the same year. In the following year another British coffee-estate in Perak inter-planted rubber and coconuts among 200 acres of coffee, and felled the coconuts a few years later. By this time (1897), twenty years after the appearance of the first seedlings in Malaya, only 345 acres were under rubber. Even in 1905 only 200 tons of rubber were produced in Malaya as against some 60,000 tons of jungle rubber produced elsewhere, mainly in Brazil.

Very significant expansion was, however, taking place in the first decade of the present century, and by 1910 the rubber boom was at its height. Ridley again contributed to this. It was he who perfected in Malaya the method of tapping which is used to-day so as to extract the maximum flow of latex with the minimum damage to the tree. The other important new element was the rise of the car industry in the West, with its heavy demands for rubber, especially for tyres. Subsequently, especially from the time of the First World War, the market for rubber was further increased by

[1] Song Ong Siang, *One Hundred Years' History of the Chinese in Singapore*, p. 449.

its use for clothing and footwear, electrical and medical equipment, and household goods and furniture.

Newly-formed companies for rubber-planting obtained land concessions in the Malay States, often using established merchant houses in Singapore as their agents and as advisers on local conditions. Most of these companies were British, but there were others from continental Europe (including an important Franco-Belgian company) as well as from Australia and America. Other companies were floated in Malaya, with substantial backing from Malayan Chinese. Until 1913, when the states of the F.M.S. were empowered separately to set aside areas reserved for the use of Malays by the Malay Reservations Enactment, land concessions could be obtained fairly easily on perpetual lease, subject to certain requirements about cultivation.

Most of the rubber-planting took place in Perak, Selangor, Negri Sembilan, and Johore, where a pattern of communications already existed. An important exception was the syndicate formed by Robert Duff, an ex-police officer, who obtained a tremendous concession of 3,000 square miles from the Sultan of Kelantan in 1900. This concession was the subject of much debate between Duff, the British government and Siam, and its size was eventually reduced. At first the company concentrated on mining, lumbering, and general trading, but from 1906 onwards it became increasingly concerned with the cultivation of rubber, and has remained so until the present time.

Manufacturing interests were represented among the early rubber companies, and these included the Dunlop Company and the United States Rubber Company. High profits were made by plantation companies which had rubber crops maturing by 1910 or 1912. The price of rubber in sterling rose from four shillings a pound at the beginning of the century to over twelve shillings a pound in 1910. By 1920 the exports of rubber from Malaya had reached an annual total of about 200,000 tons, over half of the world's supply at that time. The supply of cultivated rubber by this time exceeded that which came from the South American jungles.

It was not only the plantation companies which were concerned with rubber; once the success of rubber was apparent, it was planted by smallholders, especially Malays,[1] and in recent years smallholder crops have represented between a third and a half of total production in Malaya.

Annual Reports supply modern statistics on rubber, which now has an annual production in Malaya of over 600,000 tons. Two features of the 1920s call for a brief mention. The general depression of trade following the First World War had an adverse effect upon rubber prices. With stocks piling up and prices as low as about sixpence a pound, rubber companies in Malaya began to make economies, and the Rubber Growers' Association, which represented estate interests in Malaya, began to urge the British government to intervene by outlining a restriction scheme for all producers. The outcome was the Stevenson Committee, appointed in 1921, and the Stevenson scheme of restriction for Malaya, which took effect from November, 1922. Each rubber producer in Malaya was assigned a quota based on his output for the year ending October 1920. Any amount in excess of the quota was subject to a prohibitive export duty.

The Dutch East Indies refused to join the Stevenson scheme, and the output of rubber there was doubled between 1922 and 1928, while there was only about a 40 per cent increase in Malaya. The scheme was abandoned in 1928, but following the depression of the early 1930s, with prices even worse than in 1921, an International Rubber Regulation Agreement to restrict exports on a quota basis was signed in 1934 between the British, Dutch, French, and Siamese governments.

Despite these two depression periods and restriction schemes — and, to some extent, because of them — very valuable progress was made on the technical and research side. A Rubber Research Institute was founded in Kuala Lumpur in 1926 to carry out research projects formerly undertaken by the Department of Agriculture and the Rubber Growers' Association. Among the tasks undertaken by the Institute have been experiments in budding and grafting from selected trees, selective weeding, treatment of the soils, and the search for new uses of rubber. In recent years rubber production has been further helped

[1] Later, Chinese and Indians developed most of the larger smallholdings.

by government assistance for approved replanting schemes both for estates and smallholders. About one-third of the world's natural rubber was grown in Malaya in the 1950s.

The effects of the growth of large-scale rubber cultivation in Malaya during the present century have covered such a wide field that they are difficult to summarise. Labour for rubber plantations was recruited in south India, first through agents and an indenture system, later, after indentured labour was abolished in 1910, through a system of assisted passages. Money for this scheme was raised jointly by the estate-owners and the government of the F.M.S. in an Indian Immigration Fund. The Indian Government imposed a ban on the further emigration of unskilled Indian labour shortly before the Second World War.

The cultivation of rubber cleared vast acreages of land and eventually provided a means of livelihood for a large proportion of Malaya's workers.[1] It has provided a very valuable addition to the income of the smallholder. It is sometimes overlooked that rubber production both in estates and smallholdings has been an important reason for immigration of Malaysians (or Indonesians), mainly from Java and Sumatra, to the Malay States.

Rubber has provided industrial as well as agricultural occupations. The processing of rubber, and, to a lesser extent, the growth of factories for the manufacture of rubber goods, plays an important part in the Malayan economy. Directly and indirectly, rubber has contributed to the growth of towns, ports, and communications.

Perhaps most important of all, rubber has provided the largest single source of government revenue. As with tin, the bulk of the revenue is derived from an export duty, and the revenue from rubber has been in some years more than double that from tin. The export duty is based on a scale which varies between about 4 per cent and 15 per cent according to price; there is also, as for tin, an income-tax of 30 per cent on company profits. This very important source of income, together with the tin duty, was

[1] In 1947 over one-fifth of the men, and over one-third of the women, 'gainfully employed' in the Federation of Malaya were engaged in rubber cultivation.

largely responsible for government surpluses which were applied to public utilities and social welfare, and this still holds true today. Rubber, more than any other single item or factor, determines the standard of life in present-day Malaya. The need for quality and efficiency in the Malayan rubber industry is even greater at the present time, in view of the competition from synthetic rubber production, particularly in the United States of America.

Rubber, which now occupies about two-thirds of the total acreage under cultivation in Malaya, stands paramount in importance among agricultural crops for the export market. Brief mention must be made, however, of coconut, oil-palm, pineapple, and the present experiment with cocoa.

The coconut was important in Malaya from ancient times, both as a source of food and for other materials. It has continued to be very largely a smallholders' crop, and a great proportion of it is for home consumption. An analysis made in 1930 estimated that the consumption of coconuts in all forms in Malaya amounted to the equivalent of fifty nuts per annum per head of the population of four millions.[1] Increasingly since the 1870s, coconut has also been exported in the forms of copra and coconut oil; the value of such exports in 1957, for instance, was seventy-five million dollars. Estates have been taken up by Chinese and Europeans, but these represent less than one-fifth of the total production.

By contrast, the oil-palm was a foreign plant introduced into Malaya, and is an estate crop on European-owned estates. The oil-palm was indigenous to West Africa, but spread almost all over tropical Africa. It reached Singapore from Ceylon and Kew Gardens in the form of seeds about 1875, and was grown in the Botanical Gardens there. Other trees were grown in the early years of the present century in the Public Gardens at Kuala Lumpur. Like rubber, oil-palm was a subject for botanical experiment, but it was also an attractive ornamental plant. The first commercial planting was made by a Frenchman in Selangor in 1917, and further plantations followed in the 1920s, following the depression in rubber and the introduction of the restriction

[1] F. C. Cooke in *The Malayan Agricultural Journal*, Vol. XVIII, no. 7, July 1930.

scheme. Many of the estates were large ones; by 1933 there were thirty-two estates with 64,000 planted acres, and this acreage had increased to 79,000 by 1941. The F.M.S. government encouraged oil-palm planting as a means of diversifying the economy, and granted lands on favourable terms. Since the Second World War the expansion of oil-palm production has continued. It has remained almost exclusively an estate crop, because the organisation of collecting the fruit and extracting the oil demands good transport, storage, and handling facilities, and the use of highly mechanised plant.

Pineapple cultivation for canning was begun by Europeans on Singapore Island in 1888, and it spread to Johore, which has become the main centre of pineapple cultivation. On a much smaller scale, pineapples for canning and the export market are cultivated in Selangor and Perak. The production of pineapples for export was originally interrelated with rubber, with pineapples as a catch-crop between the rubber trees. In more recent years however, greater attention has been paid to sole cropping, which is successful under certain soil conditions. Estates and smallholders now have about an equal share of production, but Chinese smallholders were the main producers in the 1920s and 1930s.

The cocoa-tree was brought to Malaya many years before its commercial possibilities were considered. The F.M.S. Department of Agriculture had an experimental interest in the tree in the 1930s. Some practical schemes of planting have been undertaken, notably in Trengganu and Pahang since the Second World War. Cocoa follows on a long line of experimental plantation crops, including sugar, coffee, rubber, and oil-palm. It remains to be seen whether it will be a success or a disappointment.

4. THE ECONOMIC ROLES OF PENANG AND SINGAPORE

Although its importance as a port was overshadowed by the rise of Singapore, Penang remained by no means an economic backwater. Trade with Indian ports and with China still continued, although diminished by the concentration of shipping routes on Singapore. For Acheh, and other Sumatran ports, Penang

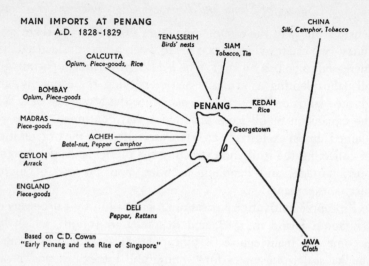

MAIN IMPORTS AT PENANG
A.D. 1828-1829

TENASSERIM
Birds' nests

SIAM
Tobacco, Tin

CHINA
Silk, Camphor, Tobacco

CALCUTTA
Opium, Piece-goods, Rice

BOMBAY
Opium, Piece-goods

PENANG——KEDAH
Rice

MADRAS
Piece-goods

Georgetown

ACHEH
Betel-nut, Pepper Camphor

CEYLON
Arrack

ENGLAND
Piece-goods

DELI
Pepper, Rattans

Based on C. D. Cowan
"Early Penang and the Rise of Singapore"

JAVA
Cloth

remained an important centre for the collection of pepper, betel-nut, camphor, rattans, and resins; opium and textiles, both Indian and European, were exported in return. From the west coasts of Burma and Siam, Penang imported rice, birds'-nests, tobacco, and tin, and for these areas Penang was a distributor of textiles, opium, and Chinese produce. Penang also developed an increasing interest in the collection of tin from the western Malay states.

Penang served as an immigration port. In the 1830s and 1840s, Chinese immigrants were arriving there at the rate of 2,000-3,000 a year.[1] During the rubber boom in the early years of the twentieth century, Penang was an important port of arrival for plantation-workers from south India.

In many ways Penang became associated with the tin industry in Perak. Penang merchants financed the development of the Larut mines and handled the tin trade. The main line of communication for both men and supplies in the mid-nineteenth century lay between Penang and the Larut river. A tin-smelter was established at Penang by Chinese enterprise in 1897, and this was taken over ten years later by the Eastern Smelting Company, which enlarged the plant and established agencies for the purchase of ore.

[1] V. Purcell, *The Chinese in South East Asia*, p. 297.

Plantation agriculture and padi-cultivation in Province Wellesley was another feature of Penang's contribution to the Malayan economy. In 1860 70,000 acres were reported to be under cultivation, including 40,000 for padi, 12,000 for coconut, and 10,000 for sugar-cane. Spices and fruit trees and tapioca were among the plants cultivated in the remainder. By 1868 the population of Province Wellesley was 80,000, of whom Malays (56,000) and Indians (10,000) were the two largest groups. At the same time the island of Penang itself had a population of about 70,000, which was predominantly Chinese in character.[1] By 1950 the population of Georgetown alone was over 180,000 and that of Penang with Province Wellesley was in the region of half a million.

In the economic development of modern Malaya, a special part has been played by Singapore. Geographical situation and a policy of free trade were the main factors in the rapid growth of the Singapore *entrepôt*, whose beginnings have already been outlined.[2] A report on the trade of Singapore for the year 1828–9,[3] barely ten years after the foundation of the settlement, shows the nature and extent of Singapore's commerce.

From England, the imports were headed by piece-goods, which were easily the most valuable part of the trade, but the list also included iron, woollens, copper-sheathing, and wines and spirits. The most costly items exported to England were raw silk and 'nankeens' from China, which were landed and reshipped at Singapore, while other commodities for the English market were coffee, sugar, tortoise-shell, 'camphor China', and pepper.

Continental Europe sent to Singapore woollens, wines and spirits, and iron, and received back cargoes mainly of Chinese and Straits produce. Copper and iron came from South America, which also provided a small market for Straits and China produce. Mauritius sent sea-snails and ebony, and bought consumer goods, including tea.

[1] C. N. Parkinson, *British Intervention in Malaya, 1867–1877*, pp. 6–7.
[2] See Chapter 6.
[3] Published in C. D. Cowan, 'Early Penang and the Rise of Singapore, 1805–1832', pp. 198–203.

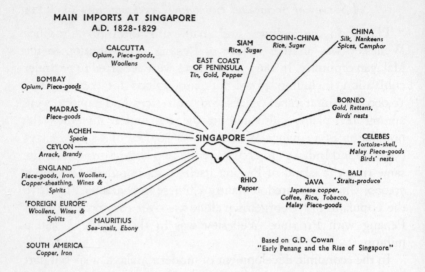

MAIN IMPORTS AT SINGAPORE
A.D. 1828-1829

CALCUTTA
Opium, Piece-goods,
Woollens

SIAM
Rice, Sugar

COCHIN-CHINA
Rice, Sugar

CHINA
Silk, Nankeens
Spices, Camphor

EAST COAST
OF PENINSULA
Tin, Gold, Pepper

BOMBAY
Opium, Piece-goods

MADRAS
Piece-goods

BORNEO
Gold, Rattans,
Birds' nests

ACHEH
Specie

CEYLON
Arrack, Brandy

SINGAPORE

CELEBES
Tortoise-shell,
Malay Piece-goods
Birds' nests

ENGLAND
Piece-goods, Iron, Woollens,
Copper-sheathing, Wines &
Spirits

RHIO
Pepper

JAVA
Japanese copper,
Coffee, Rice, Tobacco,
Malay Piece-goods

BALI
'Straits-produce'

'FOREIGN EUROPE'
Woollens, Wines &
Spirits

MAURITIUS
Sea-snails, Ebony

SOUTH AMERICA
Copper, Iron

Based on G.D. Cowan
"Early Penang and the Rise of Singapore"

From Calcutta, Madras, and Bombay, came cargoes of opium, Indian and European piece-goods, woollens, and raw cotton; in return, the main exports from Singapore to these three ports were copper, tin, gold-dust, pepper, sugar, special timber, and jungle produce. Raw silk and 'nankeens' for reshipment to England headed the list of Chinese imports, but these also included spices and camphor. Opium, birds'-nests, rattans, tin, sea-snails, ebony, Malay camphor, and pepper were despatched to China.

Copper, coffee, rice, and tobacco, as well as Malay piece-goods, were imported from or via Java, which received back Indian and European piece-goods and opium. Piece-goods were also shipped to Siam, Cochin-China, Acheh and other Sumatran ports, Borneo, Bali, Celebes, and the east coast of the Malay Peninsula. The distribution of opium from Singapore was a prominent feature of the trade with Siam, Cochin-China, the east coast of the Malay Peninsula, and island South-East Asia. From the same regions came rice, sugar, salt, gold-dust, birds'-nests, rattans, and tortoise-shell, whilst tin was the dominant commodity from the west coast of Malaya. Other trade exchanges were made with Ceylon, Cambodia, and Manila. Altogether the annual imports of Singapore were valued at seventeen million rupees, and the exports at fifteen million rupees. By comparison, the corresponding figures for Penang in the same year were five million rupees, and about three and a half million rupees. The Sicca rupee used in figures given in the official returns of the Straits Settlements at this period had a slightly higher nominal value in relation to sterling than the present Malayan dollar. By any contemporary standards, the *entrepôt* trade of Singapore in 1829 was impressive, both in value and in the extent of the collection and distribution area.

The growth of the Singapore *entrepôt* was reflected both in the size and in the racial character of the population. In 1830 the population was 16,634; in 1836, 29,984, and in 1860, 80,792. By 1901 the total figure had risen to 228,555;[1] by 1950 it was over a million. This was a multi-racial society which included Chinese, Malays, Javanese, Bugis, Arabs, Hindu and Muslim Indians, and a European community which was mainly British. Alfred Russell Wallace, who visited Singapore several times between 1854 and 1862, gave a concise description which conveys something of the atmosphere of mid-nineteenth century Singapore.

'The harbour is crowded with men-of-war and trading vessels of many European nations, and hundreds of Malay praus and Chinese junks, from vessels of several hundred tons burthen down to little fishing boats and passenger sampans; and the town comprises handsome public buildings and churches, Mahometan mosques, Hindoo temples, Chinese joss-houses, good European houses, massive warehouses, queer old Kling and China bazaars, and long suburbs of Chinese and Malay cottages.'[2]

Wallace also noted the large Chinese element in the population. In 1836 the Chinese represented rather less than half of a total population of nearly 30,000; by 1860 there were 50,000 Chinese out of a total of 80,000, and by 1901 the Chinese figure had risen to 164,000 out of 228,000. By 1950 the total population was more than a million, of whom nearly 80 per cent were Chinese. Of the typical, prosperous, Chinese merchant, Wallace wrote:

[1] Song One Siang, *One Hundred Years' History of the Chinese in Singapore*, p. 23.
[2] A. R. Wallace, *The Malay Archipelago*, p. 16.

'He has a handsome warehouse or shop in town, and a good house in the country. He keeps a fine horse and gig and every evening may be seen taking a drive bareheaded to enjoy the cool breeze.'

Enterprising and industrious as the Singapore Chinese undoubtedly were, their pattern of life was seriously shaken from time to time by the outbreak of clan fights and Secret Society feuds. Particularly violent riots occurred in May, 1854, apparently as a result of a clash between Hokkiens and Cantonese. The number of dead was estimated as 600, with a larger number wounded and 300 houses burned or plundered.

A number of circumstances imposed restrictions on the expansion of Singapore's trade. When the East India Company's monopoly of direct trade between Europe and China was abolished in 1833, private merchants were no longer under obligation to tranship at Singapore cargoes which were bound to and from China. Apart from any wider consequences, this meant the loss of commission charges formerly made by Singapore merchants for the work of landing and reshipping.

The British acquisition of Hong Kong in 1842 and Labuan in 1846 caused some decline in Singapore's share in the trade between the West and China, and also in the distributive trade of the Malay Archipelago. Direct trade between England and the treaty-ports in China was also to Singapore's disadvantage.

The weakening of Singapore's position as an *entrepôt* became apparent in the mid-1860s. There is evidence of keen competition among European merchants in 1864. Two firms went bankrupt with liabilities of over a million dollars, and there was a general breakdown of credit dealings. There was even, for a short time, a run on the banks for silver as the crisis led some traders to doubt the currency value of the bank-notes.[1] Another trade recession occurred in 1867–8.

The feelings of insecurity among Singapore merchants in the

[1] Song Ong Siang, *One Hundred Years' History of the Chinese in Singapore*, pp. 126–7.

late 1860s have already been mentioned.[1] The opening of the Suez Canal brought more shipping to Singapore from the West, but, at least to the British merchants of Singapore, it also seemed to indicate both the prospect of more direct trade between Europe and South-East Asia and the pressure of competition from other nations, including France and Germany.

The introduction of British Residents in Perak, Selangor, and Sungei Ujong in 1874 coincided with a gradual change of emphasis in Singapore's economic function which was, to some extent, already taking place. Although the *entrepôt* trade continued, Singapore became increasingly linked in many ways with the economic development of the hinterland in the Malay Peninsula. This was not a mere coincidence, for the pressure of Singapore opinion had played no small part in preparing the way for British intervention in the Malay States.

Already, before 1874, Singapore had contributed to economic developments in the Peninsula. Chinese agriculturists appeared on Singapore Island from the early years of the settlement, and they became particularly concerned with vegetable-gardening and plantations of gambier and pepper. As the numbers of these planters increased and the richness of the soil became eroded, they overflowed, from about 1840, into mainland Johore. Here, with permits issued on behalf of the Temenggong (later Maharaja) Abu Bakar, they settled in the river valleys and established further gambier and pepper plantations.

Singapore was also a point of disembarkation for Chinese immigrants. The arrival of Chinese junks in December, loaded with newcomers and with produce for sale, was one of the big events of the year in mid-nineteenth-century Singapore. Towards the end of the century, European steamships played an important part in carrying Chinese immigrants to Singapore from Amoy and Swatow.

In the export of Malayan tin, Singapore's position was paramount. Until about 1860 China and India would seem to have been the main markets, but in the next ten years there were increasing shipments to Britain and North America. By 1871

[1] See Chapter 9.

4,500 tons of tin were being shipped annually from Singapore to these two areas.[1] The opening of the Suez Canal and the increasing market for tin in the West were contributing to the growth of trade in tin between Singapore, western Europe and North America before Western enterprise had entered Malayan tin-mining at the production level.

Exports from Singapore to Britain and North America of sago-flour and gambier (for dyes) were also on the increase in the 1860s and early 1870s. This was another aspect of the growing tendency for Singapore to provide Western markets with Malayan produce. The partial decline in the *entrepôt* trade was to be compensated for by greater trade-links with Malaya.

Some changes were taking place in the port itself. The traditional anchorage for shipping was in the 'roads', while small craft entered the Singapore River. The coming of the steamship, and especially the introduction of a mail and passenger service by the Peninsula and Oriental Steam Navigation Company (P. & O.), focused attention at Singapore on a new deep-water anchorage close in-shore. This was the 'New Harbour', a narrow channel to the south of the existing town, lying between Singapore Island and Pulau Brani and Pulau Blakang Mati. From 1852 the P. & O. line had a wharf and coaling-station at New Harbour, and other development projects in this area followed. These were private-enterprise ventures, the first being the construction of a dry dock at the western end for the repair of ships. At the eastern end, a wharf was built by the Tanjong Pagar Dock Company, formed in 1863, and the same Company opened an adjacent graving dock in 1868. A third financial group, known originally as the Patent Slip and Dock Company, and later as the New Harbour Dock Company, built two docks in the same harbour, while the Tanjong Pagar Dock Company added a new Albert Dock in 1879 as a companion to its existing Victoria Dock.

Thus, during the second half of the nineteenth century, Singapore developed quite a new port, more in keeping with the age of steam. By the end of the century the Tanjong Pagar Dock Company had bought up the smaller docks and wharves, but

[1] C. N. Parkinson, *British Intervention in Malaya, 1867–77*, pp. 36–7.

A RUBBER PLANTATION IN MALAYA

further extensions were still needed. In view of the heavy expenditure involved, and the importance of the work, the government of the Straits Settlements, which had already bought shares in the Company, bought up all the assets in 1905, following considerable controversy about the repayments to be made. A dock board formed to administer the property became, in 1913, the Singapore Harbour Board.

These improved facilities for storage and shipment at Singapore assisted the export of Malayan tin and rubber (especially to the U.S.A. and Britain), but this was only one of the several ways in which Singapore contributed to the economic development of the Malay Peninsula about the end of the nineteenth and the turn of the twentieth century. Just as Chinese merchant-capital from the Straits Settlements had earlier revolutionised the scope and techniques of the Malayan tin industry, so now British merchant capital was used directly or indirectly by established Singapore merchant-houses for investment in Malayan mining and agriculture.

The Straits Trading Company, which eventually specialised in tin-smelting, was largely an offshoot of a Singapore merchant-house. Its smelting plant had been established since 1887 on Pulau Brani near Singapore, and it had agencies in the mining areas for the purchase of the ore. Other European merchants in Singapore became engaged in the shipping of tin and the supplying of machinery to the mines; they sometimes ended by participating in the actual management or ownership of the mines with which they were dealing. Even when the merchant-house retained much of its original economic function, its knowledge both of trade and of the general conditions of life in Malaya were often extremely valuable to new European companies formed for mining or agricultural enterprises in the Malay States. Such companies would be pleased to secure the services of an established merchant-house, whose name and reputation would encourage investment in the home country, and whose advice could make all the difference between success and failure. In this way many leading European merchant-houses became managing agents for one or more companies which had raised capital in say, London, for Malayan plantations or tin-mines. The Singapore firm would be employed to administer the concern and sell the produce.[1]

In a similar way, European merchant-houses in Singapore acted as agents for distant bankers during the first half of the nineteenth century. From about 1850, several Western banks opened in Singapore, and the economic development of the Malay States led a number of these banks to open agencies in new Malayan towns like Kuala Lumpur and Taiping. Chinese banks also began in Singapore at the beginning of the present century, and extended their activities later to mainland centres. The growth of banking assisted industry and agriculture in Malaya by granting credit facilities particularly in the rubber and tin industries.

Singapore, through its merchant-houses, thus contributed greatly to the establishment of Western tin and rubber companies in Malaya. Its Botanical Gardens served as a nursery and laboratory for early rubber and oil-palm plants, which were, respectively, natives of Brazil and West Africa. Ridley's pioneer work on rubber whilst he was in charge of the Gardens at Singapore had an importance for the Peninsula which it is difficult to exaggerate.

The development of industry in Singapore has been to a large degree complementary to the production of the Malayan hinterland. Tin-smelting has already been mentioned. Before the end of the nineteenth century pineapple-canning had become established in Singapore. This was a Chinese industry linked with production in Johore and neighbouring islands. By 1906 there were as many as sixteen factories producing over 700,000 cases of canned pineapples in a year. This industry suffered very severely as a result of the Second World War, but it had by 1950 regained much of its former importance in Johore and Singapore.

The milling of rubber, copra-oil, and palm-oil, and the refining of sago, are modern processing industries of Singapore which are partly connected with Malayan agriculture, although these also have their counterparts in the Federation. It must be remembered also that some of Singapore's processing industries deal with raw materials which come in some measure from other parts of South-

[1] For details of these arrangements, see G. C. Allen and A. G. Donnithorne, *Western Enterprise in Indonesia and Malaya*, Chapter 11.

East Asia. In addition, Singapore has an important modern trade in the collection and distribution of mineral oil in South-East Asia.

By the mid-twentieth century the main economic tendencies in Singapore were still partly related to an *entrepôt* trade, which, while alive and important, was nevertheless shrinking. More significant was the extent of the economic relationships with the Federation of Malaya. Economic development in the Federation has increased the import as well as the export trade of Singapore. As the needs of industry and agriculture increased in the Federation, the market for consumer goods of all kinds also expanded. By 1952 Singapore claimed to handle about 74 per cent of

Table to illustrate the importance of export duties on Rubber and Tin in the modern revenue of the Federation of Malaya.

Period: 1951–7   Figures in Millions of Straits Dollars

| Year | Export duty from | | | | Of the Total Revenue | | Notes |
	Rubber	Tin	All Sources	Total Revenue	% from Export duty	% from Rubber and Tin	
1951	—	—	352	735	47%	—	Duty from Rubber and Tin
1952	—	—	190	775	26%	—	not shown separately in the Annual Reports
1953	54	51	112	620	18%	17%	
1954	52	53	112	622	18%	17%	
1955	174	55	235	797	30%	29%	
1956	143	60	210	802	26%	25%	
1957	120	54	180	800*	22%	22%	* Approximate figure

Figures taken from Federation Annual Reports.

N.B. 1. Revenue is also obtained from Rubber and Tin by income-tax levied on the mining and estate companies, and, on a State basis, through rents and licences.
2. Rubber tends to have wider fluctuations of the market than tin, and the changes can be difficult to predict from year to year.

Malaya's direct foreign imports, and 67 per cent of the total exports.[1] Some slight reduction has recently taken place in Singapore's position as an exporter, due to increased concentration in the Federation on Port Swettenham and Penang. The main economic argument which divided Singapore from the Federation lay in the contrast between Singapore's free trade and the Federation's dependence on import and export duties.

[1] *Colony of Singapore Annual Report,* 1952.

Chapter 12

A SURVEY OF SOCIAL AND ECONOMIC DEVELOPMENTS

c. A.D. 1850–1950 (II)

1. POPULATION AND GROWTH OF TOWNS

The population of Malaya has grown at a rate commensurate with the development of large-scale industry and agriculture. No census figures for the whole of Malaya were taken before 1911; earlier, some counts were taken in the F.M.S. Early figures must be treated with a little caution, since it was not possible then to achieve the accuracy of a present-day count. When the census figures are used, it must also be remembered that until, and including, 1947 Singapore appears together with the Federation of Malaya.

After 1911 the intention was to hold a census every ten years, and this was carried out in 1921 and 1931. The scheme for 1941 was interrupted by the imminence of war, and the next census was in 1947. The most recent census followed ten years after this, in 1957. Put in very round terms, the population of what is now the sovereign state of Malaya has grown as follows:

1911	2·3 millions	1931	3·8 millions
1921	2·9 millions	1947	4·9 millions
		1957	6·3 millions

In less than half a century there has been an increase of nearly 300 per cent in the total figure, and the same process had been going on before 1911. Within the hundred years between the 1850s and the 1950s, the population of the area of modern Malaya must have increased between twelve and twenty-fold. This is much more spectacular than the rise in population which took place in Britain during a long period of industrialisation, say from

221

1700 to 1950, when the population multiplied itself about ten-fold, from five millions to fifty millions. Meanwhile, the population of Singapore increased from 80,000 in 1860 to about a million in 1950 — a twelve-fold increase in ninety years.

One major reason for the population increase was the improvement in health and the subsequent prospect of longer life. Although individual cases of long life in Malaya are attested in the nineteenth century,[1] many people died young or became old at what today would be considered a comparatively early age. Epidemics such as cholera, typhus and smallpox, together with dysentery and malaria, took a heavy toll of life, and there was, to put it in present-day language, a high infant-mortality rate. The measures taken to raise standards of health and hygiene are outlined in the following section.

The other great contributory cause of the increase in population was immigration. Several immigrant racial groups were attracted by Malaya's growing economy. Of these the Chinese, originating mainly from the provinces of South China, were the largest group. They came as merchants, shopkeepers, estate-owners, and labourers in mines and plantations. Very few became engaged in padi-planting, but Chinese have taken part in the fishing industry, both as middlemen and actual fishermen. The Chinese peasant who sailed to the 'Nanyang' in the nineteenth century was one element in a large-scale organisation run by Chinese merchants to supply labour where it was wanted. Conditions in the slow sailing junks were often appalling, the amount of personal space allowed being six feet by two feet, and even less in many vessels.

Until 1929 there was completely free immigration of all races into Malaya. An Immigration Ordnance of 1930 imposed restrictions and a quota system. This was not directed specifically against the Chinese, as it applied to all immigrants, but they were the most affected. The reasons for restricting immigration were economic. It was a time of great trade depression, and there was much unemployment in Malaya, especially among the Chinese. Many unemployed were, in fact, voluntarily repatriated to China at government expense. From 1930 to the time of the Japanese

---

[1] E.g., Sultan Abdul Samad of Selangor, who lived to be ninety-three.

invasion of Malaya, a quota system was applied to the immigration of male Chinese, the details varying from year to year, and even for different times of the year. No restriction was placed on the immigration of Chinese women and children.

Whilst there was less immigration, there was also less emigration from Malaya to China during the 1930s. In the Chinese community in Malaya, men had outnumbered women by almost two to one in 1931; the arrival of more women and less men reduced this disproportion and created more settled family units. The outbreak of war between Japan and China in 1937 deterred Chinese from returning home, and the Japanese occupation of Malaya in 1941/2 made return impossible.

Two features about modern Chinese settlement in Malaya may be noted. The great attractions which tin-mining and commerce of all kinds have had for Chinese immigrants is reflected in the large Chinese element in the towns. According to the 1947 census, the Chinese comprised 62·4 per cent of the urban population of Malaya.[1] Secondly, the numbers of Chinese have increased in greater proportion than those of the other races in Malaya. Excluding Singapore,[2] Chinese represented 38 per cent of the Malayan population in 1947, with Malays totalling 49 per cent; but the Chinese population was increasing at a greater rate. One further fact is that the number of China-born Chinese in Malaya becomes less and less as the years pass, and, though mostly descended from immigrants who arrived at varying dates up to the 1930s, Malayan Chinese have increasingly come to regard Malaya as their homeland.

Indian immigration in modern times was attracted by railways, commerce, government service of many kinds and, most of all in terms of numbers, by plantation-work. Large-scale movement from India, especially from southern India, and also from Ceylon, took place in the years of the rubber boom from about 1907 until after the First World War. As the Indian supply of labour for

[1] *A Report on the 1947 Census of Population*, p. 47.
[2] In Singapore, in 1950, Chinese totalled a little less than 80 per cent of a population of one million. Taking Singapore and the Federation together, the Chinese element was gaining a slight overall lead.

rubber-planting came later than much of the Chinese movement into tin-mining, it was also accompanied by more government assistance and safeguards. Indenture labour was abolished in 1910, and the F.M.S. set up an Immigration Fund to which all employers of south Indian labour (including the government itself) contributed, for the purpose of assisting passages to Malaya. Government regulations also protected and made welfare provisions for the Indian estate-worker.[1] Controls on emigration of unskilled workers have been placed by Indian governments from 1922 onwards, and, shortly before the Second World War, a ban was imposed on further emigration of this kind. In Malaya, the same economic circumstances which restricted Chinese immigration also applied to Indians. The Indians, who comprised 11 per cent of Malaya's population in 1947, have maintained more links with their country of origin, and a fair amount of two-way travel between India and Malaya still continues.

Chinese and Indian immigration in the modern period of Malayan history stand out clearly, in outline at least; Malay immigration is more difficult to detect and analyse. Immigrant Malays (or Malaysians, or Indonesians) merged fairly easily in the present century into Malay society in Malaya,[2] and they mostly took up agricultural occupations. Johore and Selangor were the States most affected, and the chance of a rubber-smallholding or of plantation-work attracted, in particular, Malays from Sumatra and Java. In 1931, according to T. E. Smith, nearly 28 per cent of all Malaysians in Selangor were born outside Malaya and the same was true of nearly 27 per cent of all Malaysians in Johore. By 1947 the corresponding figures were reduced to 14 per cent and 13 per cent respectively.

Other races make up only 2 or 3 per cent of Malaya's present population, but they have often had an importance out of proportion to their numbers. They include people of Arab stock[3] linked to Malaya through trade and religion and inter-marriage;

[1] Especially the provisions of a Labour Code in 1912.

[2] Sumatran Malays and their descendants merged more easily than Javanese.

[3] The number would be difficult to assess; many become Malays or Malaysians in census-returns.

Eurasians, most of whom have a long family background in Malaya; and Europeans who, as individuals, have stayed varying lengths of time in Malaya through trade, industry, plantation agriculture, and government service.

One feature of the general growth in population was the growth of townships and urban populations. By 1947 26·5 per cent of Malaya's population lived in towns and villages of 1,000 or more people, and 18 per cent lived in towns with populations of 10,000 and upwards. The urban population has continued to grow rather more rapidly than the remainder.

The history of most Malayan towns is still to be written, and it would be rash to generalise on their development until further studies are forthcoming. Detailed work has been done on early Kuala Lumpur, and Malaya's modern capital is a striking instance of a hundred years' growth from the smallest beginnings. Kuala Lumpur was, in the late 1850s, a riverside site where boats which were concerned with the newly-opened Ampang mines could conveniently come with supplies and take away tin. Nearby was a kampong of Sumatran Malays. A shop run by two Chinese in association with a Sumatran trader marked Kuala Lumpur's beginnings as a commercial centre. A small poorly-built township developed in the 1860s with the success of the tin-mining, but it suffered badly during the Selangor Civil War, and, at one stage, was almost abandoned altogether. It was very much a Chinese township under its Capitan China, who kept law and order among the Chinese and collected the revenue due to the Malay chief at Klang. The first Capitan China was one of the merchants who had opened the first shop, but the most celebrated figure in this office was Yap Ah Loy, who was Capitan China from 1868 -85.

Until the coming of the British Resident to Kuala Lumpur in 1880, Ah Loy was the real authority in the town. He was an astute business man and owned many properties, including mines, shops, houses, a smelting shed, a gambling-saloon, and the town's first market. He started a hospital for sick miners and helped to start a Chinese school. He kept law and order in a harsh mining community. Much criticism could be levelled at Ah Loy's Kuala

Lumpur. The houses and roads were poorly built; the town, including the market, was dirty and epidemics were common. Justice was of a very rough-and-ready kind. Yet, within the limits of his own times and circumstances, Ah Loy did more than anyone to establish the little township destined to become Malaya's capital.

In 1884 Kuala Lumpur's population was 4,000. Eleven years later, when the town was chosen as the administrative headquarters of the F.M.S., the population had risen to 25,000. By this time the population included Indians and Malays as well as Chinese, and a small European community, mainly British. The railway ran to Klang and to surrounding mining districts; it was soon to be linked northwards to Perak and southwards to Negri Sembilan and Johore. On a small scale the town, in 1895, was performing many of the functions of today. It possessed a railway station, railway workshops, government buildings, a police-station, a fire-station, military barracks, a building industry, banks, shops, hospitals, and schools. It was well-placed to benefit from the rubber boom about 1910, and it was at this period that the federal government buildings and railway station were designed and constructed. During the present century Kuala Lumpur has continued to grow at a remarkable rate. In 1947 the population was 176,000 and in 1957, 315,000. Kuala Lumpur has long been a centre for research institutes relating to medicine, rubber, and tin; in the 1950s it has also become a University city — and a language centre.

2. HEALTH AND EDUCATION

There were plenty of health problems in the Malay States in the nineteenth century, and evidence of them is found in contemporary accounts, including the early Journals of the British Residents and records of the Straits government. Malaria, dysentery, beri-beri and other tropical diseases were common, whilst outbreaks of smallpox, cholera, enteric fever and other plagues struck suddenly and took a heavy toll of life.

The opening-up of the country, with new mining and planting

areas, new roads and railways, and new townships, was accompanied by a heavy death-rate as virgin jungle was uncovered, malarial swamp encountered, or as the new town grew to a point where the lack of suitable water and cleansing amenities brought its own terrible dangers. To quote only a few examples: There was cholera in Larut in the spring of 1874, and the death-roll was estimated at 65. Out of 87 mining labourers who went from Lukut to Ampang in 1857, only 18 were alive at the end of a month; jungle-fever had killed the rest. The number of beri-beri cases treated in hospital in Selangor in 1894 was 2,817, and the death-rate among these was 24 per cent. In Selangor, in 1905, the number of deaths was stated to be two and a quarter times as great as the number of births, and, in 1906, almost three times as great. The project of building the new port of Port Swettenham in the first decade of the present century was almost abandoned on account of the terrifying death-rate from malaria among the labourers.

This state of affairs could not, of course, be remedied suddenly, and even when remedies had been found for many diseases, vigilance and precautions were — and still are — necessary to prevent renewed outbreaks. The development of measures to meet Malaya's medical problems may be summarised under three main headings, namely the provision of hospitals, the establishment of Town Sanitary Boards, and the application of the findings of medical research.

One of the earliest hospitals in the Malay States was that provided by Yap Ah Loy for sick Chinese miners in Kuala Lumpur. It was maintained by a tax of a dollar on every pig slaughtered in the neighbouring mining area. The patients, of whom there were twenty-eight in 1880, were provided with food, shelter, and rest, but they had no real medical attention. The early British Residents gradually provided State hospitals out of revenues, and recruited European medical staff to the State establishment. Kuala Lumpur, before 1890, had two government hospitals, each with forty beds, and a new Chinese hospital was built in 1892 by the Capitan China, Yap Kwan Seng, and maintained by voluntary contributions from the Chinese community.

The early hospitals were neither big enough nor numerous enough to meet the demand, and, in any case, many people were unwilling to enter them. The death-rate in the hospitals was very high because many people were brought there only when they were already dying.

By 1908 a wider pattern of hospital services was emerging. There were, at this time, fifty-two hospitals in the F.M.S. Each of the four States had a State Surgeon with a number of district surgeons under him. On the rubber-estates it was compulsory to provide hospital accommodation on a basis of four beds to every hundred workers, to employ a dresser, and keep a supply of drugs. These estate hospitals were subject to visits from government medical officers. The hospital service has continued to expand, providing larger buildings and increasing the number of hospitals, including several for specialist work. One of the main present-day tasks is to extend the excellent services of town hospitals into rural areas.

The establishment of Town Sanitary Boards was a very important step towards meeting the problems of urban health and hygiene. Kuala Lumpur had such a Board, or committee, in 1890, composed of Malay and Chinese leaders and members of the British Resident's Staff.[1] It was the town counterpart of the State Council. Only the Secretary of the Board was a full-time official, and he received a very modest salary. The Board supervised the cleaning and lighting of streets, the upkeep of roads and houses, the building of drains, and the administration of the market. In the 1890s it made provisions for piped water from a reservoir. It was much concerned with passing or rejecting plans for new buildings, and it made regulations for the erection of covered arcades or 'five-foot ways'. At Ipoh in 1893 the Kinta Sanitary Board began to plan out the town and provide for its cleanliness. About the same time Taiping had kerosene street-lighting and a piped water-supply.

Medical research conducted both inside and outside the Malay States made an invaluable contribution to the control of the worst diseases. For smallpox, a preventative vaccine had been dis-

[1] An Indian member, Tambusamy Pillai, joined the Board in 1894.

covered in Europe at the end of the eighteenth century. The main difficulty lay in persuading people in Malaya to be vaccinated, and much depended upon the local community leaders. In Selangor, Raja Mahmud, a friend of Swettenham, would not organise a vaccination campaign, but another prince, Raja Bot, not only co-operated, but insisted on training as a vaccinator himself. The Capitan China at Kuala Lumpur in 1890 held weekly vaccination sessions for the Chinese at his own house. A Tamil leader advocated a policy of house-to-house vaccination for his own community.

It was possible to check smallpox by vaccination and cholera by improved hygiene and water-supply, but there were still deadly diseases like beri-beri and malaria on which further research was needed.

An Institute of Medical Research was established at Kuala Lumpur in 1900 to investigate tropical diseases in both man and animals. Beri-beri figured very prominently in its early studies. Dutch medical men in Java were also interested in this disease, and a Dutch doctor, Dr. Eykman, noted in 1896 that chickens fed on polished rice were liable to beri-beri. His publication on this theme was not known to British doctors, and a similar conclusion, namely that beri-beri was due to a diet deficiency, was reached at the Kuala Lumpur Institute about 1906. With this knowledge, and the application of complementary diets to beri-beri patients, the death-rate from this disease was brought down very sharply.

The most widely known preventative measures in Malaya are those which have been concerned with malaria. In this field of research, British and Dutch medical men also played a prominent part. The researches of Ronald Ross (1857–1932), who studied malaria during his career in the Indian Medical Service, and continued his laboratory work in Britain, were put to practical purpose in Malaya. The use of drugs, especially quinine, had already been introduced into Malaya before the campaign on the various types of malaria-carrying mosquito and their breeding-grounds began. One of the worst malarial areas of Malaya was the swampy coastline of Selangor, and it was here, at Klang and Port Swettenham, that Dr. Malcolm Watson, Assistant Medical Officer in Selangor in the early years of the present century, proved the value of Ross's theories. When Dr. Watson arrived at Klang in 1901 he found the hospitals full and malaria raging; in some villages whole families died in a few weeks. By systematic drainage, he attacked the breeding-grounds, and within a year he had reduced the death-rate from malaria in Klang and Port Swettenham from 168 to 41 per thousand.

The anti-malaria campaigns were extended to other areas. A Mosquito Advisory Board was set up in 1911, a special division of the Institute of Medical Research concentrated on malaria work, and local Mosquito Destruction Boards were formed. The eventual result was the practical banning of malaria from town areas and a large measure of control in rural areas. This is a battle, however, in which the defences must never be relaxed. The work of research in tropical medicine, too, is still a very valuable and necessary side of Malaya's social services.

The Singapore Medical School, founded in 1905 and later named The King Edward VII College of Medicine, provided a flow of qualified doctors, many of whom served in the Malay States. Other doctors have been immigrants or European expatriates. Side by side with the introduction of public health services and Western-inspired medical research, traditional medicine, Malay, Chinese, and Indian, still plays a part in many people's lives. With so many medical traditions on which to draw, it is not surprising that Malaya can claim to be the healthiest country in South-East Asia.

The building and maintenance of modern schools in Malaya was at first the voluntary work of individuals or groups, including religious missionary communities. In the first half of the nineteenth century, schools were founded in Penang (1816), Singapore (1823/37), and Malacca (1826). The Anglican Chaplain of Penang, Dr. R. S. Hutchings, was the leading figure behind the Penang Free School, which was free in the sense that it was open to all races and that fees were not to be charged to those parents who could not afford them. Public subscriptions and donations from the East India Company helped to maintain the school. This was a boys' school; a brave attempt to run a girls' school was made between 1817 and 1821 and again between 1828 and 1851, when it was finally given up. The Singapore Institution of 1823 was Raffles's idea, though he consulted Dr. Hutchings of Penang and Dr. Morrison, a missionary and Chinese scholar. Money again came from subscriptions, and was to have come from the East India Company, but the scheme was soon abandoned after Raffles's departure from Singapore. The East India Company withheld money, regarding Raffles's idea as impracticable; it was, however, prepared to make grants to less ambitious local schools. The buildings were not completed, but the site obtained a new lease of life in 1837 when it became a boys' school, the Singapore Free School, set up by a trusteeship and modelled on the school in Penang. From 1844, a girls' school was incorporated on the same site; this moved to other buildings in 1871. The Malacca Free School (from 1878, Malacca High School) was founded in 1826 and was, like the Penang school, an Anglican foundation, supported and managed by a committee of prominent local residents and aided by funds left over by a former Dutch school.

Mission schools, organised mainly by the Christian Brothers, a French order of nuns (Les Soeurs du Saint Enfant Jesus), and the American Methodist Church, were opened in the Straits Settlements during the second half of the nineteenth century, and, before the end of the century, in the Malay States. These included St. Xavier's, Penang, St. Joseph's, Singapore, and the Penang Convent School, all founded in the 1850s; the Anglo-Chinese School, Penang (1891), the Methodist Boys' School, Kuala Lumpur (1897), the Convent School, Kuala Lumpur (1899), and in 1904 St. John's, Kuala Lumpur. Other mission-schools followed. In the meanwhile, from a fund raised in Kuala Lumpur to commemorate Queen Victoria's Jubilee, the Victoria Institute was endowed and founded (1894).

All these were trustee- or mission-type schools. They began mainly with voluntary funds, but they received some government support in the form of grants from the Straits and F.M.S. governments. Before the First World War some headway had been made in the provision of government schools using the language medium of English or Malay. Kuala Lumpur, for instance, had its first 'Government English School' about 1890. In 1919 there were seventeen of these Government English Schools as against sixty-three schools of a trustee or mission type, aided, but not established or controlled, by the government. The government schools, both in the medium of English and Malay, were mainly small ones at first; the Government English School in Kuala Lumpur had forty pupils in 1892; in the same year the Malay school (Raja School) in Kuala Lumpur, founded for the sons of Malay aristocracy, had eleven pupils. A notable exception was the Malay College at Kuala Kangsar, dating from 1905, which was a residential school for the sons of princely Malay families, aiming mainly at preparing boys for a career in government service.

Indian vernacular schools had their beginnings largely on the rubber estates where, by the Labour Code of 1912, estate-owners were obliged to provide schools for their workers' children between the ages of seven and fourteen, in cases of ten or more children, and were aided by a government grant. The efficiency of these schools and, even, in many cases, their functioning at all, was a very doubtful matter until at least well into the 1920s. In urban areas, Indian communities, where large enough, made some efforts to provide vernacular schools; but poor conditions of pay and service for teachers who were recruited from India and Ceylon resulted in low standards of education.

Early Chinese vernacular schools were founded by the efforts of the Chinese communities, mostly without any government help. In Kuala Lumpur, by way of exception, the government built the first Chinese school, but Yap Ah Loy provided a schoolmaster at his own expense, and other leading towkays supported the school. The Chinese literary tradition was fostered before 1911, and all ten text-books in use at the Kuala Lumpur school in 1895 were Chinese classics.

In the twenty years between the First and Second World Wars a great deal of progress was made in Malayan education. The main steps can only be briefly summarised here.

Several of the old trustee schools were taken over by the governments, mainly for financial reasons. These included the

Penang Free School and the Victoria Institute. (Trustee schools in Malacca and Singapore had been taken over by the Straits government at earlier dates.) Non-government English schools became eligible for increased grants, known as grants-in-aid, which paid the salaries of teachers on an approved scale and contributed to the cost of new buildings and maintenance. Many more Government English and Government Malay Schools were opened, and a Malay Training College was founded at Tanjong Malim in 1922. The number of Indian and Chinese vernacular schools increased and grants were made available to them, subject to some degree of government inspection, which the Chinese did not always welcome. Kuo-Yu became the medium of instruction in Chinese schools.

A small beginning was made in the field of technical education when a technical school started by the Public Works Department in Kuala Lumpur was taken over by the Education Department in 1926. A School of Agriculture was founded at Serdang (Selangor) in 1931. Teacher-training was established from 1907 onwards in Normal Courses which consisted mainly of holding a practical teaching job and pursuing associated studies under the guidance of experienced teachers. This Normal-training was extended from a two-year to a three-year period in 1928. In the same year the Raffles College of Arts and Science was established in Singapore with a two-million dollar subscription and government aid, and graduates of the College could take a one-year diploma course in Education. A Training College for Malay men has already been mentioned; a Malay women's Training College was opened in Malacca in 1935.[1]

Shortly before the Second World War committees began work on the idea of a university in Singapore, with the King Edward VII College of Medicine and Raffles College as its nucleus. Details were still being worked out when the Japanese invasion took place, but the project was revived again after the war. In October 1949 the University of Malaya was established at

[1] Education for girls lagged behind that for boys in Malaya as elsewhere, but progress in the education of Malay girls has been one of the striking features of Malayan education in recent times.

Q

Singapore and, more recently, a Kuala Lumpur division of the University has been developed. A Chinese 'Nanyang' University, also at Singapore, is another recent development; it is at present faced with problems of finance as well as with the need to raise academic standards.

Finally, a brief word is due on the administration of education, which has been as complicated as the other branches of administration in Malaya since 1895. In the Straits Settlements an Inspector of Schools was appointed in 1872, and his title was changed in 1901 to that of Director of Public Instruction. His headquarters were at Singapore, with assistant officers at Penang and Malacca. In the F.M.S. Perak lead the way with a Department of Education set up in 1890. A Federal Inspector of Schools for the F.M.S. was appointed in 1897, but in 1906 the F.M.S. and the Straits Settlements were amalgamated under one Director of Education. In 1927, when some decentralisation took place in the F.M.S., the Director's work became much more advisory, and each State was in charge of its own Education service. The Unfederated States recruited Education officers from the Straits Settlements, the F.M.S., and from outside Malaya, including Britain, and worked out their own programmes, not uninfluenced by what was happening in other Malay States.

Under the Federation of Malaya Agreement, the Federal government became responsible for educational policy which was then carried out at State and Settlement level, aided by funds from Federal revenue. On the introduction of the Member system in the Federal Legislative Council, the post of Member for Education was created. After the 1955 elections Dato Abdul Razak became the first Minister for Education in the Alliance government.

Education is a subject of the greatest importance in mid-twentieth century Malaya, and a vast programme of expansion is being carried out, with the inevitable accompaniment of heavy expenditure. Included in this programme are more schools of all kinds, more teacher-training and university facilities, and more technical education. Attention is being given to the less-developed East Coast, and to ensuring that the Malayan boy or girl will have the best education possible. Prominent among the aims of the present education programme is the creation of a Malayan consciousness and unity.

(A) *Population Figures in Census Returns*

	1911	1921	1931	1947	1957
Federation of Malaya	2,339,051	2,906,691	3,787,758	4,908,086	6,276,915
Singapore	305,439	420,004	559,946	940,824	1,445,929

(B) *Main Racial Groups in Census Returns (in thousands)*

Malaya, including Singapore.

Year	1911	1921	1931	1947
Malays	1420	1630	1930	2540
Chinese	920	1180	1710	2620
Indians	270	470	620	610

Based on:
Tufo, M. V. del, *Malaya, 1947*, Census Report
Smith, T. E., { *Population Growth in Malaya*
{ *The 1957 Census, A Preliminary Report*
Singapore, Colony of, *Annual Report*, 1958

Chapter 13

POLITICAL AND
CONSTITUTIONAL CHANGES

A.D. 1895–1941

In 1893 Swettenham submitted to the Governor of the Straits Settlements, Sir Cecil Clementi Smith, a scheme for the federation of the four states which had British Residents. This draft scheme was forwarded to the Secretary of State for the Colonies, and Smith's successor, Sir Charles Mitchell, received instructions to report on its proposals. For nearly two years the matter remained undecided, but in 1895 Mitchell recommended that if the Malay Rulers would agree to it, the plan for federation should be accepted. The Colonial Office confirmed this recommendation.

Several reasons prompted first Swettenham and, later, Mitchell to urge the advantages which would follow federation. Communications between the four states and between their four Residents were limited and uncertain. All the Residents were attempting to follow a similar broad policy, but there was little or no opportunity for consultation between them, or for passing on the benefits of experience gained. Too much power was said to be left in the hands of one man, especially as it was difficult to maintain effective control over the Residents from Singapore. With some form of centralisation it would be possible to secure uniformity in matters such as justice, taxation, and land-settlement, as well as to plan communications on a wider, inter-state, basis.

Swettenham proceeded to seek the approval of the four Rulers to the proposals for federation. These proposals included the appointment of a British 'Resident-General' to supervise the administration of the four states, and to act through the individual

Residents. The Resident-General was to be under the supervision of the Governor of the Straits Settlements, who would also be known as High Commissioner for the Federated Malay States. There was to be a Federal civil service with departmental heads, but no Federal Council with powers to make laws or to take financial decisions. Although the aim was uniformity, all legislation was to be passed, in similar terms, in each of the four State Councils, and the theory was maintained that the powers of the Rulers within their own states, together with those of the individual State Councils, were not curtailed.

The Rulers accepted these proposals; in fact, according to Swettenham, they gave them their cordial approval. Their status was apparently not impaired, they believed that their prestige and dignity would be enhanced by federation, and they saw advantages in the better opportunities for economic development and in the lessening of inter-state frictions. The Sultans of Perak and Selangor were prepared to agree, as Rulers of the richer states, to some measure of financial help for the development of Negri Sembilan and Pahang.

The Federated Malay States thus came into being on July 1st, 1896. Kuala Lumpur, on account of its central position, was chosen to be the headquarters of the Resident-General and of the departmental heads, and it thus became the Federal capital. Yet there was no true federation. Arrangements were made for holding periodic conferences of the four Malay Rulers together with some of their Chiefs and members of their State Councils, but these conferences had no legislative powers. There was no definition of the division of authority between State and Federation. One of the reasons put forward for federation was the danger of leaving too much power in the hands of an individual Resident, but the new scheme put even more power in the hands of one man, the Resident-General. Swettenham himself was the first holder of this office, and although responsible both to the Governor at Singapore (as 'High Commissioner') and to the Secretary of State for the Colonies, he had considerable freedom of action, and he soon began to build up a series of departmental headquarters in Kuala Lumpur.

The first Conference of Rulers took place at Kuala Kangsar in July 1897, just a year after the introduction of the new system. It lasted for a week, and it was impressive both as an assembly of a kind which had never met in the Malay States before and as an advisory body. Its proposals were passed to the State Councils for their enactments. Despite the assurances given in the terms of the Federal constitution, the State Councils were thus losing much of their importance and power as separate units. On the one hand, day-to-day policy was controlled by officials in Kuala Lumpur working through subordinates in their own departments in the separate states; on the other hand, the agreements on general policy were being made at this advisory conference and the State Councils were simply rubber-stamping these decisions. The trend was all towards greater centralisation.

The second Conference of Rulers was held in Kuala Lumpur in 1903, and it was marked by the arrival of three Sultans by railway train; the Sultan of Pahang made the journey by sea. By this time Malay leaders were realising that increased centralisation of government considerably reduced Malay participation, and the Sultan of Perak, while praising the British contribution in the administrative field, spoke against overcentralisation and its effects.

There can be no doubt that the economic effects of federation — or, to be more accurate, of administrative union — were beneficial and wide in scope. The existing railways and roads were soon linked up by a trunk line and a trunk road in the western states and, a little later, a railway was planned to run through parts of Pahang. A unified Land Code and Mining Code was introduced, government survey work was undertaken, especially in Perak, and scientific research in agriculture, forestry and medicine began on a federal basis.

Swettenham[1] was proud of these achievements. The population of the four States was reckoned as 424,218 in 1891, ten years later (after five years of the Federation) it was 678,595. Between 1895 and 1905 the revenue of the four States rose from 8½ million dollars to just under 24 million dollars, and postal and telegraph

[1] See his *British Malaya*, pp. 299–301.

services had increased tremendously to include over 2,000 miles of telegraph wires and the handling of about 10 million postal covers in a year. The same story of expansion was also shown in the statistics for roads and railways, hospital patients, and the number of pupils attending schools, which was recorded as 13,000 in 1904.

Not all of this economic and social development was due to federation. Tin-mining, plantation agriculture and population would all have increased in any case, but administrative unity helped, in particular, the development of communications and the introduction of valuable research work in matters of common interest.

Political aspects of federation were more open to criticism. The State Councils had been weakened in practice, if not in theory. The Rulers themselves, despite the idea of the advisory conference, tended to be rather left out of the administrative scene; no arrangements were made for holding the conferences at regular intervals and, in an interval of several years, much happened. The Resident-General became a policy-maker almost in his own right. It was not only Malay leaders from the State Councils (as well as the Sultans) who felt they should have some say in the government; the mining, trading, and planting concerns began to press for some established form of representation in the government so that their views could be given, especially on subjects which affected them directly.

To meet this political discontent, a Federal Council was set up in 1909 through the initiative of Sir John Anderson of Singapore and with the agreement of the Rulers. The High Commissioner (i.e. Governor of the Straits Settlements) was its President, and the other members were the four Rulers, the Resident-General, and the four Residents, as well as four 'unofficial' members who were to be nominated by the High Commissioner and approved by the British Crown. The High Commissioner was empowered to add to this Council, if he thought it desirable, heads of administrative departments, but any additions of this kind were to be counterbalanced by the same number of new 'unofficial' members taken from trade, industry, or agriculture. The Resident-General's title was changed to that of Chief Secretary to mark his subordination to the High Commissioner.

This Federal Council was to meet once a year and to deal with the draft estimates of revenue and expenditure of each State. It controlled all important policy, leaving on the agenda of the State Councils only 'matters of the Muslim religion, the consideration of death sentences, and the banishment of alien criminals'.[1] A clause in the Council's constitution gave the High Commissioner discretion to leave to the State Councils any matters which he considered should properly be dealt with only by them. In effect, however, all important policy decisions were made in the Federal Council, which apportioned the combined revenues of the four states and then informed the State Councils of its decisions.

The Federal Council was a curious piece of constitutional machinery. Its president was the Governor of a neighbouring colony, and its unofficial members required the approval of the British government and not that of the Sultans. The four Sultans sat on the Council as ordinary members with no powers of veto, and its business went on whether they attended or not. Its legislation was signed by the High Commissioner. The Sultans were entitled to a voice in the discussions and debates of the Council, but, as traditional Rulers, this would have brought them a loss of dignity and esteem, and they either sat silent or ceased to attend altogether. The Federal Council did serve, to some extent, as a channel for the views of the 'unofficials', of whom three of the first four were British and the fourth Chinese. The State Councils and the Sultans were, however, weakened more than ever and Malay representation was diminished.

The Federal Council hinged the Federated Malay States more closely to Singapore through the presidential status of the High Commissioner and the influence of his representative, the Chief Secretary. This latter new title was not popular in Malay circles because it seemed to emphasise a subordinate link between the F.M.S. and Singapore. In the Federal Council the main voices were those of the Chief Secretary and of the unofficial members;

[1] R. O. Winstedt, *History of Malaya*, p. 251.

the High Commissioner mainly limited himself to the role of chairman.

Political grievances in the F.M.S. were rather overshadowed by the general peace and prosperity until the depression years of the early 1920s. At this time, trade and revenues took a serious drop and a more critical attitude to government developed. From 1909 onwards many British officials in the F.M.S. and the Straits Settlements had considered it likely that the 'Unfederated' States would sooner or later come into the Federation, but these states, together with Johore, although subject to British advice and protection, had their own Councils with a very considerable measure of independence. The existence of these Councils stirred the Sultans in the F.M.S. to urge the restoration of former powers to their State Councils. At the same time, it was thought in the Straits Settlements that a process of decentralisation in the F.M.S. might encourage the other states to federate also.

In this atmosphere, a reorganisation of the Federal Council was carried through by Straits Governor, Sir Lawrence Guillemard, in 1927. By this time the unofficial members of the Council totalled eight, including five Europeans, two Chinese, and one Malay. Guillemard increased the number of official members to thirteen and that of the unofficial members to eleven. Further heads of departments were given seats on the Council, but the Sultans were withdrawn, and the inclusion of four new Malay members gave a little more outlet for Malay opinion. The four Sultans now held annual meetings with the High Commissioner and Chief Secretary and, in practice, the Residents usually discussed the business of forthcoming Council meetings with the Sultans.

In the early 1930s further changes were made. The Chief Secretary became known as a Federal Secretary, and his status was lowered so that he lost authority over the individual Residents and remained mainly a co-ordinating officer. Some life was put back into the State Councils; the control of agriculture, education, medicine, and public works, was put on a State basis and the State Councils drafted their own budget proposals for the Federal Council. Control of police, customs, military defence, and general finance, remained, however, matters for the Federal Council. Laws were to be made again by the State Councils and not by the Federal Council. Links were made between State Councils and Federal Council by the appointment of the two Federal officers for finance and legislation to membership of all the State Councils, and by the appointment to the Federal Council of unofficial members who had previously served on State Councils.

This uneven and complex mixture of State and Federal relationships remained until the Japanese invasion of 1941–2. The policy of the British Colonial Office contained elements of contradiction. There was a conflict between trying to preserve the rights and prerogatives of the Sultans and the individual States and, at the same time, seeking to provide efficient government for the four Federal States, which might best be achieved by centralisation. Apart from the question of efficiency, the nature of the government was a matter of concern to several interested parties — the Malay Sultans, the European and Chinese planters, miners and merchants, and political and commercial interests in the Straits Settlements. Any change was liable to arouse some opposition in one quarter or another, and the result was perhaps rather an untidy compromise. No widespread political movement existed to demand radical changes or to press for a government based on wider representation. During the 1930s, however, the State Councils began to change a little in their appearance; European and Indian unofficials were made members as well as Malays and Chinese, and the Malay members included young men with a modern education and outlook.

Whilst this uneven constitutional pattern was being woven in the F.M.S., changes occurred in the other Malay States. These can be examined in two parts; firstly, the transference of protectorate over the four northern states from Siam to Britain in 1909, and, secondly, the constitutional development of Johore.

A long background of motives and negotiations preceded the Anglo-Siamese Treaty signed at Bangkok in March, 1909, and the wider issues can only be summarised here. In the late years of the nineteenth century there were frontier issues between Siam and France and between Siam and Britain. By 1867 the French protectorate over Cambodia was firmly established, and over the next thirty years there followed a long-drawn-out series of incidents and negotiations between France and Siam in relation to disputed territories, particularly in what is today Laos, and in the Lower Mekong basin. The French brought very considerable military and diplomatic pressure to bear on Bangkok in support of their claims.

The Franco-Siamese issues were of real interest to Britain because Siam was bounded on the west by British Burma, whose extent was increased by the annexation of Upper Burma in 1886. The extension of French control in Laos was creating the strong possibility of a common frontier between British and French-controlled territories lying, roughly, to the north of Siam between French Tongking and British Upper Burma. Another reason for British concern was a French idea of a canal across the Kra Isthmus. In the 1880s and 1890s, British policy was aimed at attempting to modify French demands on Siam; to avoid, or at least limit, a common frontier with French Indo-China, and to negotiate with Siam a peaceful settlement of Anglo-Siamese frontiers. In this way Siam might play the part of a buffer-state between British and French interests just as, perhaps, Afghanistan served as a buffer state between British and Russian interests.

The Siamese government only yielded to French demands when under very great pressure, and saw a way of retaining independence by playing off France and Britain against each other. Siam also sought some compensation for losses of territory in the east by securing a firmer hold on the southern provinces in the Malay Peninsula and obtaining legal recognition of her rights there from Britain. The establishment of British protection over the four central states of Malaya gave Britain a closer interest in any actions of the Siamese to the north, and some British officials, including Swettenham, were in favour of the extension of British protection to the Malay states claimed by Siam. The Colonial Office took a much more cautious line and approached Bangkok in matters concerning Perlis, Kedah, Kelantan or Trengganu. One instance of this was the liaison with the Siamese government in 1895, when a military force entered Trengganu and Kelantan in pursuit of rebel Malays from Pahang; another example of this attitude was the refusal of the British Foreign Office, in 1900, to give outright support to a British speculator, Duff, who claimed a title to a large land-concession from the Sultan of Kelantan. Duff was asked to go to Bangkok and secure ratification from the King of Siam.[1]

In 1896, after British attempts to negotiate with France for a buffer state in the Upper Mekong region had broken down, an Anglo-French agreement was signed by which France gained territories from Britain lying east of the Mekong, and formerly part of the Shan States of Upper Burma, but both Britain and France guaranteed the integrity and independence of central Siam, based on the Menam valley. This had the effect of checking any French aspirations on the Menam, protecting British trade interests in Siam, and leaving open the chances of Anglo-Siamese negotiations concerning the southern boundary. As a further safe-guard to the Anglo-French agreement, Britain made a convention with Siam in the following year by which Siam agreed not to cede any territory south of the eleventh parallel or to give any special advantage in trade or land in that region without British approval; in return, Britain would support Siam if any third power tried to gain influence in the area by pressure of any kind.

The price of this British policy of keeping the French out of Siam was co-operation with Bangkok in Siamese claims to authority in the northern Malay states. In 1899 an agreement was made about the frontier boundary of Pahang and Trengganu by reference to Bangkok and not to the Sultan of Trengganu. In 1902 an Anglo-Siamese agreement provided that the Sultans of Kelantan and Trengganu should conduct foreign affairs only through the Siamese, that Siam would appoint an Adviser and an Assistant Adviser to each of these states, whose advice was to be taken on all matters of administration except those touching Malay custom or religion, and that these appointments should have British approval. So long as peace and order and good government were maintained, the Siamese would not interfere in the internal affairs of the two states.

[1] A. Wright and T. H. Reid, *The Malay Peninsula*, p. 160.

Swettenham, who was Governor of the Straits Settlements at the time, paid visits to the Sultans of Kelantan and Trengganu to discuss this Anglo-Siamese agreement. There was no doubt where Swettenham's sympathies lay. He had previously been in favour of direct negotiation between the British and the northern Malay states, and before he finally left Singapore in 1904 he showed himself sympathetic to applications for British protection from the Malay populations of Patani, Sai, and Reman, who complained of various forms of Siamese oppression.

The Sultan of Trengganu refused to sign the 1902 agreement, but the Sultan of Kelantan, who was always in a weaker position, complied. An Adviser and Assistant Adviser were appointed by Bangkok to Kelantan in 1903; both were British officials who had been in the service of the Siamese government for a number of years, and they spoke no Malay.

Britain and France agreed to bury existing differences in 1904 when they made the famous 'entente cordiale' which was to make them partners in the First World War. After this date, both countries conducted further negotiations with Siam concerning boundary questions. There were Franco-Siamese agreements in 1904 and 1907, and Anglo-Siamese talks, which began in 1904, eventually led to a treaty in 1909 which placed not only Kelantan and Trengganu but also Kedah and Perlis under British protection. By this Anglo-Siamese Treaty the Siamese transferred to Britain all their rights over the four states, leaving the British government to negotiate its own treaties with each of the individual states.

In return for these vaguely-defined powers, Britain gave up the right to have jurisdiction for British citizens in Siam which had existed through a consulate system since 1855, a new Anglo-Siamese boundary was defined and, by a separate treaty at the same time, the Federated Malay States made a loan of four million pounds to the Siamese Railway Department for the construction of railways in Siam. The 1897 agreement, which had subjected Siamese concessions south of the eleventh parallel to British consent, and had offered British help in the event of third-power pressure in this area, was now abrogated, but Siam gave a

THE MALAY STATES
A.D. 1909 - 41

SIAM

PERLIS

KEDAH

PENANG

PERAK

KELANTAN

TRENGGANU

SOUTH

CHINA

SEA

F. M. S.

PAHANG

SELANGOR

STRAITS OF MALACCA

Kuala
Lumpur

NEGRI
SEMBILAN

MALACCA

JOHORE

SUMATRA

SINGAPORE

Federated Malay States
Unfederated Malay States
Straits Settlements

Scale of Miles
0   20   40   60

further undertaking against granting strategic concessions to any third party on the west coast of the Gulf of Siam.

British influence over the four states concerned in the 1909 treaty was increased only gradually. Much depended at first on the existing nature of Siamese control. Kelantan, which had had an Adviser and Assistant Adviser appointed by Siam since 1902, was more closely linked with Siam than any of the other states. Other officials had already been recruited from the F.M.S., and Kelantan had the nucleus of a British civil service, admittedly linked with Bangkok. This administration now became divorced from Siam, and a State Council was set up under the presidency of the Sultan. Apart from the British Adviser, the Council was almost exclusively Malay, but a small number of British administrators acted as heads of departments.

Trengganu had long resisted Siamese claims to suzerainty, and the Sultan showed no great haste about accepting British advice. He complained, in the first instance, that Siam had not informed him of the terms of the Anglo-Siamese treaty. In 1910 Trengganu agreed to accept British protection and control of foreign affairs, together with a British agent with very limited powers. A State Council was later instituted, together with administrative changes which brought the state more into line with systems in Kelantan and Pahang. A British Adviser was accepted by treaty in 1919, but, as in Kelantan, the State Council was essentially Malay. Its president was the Mentri Besar, while the Sultan remained legal head of the state. A small number of British officials were recruited for the administration, and the Adviser was consulted on all important matters of state, though he was not strictly a member of the Council, whose meetings he attended.

Kedah also delayed in making a definitive treaty with Britain for many years, although British advice and assistance in the administration began in about 1910. By a treaty of 1923 the Sultan accepted a British Adviser, but he was to be informed beforehand of any British appointments. A State Council was provided, and it consisted of the Sultan as president, three Malay members appointed by the Sultan and approved by the High Commissioner for the F.M.S., and the British Adviser. Additional members were to be appointed on the same principle of joint agreement. It was expressly stated in the treaty that no attempt should be made to merge Kedah with any other state or colony without the consent of the Sultan in Council.

Similar developments took place in the small state of Perlis. As a result of the Anglo-Siamese treaty, a British Adviser replaced a Siamese Adviser, who had been mainly concerned with financial matters relating to a loan from Bangkok. The Siamese debt was eventually paid off, twenty years later, and the role of the British Adviser, whose influence had long extended into the general administration, was regularised by a new treaty in 1930. Government was conducted by a Sultan in Council; a British Adviser took a leading part in the administration and there were other British officers, but the civil service was predominantly Malay.

In all these Malay states, the British share in the administration was less than in the F.M.S., and the connections with the Straits Settlements were less marked. There was much more of a Malay administration with British guidance as compared with the largely British administration, with certain Malay prerogatives, in the F.M.S. The Rulers of these states had no wish to join the F.M.S., because this would have entailed some loss of independence; in particular, their finances would have been subjected to decisions taken at Kuala Lumpur. They had the advantage of British advice, and they could recruit British professional and technical assistance while still retaining a very considerable measure of self-government. Though willing to make internal changes from time to time, the Malay Sultans of Perlis, Kedah, Kelantan and Trengganu, together with their State Councils, were anxious to preserve the separate identity of their own states.

Finally, the case of Johore remains to be considered. The nearness of Johore to Singapore made some measure of British influence inevitable,[1] yet the government of Johore retained its individuality, and it was remarkably moulded by the careers of three descendants of that Temenggong who signed the Preliminary Treaty with Raffles at Singapore in 1819.

In an earlier chapter[2] reference has been made to a long-drawn-

---

[1] This could also be said of Kedah and Penang.　　　　[2] See Chapter 8.

out dispute which arose in the middle of the nineteenth century between Tunku Ali, son of Sultan Hussein, and Temenggong Ibrahim, son of Temenggong Abdu'l Rahman. Both were at the time pensioners of the East India Company, and the real issue was the control of Johore and its revenues. Tunku Ali also pressed for recognition as Sultan of Johore from the Company, whose agent, Raffles, had given recognition to his father. The policy of Singapore was at this time directed from India, and Bengal was not very much interested in Ali's case, which seemed to offer no advantage from the Company's point of view. Ali's entitlement to property and pension was maintained, but, in view of Ibrahim's *de facto* rule in Johore, the matter of a Sultan's title was passed over. Eventually it was settled on a basis of expediency in 1855, when negotiations between the two princes and the Straits authorities ended in a treaty which allowed Ali the title of Sultan, a cash payment, and an increased pension, together with a personal domain on land between the Kesang and Muar rivers. Ibrahim and his successors became the rulers of Johore, subject only to acknowledging a title and paying a pension to Ali and his descendants.

Temenggong Ibrahim continued to live at Singapore, but he received the revenues of Johore, and he arranged for the building of a town at Tanjong Putri, which was to be later known as Johore Bahru. It was Ibrahim's eldest son, Abu Bakar, who, succeeding to the title of Temenggong on his father's death in 1862, gave to the capital of Johore (in 1866) its modern name. He had great business sense and a good mind for detail; he encouraged immigration and plantation agriculture in Johore and established new land laws and new customs posts. In 1868, after a visit to Europe and some sounding of Malay opinion on the subject, Abu Bakar assumed, with the agreement of the Straits Governor, the novel title of Maharaja, reminiscent of the old title of Sri Maharajah borne by some of the early South-East Asian kings. On several occasions Abu Bakar acted as an intermediary between the British authorities and other Malay states, and in the 1870s and 1880s, by his relationships with parts of the later Negri Sembilan and with Pahang, he seemed to be aiming

R

diplomatically at restoring some form of Johore leadership over neighbouring Malay states. In this he was unsuccessful, but in 1878 he secured control of the Muar district, where Sultan Ali had died in the previous year. This was achieved through an election held by Muar chiefs, who were made clearly to understand the Maharaja's aims, and knew that the Singapore authorities were in favour of them. Ali's successors were entitled to 500 dollars a month from the Maharaja under the terms of the 1855 treaty; this was now increased by a further 750 dollars to compensate for loss of territory. In 1885 the dynastic issue was finally settled when the Maharaja took the title of Sultan, signed a treaty of alliance with Britain, and accepted a British officer as a consular official.

Abu Bakar took great interest in planning Johore Bahru, especially the royal palace and its gardens. He encouraged plantations and market gardens both near Johore Bahru and near the new town of Muar, which he founded in 1884. Singapore Chinese were the main producers, and crops included coffee, tea, cloves, gambier, and pepper. In 1892 the Sultan was honoured by the Chinese Emperor with the award of the first-class order of the Double Dragon for his justice to the Chinese in Johore.

Shortly before his death in 1895 Abu Bakar issued a written constitution for the state; it was drawn up by British lawyers. This provided for a Council of Ministers, all Malays and Muslims, who would advise the Sultan. In addition, there was a Council of State whose members were not necessarily Malays, but who were required at first to be Johore subjects. The Council of State consisted of members appointed by the Sultan with the advice or agreement of his Council of Ministers, who were themselves ex-officio members. The powers of this Council of State were similar to those of a Legislative Council in a British colony; it made laws requiring the Ruler's consent, which, under certain conditions, he was obliged to give. An amendment in 1912, in the reign of Abu Bakar's son, Ibrahim, introduced a third body, an Executive Council whose members were appointed by the Sultan; this was the counterpart of Executive Councils in British colonies. It met weekly, usually under the Sultan's chairmanship, dealt with routine administration and proposed new legislation. The Council of Ministers tended to become confined to dealing with the narrower field of exclusively Malay and Muslim matters.

Two further changes occurred in 1914. The Council of State became open to members who were not Johore subjects, including British officials, and Sultan Ibrahim, to meet the problems of a growing population and economy, took a British General Adviser whose function was similar to that of the Advisers in the other States outside the F.M.S. Under the Sultan, a Malay Mentri Besar remained at the head of the administration, and Malay and British officials shared senior departmental work. Close links—but not dependence—were maintained with the Singapore authorities.

This brings the outline of constitutional development in Malaya to the situation which existed in 1941, at the time of the Japanese invasion. It was a complex scene. On the fringe lay the Straits Settlements, Penang, Malacca, and Singapore, a British colony divided in three pieces and governed from Singapore, subject to the Colonial Office. At the centre lay the Federated Malay States with a large measure of British administration based on Kuala Lumpur, but with some rehabilitation of the State Councils since the early 1930s. To the north lay the states over which Siam had formerly claimed suzerainty — Perlis, Kedah, Kelantan, and Trengganu — and which now had treaties with Britain as the protecting Power, as well as British Advisers and a small number of other British officials. To the south lay Johore, which had had close associations with Britain from the time of the founding of Singapore but had maintained considerable independence and Malay control through the progressive policies of the Rulers descended from the Temenggong family. For lack of a better word, perhaps, the four northern states, together with Johore, were commonly named the 'Unfederated' States, to distinguish them from the F.M.S. Federated, Unfederated, and Straits Settlements — politically, this was the Malaya of 1941.

Nationalist movements were widespread in South and South-East Asia long before the Second World War. The Congress Party in India was aiming for self-government from as early as 1906. The military and economic nationalism of Japan served as another kind of example for the achievement of Asian political ambitions and prestige. The Chinese revolution of 1911, and the subsequent measures to create a modern republican China, drew the attention of overseas Chinese. In Burma, in Indo-China, in the Netherlands East Indies, and in the Philippines, political groups, in open or in secret, and by peaceful means or violence, were working to achieve the end of colonial rule. The Japanese conquest of the region in the Second World War did not create nationalism in South-East Asia; it simply hastened the growth of a plant whose roots were already well established.

To a large extent, however, Malaya's case was exceptional. Nothing which could be termed a large-scale political movement for political independence had as yet come into existence. A number of individual Malayans were, of course, affected by nationalist ideas which were current in other parts of Asia. Western-type education, with its emphasis in history, literature and law, on patriotism, political freedom and the democratic society, contributed considerably, in Malaya as elsewhere, to the idea of applying these principles in an Asian country. British administrators in Malaya were neither completely unaware of, nor completely unsympathetic to these aspirations, but the prospect of a united and independent Malaya still seemed a very long-term one. In the absence of a strong political party with a nationalist platform, or an organised popular movement, the case lacked urgency. Moreover, there were several difficult obstacles in the way.

To begin with, there were the political and administrative divisions of Malaya. Unity could only come by agreement between no less than eleven different governments. Secondly, Malaya was not directly under British rule, apart from the Straits Settlements. Different states and groups of states had different treaty relationships with Britain. While British administration was strongly entrenched in the F.M.S., the Unfederated States retained a considerable measure of independence and were suspicious of any suggestions of union or federation which might reduce this. Even in the F.M.S., the forms of Malay political power were preserved and there was a fair amount of consultation on both sides. As compared with India, the Netherlands East Indies, or even Burma or French Indo-China, the British protectorate over the Malay States (excluding the Straits Settlements) had been a comparatively short one. It began in 1874; it was not fully extended to the four central states until about 1890; the four northern states made their treaties at various dates after 1909, and Johore took a General Adviser in 1914.

The period of British protection was marked by three other factors which would have a delaying effect on nationalism. Broadly speaking, it was a period of prosperity, apart from hardships caused by trade depressions after the First World War and again in the early 1930s. Secondly, until 1931 it was a period of emigration and immigration on a large scale. Although the overall population increased enormously, a high proportion of it was temporary, and did not regard Malaya as a permanent home. Thirdly, for educated and intelligent Malays, at least, there were opportunities of appointments to government service at a high level. Obviously, without the presence of British administrators, these opportunities would have been greater, but the fact that they existed at all not only brought able men into the administration, but also reduced the possibility of an active discontent stirred by potential political leaders who could find no place in the existing régime.

The divisions of Malaya before the Second World War were racial as well as political. Although Malaya provided a fine example of racial harmony, the small balance in numbers which existed between Malays and Chinese, and the existence of a very considerable Indian minority, put further difficulties in the way of potential national unity. There were loyalties and patriotisms in the Malaya of 1941, but they had many outlets which had no bearing on the vision of an independent Malaya. The Malay's loyalty was traditionally felt and given towards his own Sultan and State. The politically-minded Chinese looked towards China and mainly supported in spirit or in deed the Kuomintang party; a much smaller number of Chinese, with a sprinkling of other races, were members of the illegal Malayan Communist Party. The Congress Party in India unwittingly channelled away from Malaya Indian sympathies and aspirations.

Although Malaya was by no means a political vacuum, politics did not loom large on the pre-war scene. In general, standards of living were higher in Malaya than in neighbouring countries; the governments were stable, and there was no widespread pressure, or even desire, for radical changes.

DATES OF EVENTS

1895	Sultan Abu Bakar's Constitution for Johore.
1896	Federated Malay States
1902	Anglo-Siamese agreement concerning Kelantan and Trengganu.
1909	Anglo-Siamese Treaty concerning Perlis, Kedah, Kelantan and Trengganu. (Followed by separate treaties between these States and Britain.)
1909	Federal Council in F.M.S.
1912	Executive Council in Johore.
1914	{Membership of Johore Council of State widened. {British General Adviser in Johore.
1927	Federal Council reorganised in F.M.S.
Early 1930s	{Further changes in Federal Council (F.M.S.). {State Councils partly rehabilitated (F.M.S.).

Rulers of Johore: The Temenggong Family

	Accession
Ibrahim [Son of Temenggong Abdu'l Rahman]	1825
[Son] Abu Bakar [Maharaja, 1868: Sultan, 1885]	1862
[Son] Ibrahim	1895

Chapter 14

THE IMPACT OF JAPAN

A.D. 1941–1945

On December 8th, 1941, the peace of Malaya was shattered by a Japanese military invasion which began when troops landed on the Kelantan coast near Kota Bharu. It was the end of an era.

A long war between Japan and China had been sparked off in Manchuria in 1931, and by 1937 the Japanese government, under strong militarist pressure, was committed to an all-out invasion of China. By 1940 the Japanese were in control of the greater part of China; only the western provinces were held by the armies of defence.

In the struggle against Japan, Nationalist China was helped by Britain in several ways. First Hong Kong, and later Burma, offered gateways for imports vital to the Nationalist cause. The British embassies and Concessions in China offered political asylum to Chinese who sought it, and China Relief Associations in Britain made voluntary contributions to the Chinese war efforts. Britain refused to recognise a puppet government set up by the Japanese at Nanking in March 1940. The Japanese countered these measures as far as possible by action against British subjects and interests in China, and these incidents added to the increasingly sharp relationships which had developed between Britain and Japan in the 1930s. In the first place, Anglo-Japanese rivalries were based on the growing strength of the Japanese navy after the First World War and the threat which this seemed to represent to Britain's interests in the Far East; secondly, Japan and Britain had similar economic problems and were competing in world markets, especially in textiles. This was emphasised in the depression years of the early 1930s.

In 1936–7 Japan entered into an alliance first with Hitler

Germany and then with the Mussolini régime in Italy. The weakness of Britain and France in the face of Hitler's demands in 1938 encouraged the Japanese to initiate further military campaigns into south China, which included within a few months the seizure of Canton, the island of Hainam and the Sinnan Islands, including Spratley, in the South China Sea. This gave the Japanese island bases within very easy reach of the coastline of French Indo-China and, in the case of Spratley, at little greater sailing distance from Singapore than, say, North Borneo.

War broke out in Europe in September 1939, and in the following June France was overrun by German armies and defeated. Britain stood alone against Germany and Italy; Soviet Russia and Germany had signed a Non-Aggression Pact two weeks before the German attack on Poland which marked the outbreak of war. Japan was quick to take advantage of the European situation by first making a treaty of friendship with Thailand in June 1940, and then, using the alliance with Germany as a lever, securing from the German-controlled government of France rights for troop-movements and bases in French Indo-China. By September 1940 Japanese forces occupied the northern part of French Indo-China, and at the same time Japan made a three-Power Pact with Germany and Italy, each promising total aid to the others for a period of ten years. This was little short of a declaration of war against Britain, and it brought British-protected Malaya, as well as the Straits Settlements, into a danger zone. For the time being, however, Japan was occupied with the attitudes of both Soviet Russia and the U.S.A. A Neutrality Pact was secured with Russia in April 1941, and the attempt was made to keep talks going with America.

The German attack on Russia in June 1941 was so successful at first that the Japanese became prepared to risk the entry into the war of the U.S.A. In July they occupied the whole of Indo-China. Washington applied economic sanctions and prepared for war. On December 7th, 1941, Japanese aircraft, without warning attacked the American Pacific Fleet based at Pearl Harbour in the Hawaiian Islands. On the following day Japanese landings were made in Kelantan and Patani.

In a sense, Japan's attack on Malaya was an attack against Britain. There had been the long-standing naval and economic rivalry, followed by Britain's attitude in relation to the Sino-Japanese war. Moreover, Britain had shown weaknesses — diplomatic ones at Munich, and sometimes also in the face of Japanese demands in China, and military ones in the battle for continental Europe in 1940–1. Malaya represented an area of British political influence, exercised directly and indirectly; it was a very important centre of British financial investment, and it was a vital source of tin and rubber for Britain's war-effort.

In a general way, too, the Japanese attack was based on anti-Western emotion. Japan, by adopting Western technology and military techniques, had now become powerful enough, in the hands of militarist leaders, to challenge a Western Power to a trial of strength.[1]

Yet there were other motives involved as well. Considerable funds were raised by Malayan Chinese for assistance to China in the war against Japan. The Japanese attitude to the Malayan Chinese was related to the war in China, and in 1942 many Chinese in Malaya paid with their lives for their former connection with the China Relief Fund.

Perhaps the strongest motive of all lay in the military and imperial ambitions of the Japanese war leaders, who created a vision of an Eastern Asia under Japanese leadership, together with wide opportunities for Japanese emigration into parts of South-East Asia. Japanese slogans made great use of an 'Asia for the Asians' theme, and of a promised 'Co-prosperity sphere' in South-East Asia, but so long as a military clique remained dominant in Tokyo, 'liberation' from Western rule could only mean a large measure of subjection to Japan.

The open warfare in Malaya, including Singapore, lasted only ten weeks. The Japanese, with superiority of numbers and of air power, and showing greater adaptability to the terrain, made rapid progress, receiving serious checks in only two or three places. The defending units, Malay, Indian, Australian, and British,

[1] An early example of this was the check to Russia in the Russo-Japanese War, 1904–5.

fell back on Singapore, where Chinese volunteers added a brave element in a desperate situation. On February 15th, 1942, Singapore, with its water-supply cut, surrendered.

The Japanese achieved a dramatic and spectacular victory, and the fall of Singapore, in particular, caused a great shock in Britain and in the United States. In retrospect, many reasons can be offered for Malaya's lack of an effective defence. One was the relative (but not total) lack of preparation against such an attack. The fall of France and the rapidity of the Japanese advance towards the Malay Peninsula were not foreseen. Japanese striking-power had been underestimated. The defence of Malaya had been regarded in Britain largely as a naval matter, through a war fleet based on Singapore; it would seem that insufficient attention had been given to providing this fleet with adequate air cover, and to giving it balance in terms of different types of naval vessels. Two modern British warships, the strongest naval units, were sunk by Japanese aircraft off the east coast of Malaya after they had attempted to reach Kelantan in time to prevent the invasion. At the time of the Malayan campaign, Britain was in an extremely difficult position, still recovering from losses in France, heavily committed in North Africa, and sending aid to Russia. The United States was only just in the war, with her Pacific Fleet crippled.

More might perhaps have been done to recruit Malayans into armed forces for the defence of their own territory, instead of leaving this largely to British forces. There was a Malay Regiment, and after the outbreak of the war in Europe a Malay navy was established on a small scale. A Local Defence Force was formed in 1940, and a number of auxiliary services — including Auxiliary Medical, Fire and Transport services were organised. Much of this may have been 'too little and too late', yet it would have been no easy matter to raise armed forces in Malaya before the Second World War. There was no popular demand for such a step, and there seemed no need for it. For effective defence, the close co-operation of several governments would have been involved, and, not least, there was the question of expense. Outside Malaya, a British-sponsored plan for Malayan armed forces would have met with sharp criticism, even in Britain and the

United States, and it might have given provocation in other quarters. It is, however, clear that, in the light of later events, British plans for the defence of Malaya were inadequate; Britain, too, was inadequately prepared for the dangers of the Second World War.

Military considerations naturally dictated the nature of Japanese government in Malaya between 1942 and 1945. Europeans who had been in the administration of the various governments were interned in prison camps. In the Straits Settlements, the Japanese took direct control; in the Malay States, the forms of government remained but their powers were subject to the advice of Japanese political agents and the requirements of Japanese military commanders. The police came under the control of the dreaded Kempeitai. Labour was conscripted by force for work at the ports, for military installations, and for the Burma-Thailand railway.

The Malayan Chinese received particularly ruthless treatment; the Malays suffered in the general economic hardships and were subjected to arbitrary demands for supplies, yet, on the whole, the Japanese attitude towards them was less harsh;[1] Indians were prominent among the conscripted labourers. Eurasians had to suffer for the Western elements in their heredity.

It was Japanese policy to humiliate Europeans and to stamp out Western influence. In some places monuments were removed, and the Japanese language was introduced into schools to replace English. The Japanese victory and the anti-Western propaganda which followed it undoubtedly caused a lowering of British prestige in Malaya, but the nature of Japanese rule, even allowing for the contingencies of war, had little attraction for the people of Malaya.

Economically, there was very great hardship. The standard of living in Malaya was (and is) linked with production for export, especially rubber and tin. When the Japanese moved southwards in 1941-2, tin-mining equipment and rubber-processing plants were heavily damaged as they were about to fall into Japanese hands. This, in itself, might only have had limited effects on Malaya's two main industries; more significant was the fact that

[1] There were, however, instances of collective punishment against Malays.

Malaya was cut off from the normal export markets and production could now only be measured by Japanese requirements. Although both tin and rubber were important materials in wartime, transport was also a vital factor and the needs of Japanese industry could often be met in controlled territories nearer to Japan than Malaya. The loss of markets for tin and rubber also meant to Malaya a loss of consumer goods of all kinds, which were normally imported. More serious still was the shortage of imported foodstuffs, including rice, much of which came from Japanese-controlled areas but for which the Japanese were incapable of providing adequate transport or marketing arrangements. Town-dwellers in Malaya, including a large proportion of Chinese were very badly hit by this food shortage, and many moved out to take refuge on the fringe of the jungle. Here they hoped to receive less attention from the Japanese and to grow a little food for themselves. This marked the beginnings of what became known in post-war years as a 'squatter-problem'. An uncontrolled issue of paper-money created a worthless currency and caused inflation, adding to the general economic chaos.

Before the Japanese invasion the health services in Malaya had been built up to a very high standard. The looting of hospitals by the Japanese for medical stores and equipment, the neglect of preventative measures against tropical diseases, together with diet deficiencies caused by food shortage, led to outbreaks of epidemics and diseases on a scale such as had not occurred in Malaya for many years.

On the political side, the Japanese authorities attempted to combine the administration of Malaya and Sumatra through a headquarters at Singapore. This would seem to have been partly aimed at gaining Malay support for a union which would strengthen Malay and Muslim influence as against that of other communities, but it had little marked success, and by 1944 the scheme was dropped. The Japanese attitude on this matter may, however, have assisted the gradual rise of a pan-Malay movement with links between Indonesia and Malaya.

Another Japanese administrative measure was the establishment in 1943 of Malay local councils whose members were partly appointed by the Japanese and partly elected by the village head-men. The function of these Councils was, at the most, advisory. It is very significant that no party or group existed in Malaya whom the Japanese, as their own defeat drew near, could recognise and sponsor as a new 'independent' government.

Resistance to Japanese rule in Malaya took many forms, including the organisation of armed groups in the jungle which made attacks on Japanese installations and communications. The jungle-fighters represented a mixture of many elements and motives. Racially, they were largely Chinese, and, in view of the Japanese attitude to the Chinese, this was not surprising. There were also, however, Malays as well as individuals of other races, including a number of British officers left behind to organise such resistance or, later, parachuted-in to prepare for the final attack against Japanese-held Malaya.

The main force of the armed resistance movement took the name M.P.A.J.A. (Malayan Peoples' Anti-Japanese Army). It was divided into State groupings and was Communist-led. The Malayan Communist Party (M.C.P.) had been formed about 1927. Its members were almost all Chinese and its activities were organised along the lines of a Secret Society. As it did not register publicly its constitution and aims, it was an illegal body, and it gained no widespread support. Its activities, however, were not insignificant. In the years immediately preceding the Second World War, and in the period of nearly two years before Soviet Russia was involved in the war, the M.C.P. was active in labour troubles and disturbances in plantations, mines, and docks. In June 1941 Soviet Russia was invaded by German armies, and Britain and Russia became wartime allies; the M.C.P. changed its attitude with this event and supported the war-effort, including production, in Malaya.

During the Japanese occupation, Communists were specially sought out as active opponents of the Japanese régime and its plans, and they took to the jungle both in order to survive and to preserve their organisation. They represented a tough and dedicated group, and their ranks included men capable of leader-ship. They led the resistance-movement not only with the aim of

overthrowing the Japanese, but with the further and more important objective of establishing a Communist republic. The British
authorities made an alliance of convenience with the M.C.P.
leaders, by which British officers and supplies would be sent
as and when possible, on condition that weapons would be
handed in at the end of the war and that the men of the M.P.A.J.A.
would return to normal civilian life.

Representing as it did a general Malayan attitude towards the
Japanese occupation, the M.P.A.J.A. received support both in
new recruits and in supplies of food and clothing from outside
the jungle. In the early stages of the Japanese occupation, the
number of jungle fighters may have been about 3,000; by 1945 it
had increased to about 7,000.

The end of the war in Asia and the Pacific occurred in an
unforeseen manner. In 1944, and in the early months of 1945, the
Japanese received several military setbacks and the area of
Japanese control began to shrink significantly. The dropping of
two atomic bombs on Japan in August 1945, however, brought
the Japanese surrender with dramatic suddenness. In occupied
territories like Malaya there was inevitably a time-lag between the
Japanese surrender and the arrival of armed forces to make this
surrender effective. This created a disturbed and confused interval, marked by incidents of lawlessness and pent-up bitterness,
and also by an attempt on the part of the M.P.A.J.A. to establish
political control before British forces arrived. The M.P.A.J.A.
emerged from the jungle as heroes, but when some leaders began
to use methods of obtaining control which were reminiscent of
those employed by the Japanese, local attitudes hardened. The
arrival of British military forces in September 1945, and the
establishment of a British Military Administration, was followed
by negotiations with the M.P.A.J.A. Weapons were handed over
to the British at ceremonial parades, and each man received a
gratuity of 350 dollars on demobilisation. This marked the end of
the M.P.A.J.A., but not the end of its leadership and organisation,
nor of its supplies of arms. Arms were hidden in the jungle for
some future date when they might be used in a Communist revolt.
Meanwhile the M.C.P. became a legal party, and began to work

for a Communist republic in growing trade-union movements.

The British were generally welcomed back in Malaya, and the M.P.A.J.A. had not been able to gain sufficient support to risk a trial of strength. Malaya in the late months of 1945 was, however, in a very sorry state.

The Japanese had created a certain amount of friction between Malays and Chinese, and in some places serious clashes occurred. These incidents arose out of the bitterness and misery of a long period of foreign military occupation of a harsh nature, and they had their counterparts in the post-war atmosphere of European countries which had suffered a long German occupation. It was unfortunate that in Malaya, largely due to Japanese policy, these troubles took on this communal aspect, but, although they were serious enough, they did not become very widespread. The British Military Administration took firm measures on this issue.

There was a general absence of organised law and order. The police forces had declined both in morale and efficiency, and the extent to which they had been associated with Japanese rule left, in some cases, their continued authority open to question. There was a wave of crime, accompanied by violence such as Malaya had not previously seen in peacetime during the present century. Behind this lay a psychological attitude of lawlessness which had been engendered by nearly four years of opposition, passive or active, to hated authority.

Much work was required to restore what had once been normal health measures. Breakdown and neglect of public health services under the Japanese brought its own toll of diseases and epidemics, and the need for anti-malaria work was especially urgent. Added to this problem was a very serious food shortage which, for many reasons, could only gradually be remedied.

A vast programme of reconstruction was required for the re-establishment of the tin and rubber industry. This entailed not only large sums of capital, but also a supply of skilled personnel for the managerial and technical posts of the companies concerned, and this was not easily available in 1945. A real problem in the sphere of unskilled or semi-skilled labour existed in Malaya in 1945–6. According to local conditions, there was either unemployment or a labour shortage; alternatively, men were either physically unfit or engaged in troubles of their own.

One element in the Malayan atmosphere of late 1945 which may not have always made itself apparent was the loss of confidence in British protection which came from memories of four years earlier. The welcome to the British was sincere, but, inevitably, a country which had passed through great trials and hardships could never be quite the same as before, and one aspect of this was a greater political consciousness. No group, of course, was more politically conscious that the M.C.P., which had gained both strength and recognition through the war. In November 1945 a Malay Nationalist Party (M.N.P.) was formed with Indonesian sponsorship as a political mouthpiece for Malays. In the following month another party was formed, mainly by Chinese of the professional class, and named the Malayan Democratic Union[1] (M.D.U.); it aspired to be the party for non-Malays. The emergence of these political parties was an early indication that politics had come to matter in Malaya to a much greater extent than in pre-war days.

DATES OF EVENTS

1937	Japanese invasion of China.
1940	Japanese pact with Germany and Italy.
1941 (July)	Japanese occupation of all French Indo-China.
1941 (Dec.)	{Japanese attack on Pearl Harbour. / Japanese invasion of Malaya.
1942 (Feb.)	Japanese capture of Singapore.
1945 (Aug.)	Japanese surrender.
1945 (Sept.)	British Military Administration.

[1] There appears to have been Communist influence at first in both the M.N.P. and M.D.U. See V. Purcell, *The Chinese in South-East Asia*, pp. 379–80 and 411–12.

KUALA LUMPUR MOSQUE AT THE RIVER JUNCTION

Chapter 15

THE ACHIEVEMENT OF NATIONHOOD

A.D. 1946–1959

B ritish policy aimed at restoring civil government as soon as possible, and a new plan for Malaya was drawn up in London before the end of the war. The general policy behind the plan was made known in October 1945, and the details were published in a Government White Paper in January 1946. One major aim was to avoid the pre-war pattern of several governments, with its lack of liaison for common defence. It was therefore proposed to unite the former Federated and Unfederated States, together with Penang and Malacca, under a centralised government known as the Malayan Union. Singapore, on the grounds of its economy, racial structure, and strategic importance, was considered to be a separate case, and was to remain a British colony, at least for the time being.

The chief official of the Malayan Union was to be a British-appointed Governor, and his central administration would leave little or nothing of political importance to the Sultans and the State Councils. State Councils were to be retained, but the main burden of government would rest on an Executive Council and a Legislative Council, the details of which were to be worked out after further consultations in Malaya. The Sultans were to be members of two advisory Councils, one at State level over which they would preside, and the other at Union level over which the Governor would preside, but these were only concerned with Muslim matters. In fact, the Sultans were to retain their titles and their income, but would lose their political influence.

The Malayan Union thus seemed to give to the protected States of Malaya (as well as to Penang and Malacca) a government similar to that which obtained in British colonial territories. It was,

however, an important intention of the Union scheme that British
government would eventually be replaced by democratic self-
government in Malaya. With this aim in mind, the Union proposals offered Union citizenship on a wide basis. Put perhaps in
general terms, the intention of the citizenship clauses was clear
enough. All who were citizens would have equal rights, including
admission to government service and, in due course, a vote in
government elections. The Malays would retain their Land
Reservations. All who were born in the territory of the Union or
in Singapore were entitled to citizenship, as well as those who had
lived there for ten of the fifteen years preceding 1942. Future
immigrants could apply for citizenship after five years' residence.
Citizenship rights were open to people of any race or creed.

Before these proposals were published, Sir Harold MacMichael
was sent from Britain as special envoy to the Malay Sultans, to
obtain their agreement for the British Crown to legislate for a
new constitution.

The Sultans were in a very unsure frame of mind following the
long period of Japanese authority, and, as they were pressed for
an urgent reply, they had little time for consultations. In fact, they
all signed their agreement.

It has been said of the Malayan Union plan that its proposals
were 'well-intentioned, but ill-timed and badly-presented'.[1] The
scheme was drawn up under stress of wartime, and the consent of
the Malay Rulers to a transfer of sovereignty was hastily obtained.
It may have seemed to some of the Sultans that their agreement
was a necessary condition of the continued recognition of their
titles by Britain.

The publication of the Malayan Union proposals aroused
widespread political consciousness among the Malays, and this
took a positive form in the support given to the United Malays
National Organisation (U.M.N.O.), founded by Dato Onn bin
Ja'afar of Johore in March, 1946. This movement had the immediate purpose of resisting the introduction of the Malayan
Union and the longer-term purpose of preparing the Malays for
their part in eventual self-government. Dato Onn toured the

[1] B. Harrison, *A Short History of South-East Asia*, p. 255.

country with great success; demonstrations of national mourning were organised by U.M.N.O. for the loss of status by the Malay Sultans and the loss of rights by the Malays as a whole. The Malay Sultans openly regretted and excused their signatures given to MacMichael, and declared their intention of avoiding any public meeting with the newly-appointed Governor, Sir Edward Gent. In Britain, the Malayan Union plan was attacked by speakers in the House of Lords, by lobbying in the House of Commons, and by letters to national newspapers from former high-ranking officials of the Malayan civil service, including Sir Frank Swettenham, who considered that the proposals imposed too much British control and undermined the special position of the Malays which had been protected in pre-war years. No open support was given to the Union by any group in Malaya, although for many Chinese, at least, the scheme would have been acceptable.[1]

In the face of opposition in Malaya and informed criticism at home, the British government decided to have second thoughts. The Malayan Union was never fully established. In its place a kind of provisional caretaker government carried on while reports were sought first from a Working Committee, consisting of Malays, and later from a Consultative Committee on which other races were represented. The Malayan Union plan had, in the meanwhile, given a tremendous impetus to Malay political consciousness, and created a measure of distrust between Malay leaders and Britain; it had also raised the issues of political unity for the Malay States, and the claims and rights of Malayan citizenship.

As a result of British consideration of the two reports, the Federation of Malaya Agreement was arrived at, and its terms were put into practice in February, 1948. The territories which it covered were identical with those of the abandoned Malayan Union; Singapore remained a separate Crown colony. A federal government was established under a British High Commissioner, whose appointment required the approval of the Malay Sultans. The main organs of federal government were an Executive Council

[1] According to V. Purcell, there was general apathy among the Chinese regarding the Union (*The Chinese in South-East Asia*, p. 390).

which included both official and unofficial members, the latter chosen from the various races, and a Legislative Council which had a large majority of unofficial members, including a predominant Malay element. Provision was also made for State governments, headed by the Sultan (or Resident-Commissioner in the cases of Penang and Malacca) and consisting of both an Executive Council and a legislative Council of State. Such matters as Local Government, Health, Education, Agriculture, and Lands, were entrusted to the State governments, but the Federation could also make enactments on these subjects so far as it was necessary to ensure policies common to all the States. British Advisers remained, but the Rulers' chief official was the Mentri Besar.

The Sultans were to be members of a Conference of Rulers which would meet at least three times a year. The approval of this Conference was required for any amendments in the Constitution or in the immigration laws, and for the appointments of senior government officials.

Citizenship of the Federation was much more restricted than that which had been proposed under the Malayan Union. The clauses were rather complicated, but the main provisions were as follows. There were two types of citizenship, one automatic, the other by application. Those who became citizens automatically included the subjects of the Sultans in all the States, British subjects born in either of the Settlements who were permanently resident in the territories of the Federation, and British subjects born anywhere within the territories of the Federation whose fathers had either been born there or had resided there permanently. Other 'automatic' citizens were persons born within the territories of the Federation who habitually spoke Malay and conformed to Malay customs, persons permanently resident in the territories of the Federation whose parents had both been born there, and any person whose father was a Federal citizen at the time of the person's birth. Those eligible for citizenship by application included persons born within the territories and resident there for not less than eight years out of the twelve years preceding the application, and others who were resident in the territories for not less than fifteen years out of the twenty years preceding the application. In both cases the minimum age was eighteen, and a good character was required as well as a knowledge of the Malay or English language, together with a declaration of permanent settlement and a willingness to take the citizenship oath.[1]

The Federation was something of a compromise, but weighted on the Malay side. Malay influence was preserved through the Sultans and predominant Malay representation in the State and Federation governments as well as by the citizenship clauses. At the same time, citizenship rights would become increasingly available to non-Malays, and this, together with the application of an election system to a majority of seats in the Legislative Council, would eventually make for a more representative government.

Most Malays were probably satisfied with this constitution; non-Malays had more complaints. Not all Chinese saw good reasons for the separate treatment of Singapore, with its predominantly Chinese population; there was also the controversial question of citizenship. There were outward signs of Chinese resentment of the proposed Federation when Chinese organisations called for a token stoppage of work in October 1947, and when only a small fraction of eligible electors registered in Singapore during 1947 to vote for the new Legislative Council there in 1948. Among the Indian community also there were feelings that insufficient attention had been given to the political status of the Malayan Indian.

Despite feeling and action among non-Malays, it seems probable that the majority of Malayans were prepared to give the Federation a fair trial. Yet, within a few months of its birth the new Federation was faced with very serious problems of law and order. Armed violence became an everyday occurrence. There were attacks on police-stations, rubber plantations, tin-mines, and communications. There were killings in which the main victims were Europeans and Chinese.

Outbreaks of violence had not been uncommon in Malaya

[1] Those who became citizens by registration were not bound to forswear allegiance to any other country. This proviso for 'dual citizenship' was withdrawn by the terms of the Federal citizenship law of 1952.

since 1945, and it seemed possible, at first, that the attacks and murders in 1948 were the work of robber-gangs. Increasingly, however, the evidence pointed to nothing less than an armed revolt against the Federation government organised under Communist leadership. A mounting number of murders led to the proclamation by the government of a State of Emergency on June 18th, and six days later the Singapore government made a similar declaration.

The question arises, why did an armed Communist revolt break out at this time? The M.C.P. had, of course, never lost sight of its fundamental aims, and its members had used their influence in other organisations as well as in the sphere of labour relations. Even as early as January–February 1946 the General Labour Union under Communist influence attempted trials of strength with the British Military Administration. One incident was the calling of a widespread strike in support of the unconditional release of thirty former members of the M.P.A.J.A., who had been arrested for various crimes. Another was a plan by the same Union to declare February 15th a public holiday to celebrate the defeat of the British by the Japanese at Singapore in 1942. The B.M.A. dealt firmly and effectively with both of these challenges.

During 1947 strike action had been frequently associated with Communist activities, and the establishment of a Pan Malayan Federation of Labour reflected largely a Communist move to amalgamate all trade unionism into one organisation and then control it. The use of armed attacks by Communists from March 1948 onwards did not, of course, imply any change of objectives; it did, however, represent a very fundamental change of strategy and tactics for which some explanation must be sought.

There has been a strong argument that the inspiration for armed attack came from a Russian-sponsored meeting of Asian and Australian Communists held at Calcutta in February 1948, with South-East Asian countries both represented and discussed. In this connection, it is noteworthy that Communist-led armed outbreaks also took place in India, Burma, and Indonesia, during the first half of 1948.

Communist tactics in the trade-union movement in Malaya

were checked by new laws which were passed early in 1948 to counter a wave of strikes, many of which were based on trivial pretexts. By these laws, trade-union officials were required to have had at least three years' experience in the branch of labour which they represented. Men previously convicted of certain crimes, such as extortion and intimidation, were barred from holding office in the unions. Any federation between the trade unions was permissible only between unions concerned with similar industries or occupations. These measures may have given the Communist leadership an added motive to resort to open warfare.

Many other circumstances could be taken into account. Banditry and violence were not in themselves uncommon at the time, and labour disputes had sometimes been accompanied by violence and deaths. Quite frequently, and for various reasons, crimes of violence went unpunished, and this may have encouraged the Communist leaders to think that a quick campaign of terrorism might succeed. The current successes of Mao Tse-Tung's forces in China may have supplied an added inspiration.

The Federation was a new government, faced by plenty of problems, and its strength was unknown. It might have proved to be much weaker in a trial of armed strength than the B.M.A. had been two years earlier. There was also the question of Chinese sympathies and loyalties. Most of the Communists were Chinese and, in making a bid for power, they may well have hoped to gain a large measure of support from the Chinese community, which had, for the time being, so little participation in the new government, whose strongly Malay character gave the Chinese added cause for discontent.

The armed revolt was led by men who had been leaders in the M.P.A.J.A., and once again they used the jungle as their base and resorted to supplies of arms which had been hidden there three years previously. These men had enjoyed a short taste of power in 1945, and had maintained contact through an Old Comrades' Association. By terrorist tactics, they aimed at breaking down the existing machinery of government as well as creating economic chaos. An immediate objective was to create limited areas of Communist control from which further conquests could be made until the whole country had been gained. The attacks on Europeans were part of the policy of bringing the tin and rubber industry to a standstill, and at the same time driving out British personnel altogether. The attacks on Chinese were directed partly against those associated with the Kuomintang party, and partly towards gaining the support, passive or active, of the Chinese community as a whole, through the use of intimidation methods.

After declaring the Emergency, the Federal government took several firm measures. The M.C.P., M.P.A.J.A., together with its Old Comrades' Association, and other Communist-infiltrated associations, were banned. Police and military forces were increased,[1] and measures taken to protect mines and plantations. At a critical period in 1948-9 the determination of mine-managers and rubber-planters to stand fast and defend their lives and property was of great importance; equally significant was the recruitment of volunteers as kampong-guards and their work in protecting the villages.

On the other side, the Communists called for the support of all M.P.A.J.A. men, and called on workers everywhere to withdraw their labour. They used fresh titles and approaches becoming, for instance, early in 1949, 'The Malayan Races Liberation Army' and attempting in this way, and by anti-British slogans, to give their movement a nationalist appearance. They also developed a vast supply organisation known as the 'Min Yuen' (literally 'Masses' Movement') for the collection of money and supplies of all kinds. The members of the Min Yuen were not necessarily willing supporters of the armed revolt; fear and intimidation played a large part in determining their actions. A particularly important source of contact and supply to the men in the jungle was the Chinese 'squatter' population, about half a million in number and, for the most part, living on the jungle-fringe.

The Communist fighting forces were not very large, but their hit-and-hide tactics gave them the advantageous element of surprise, and the jungle provided almost perfect cover. Although they failed to establish areas of control, they remained a dangerous

[1] Troops were sent from Britain and Commonwealth countries.

and destructive body whose presence and activities cast deep shadows over the general life of Malaya for several years. Emergency Regulations inevitably imposed hardships on everybody, and as time passed with no appreciable improvement in the situation, these measures became more stringent. The fighting war was difficult enough, but even more complex was the problem of the Min Yuen. An Emergency Regulation issued in 1949 empowered the government to arrest and detain people in any area where there was evidence of aid being given to the Communists. This led to detention camps holding mainly Chinese, and with innocent and guilty side by side. Among the Chinese, they were a source of much bitterness. Food supplies were also checked and controlled and, at times, collective punishments instituted. Repressive measures like these were apt to lose sympathy for the government, especially when, as was almost inevitable, mistakes were made. On the other hand, the authorities were fighting a grim war to retain control of Malaya against an armed minority which did not scruple about the means it used.

As a community, the Chinese were in a particularly unfortunate position. They were the main victims of Communist murders and intimidation, and they were also the main victims of government searches, reprisals, and detentions. They had only a very limited political stake in the Federation government. The recognition of Communist China by Britain in January 1950 added to their dilemma. It was good news to the Chinese Communists, who saw in it a weakening of their opponents' position; to the majority of Chinese in Malaya, it raised the questions of how strong the British anti-Communist outlook was in relation to Malaya, and of how far their relatives in China might eventually be affected by any action which they took on behalf of the government in Malaya.

Fortunately, the authorities developed constructive measures as well as repressive ones. One of these was formulated by a Director of Operations, General Briggs, who was appointed in April 1950 to relieve the High Commissioner of responsibility for the military operations. The boldest part of the 'Briggs Plan' was the proposal to move the large Chinese squatter population — estimated at half a million — to resettlement areas, later known as

'New Villages', where guards could be maintained. By this measure it was hoped to cut off the Communist fighters from their major supply-bases. This resettlement was a most difficult and delicate task, for many reasons. First, the co-operation of the State governments was required, because the use of land was involved. Here, the policy of Malay Land Reservations had to be modified in a way which meant giving good land for Chinese settlement. Secondly, there was the physical task of planning and building following the difficult work of surveying and mapping. Thirdly, materials had to be requisitioned and transported to the sites. Lastly, and most complex of all, was the problem of moving the squatters to the new sites, at the same time ensuring that they had the means of earning a living in their new environment. When all this had been done, there remained the problem of staffing the new areas with administrators and police, and of providing them with welfare amenities.

Resettlement was a serious set-back to the Communists. How far the New Villages succeeded in establishing among their inhabitants confidence in, and support for, the government in the early years of their existence was more debatable. Much depended on local circumstances, including the character and ability of both the resettlement officer and the police guard, as well as the suitability of the land for vegetable-growing, and the nearness to work in plantation or mine. Conditions varied from place to place, and with them so did the measure of satisfaction or resentment felt by the ex-squatters themselves.

Resettlement took a considerable time, and difficulties of materials and transport were often encountered. In Johore alone, the work was only roughly completed at the end of a year. In the meantime, the Communists devised ways and means of keeping in touch with the Min Yuen, even in the resettlement areas themselves. General Briggs introduced measures for a stricter control of food supplies and distribution to prevent food reaching the jungle; the details were very carefully worked out but, in practice, they needed a tremendous amount of supervision — more than could often be given.

In October 1951 the British High Commissioner, Sir Henry

Gurney, was assassinated in an ambush on the road between Kuala Lumpur and Fraser's Hill. He had been a brave and sincere man who had toured the country, keeping in close contact with all aspects of the Emergency, and winning wide respect. His death was generally mourned, but public morale was lowered. Early in 1952 Sir Gerald Templer was appointed High Commissioner, with full and direct responsibility for the Emergency; a deputy High Commissioner, Mr. Donald MacGillivray, was to assist in the administrative work. These appointments indicated strong leadership on the military side, and a division of duties which would free the High Commissioner from much of the normal administration so that he could devote almost all his energies to the Emergency.

The new High Commissioner brought great energy and strong leadership to his work, imposing heavy collective punishments on townships and villages which were known to be centres of assistance to the Communists. General Templer was associated with a tough military policy which has had its critics, though others have considered it justified both by circumstances and by results. He also encouraged the New Villages, introduced the idea of 'White Areas', where restrictions were lifted, and presided over some reforms in the constitution and the administration. When he left Malaya in June 1954 there was a very considerable improvement in the military situation, and constructive political developments were taking place. The reduction of the scope of Communist fighting was perhaps largely due to a change of policy on the part of the movement's leadership, dating from October 1951. This required a restriction of violence and an emphasis on regrouping, political activity and penetration into other organisations, including the Home Guard, the Malay Regiment, and the Civil Service. Thus, although it was not known to the government at the time, the fighting war was dying down even before General Templer's arrival.

The Federation of 1948 was intended to pave the way for eventual democratic self-government in Malaya.[1] The tensions

[1] Newly independent countries were arising in Asia about this time — 1946–8; the Philippines, India, Pakistan, Burma, and Indonesia.

and restrictions of the Emergency at first delayed political progress along these lines, yet some developments were noteworthy. Some political parties continued to function, and new ones appeared. In February 1949 the Malayan Chinese Association (M.C.A.) was formed under the leadership of Mr. Tan Cheng-lock, a member of a family which had been in Malaya for several generations. This gave the Chinese a legal political mouthpiece, and helped to answer any charge that there was general Chinese sympathy with the armed revolt. One major activity of the M.C.A. was its contribution to welfare work and amenities in the New Villages; by August 1953 the M.C.A. had given more than two and a half million dollars to this work by running lotteries among its members. Not surprisingly, the membership of the M.C.A., and its leaders in particular, merited the bitter hostility of the Communists. Some M.C.A. officials were murdered, and Mr. Tan Cheng-lock himself was wounded when a grenade was thrown during a meeting of the Association at Ipoh.

Dato Onn left U.M.N.O. in 1951[1] to start a new party to which he hoped to win members from all the racial communities. He considered at this time that the purely Malay character of U.M.N.O. was not helping the progress of Malaya to independence, and he named his new party the Independence of Malaya Party (I.M.P.). His programme included a united Malaya, reduction of the Sultans' powers, a common citizenship, and admission of Chinese and Indians into the administration. Onn received comparatively little active membership from Malays and Chinese, but he had support from the Malayan Indian Congress (M.I.C.). The M.I.C. was a political party formed in 1946 to speak for the interests of Malayan Indians; for a year or so after the beginning of the Emergency it suspended activities, but by 1951 it was a revived and active organisation. Onn was disappointed at the response to the I.M.P., and stated later that he thought that its founding was premature. Early in 1954 he established another non-communal party, Party Negara, in a second attempt to cut across the existing parties.

---

[1] His place as leader was taken by Tengku Abdul Rahman, a member of the royal house of Kedah and, by training, a lawyer.

In 1951 the 'Member' system was introduced into the Legislative Council. Nine of the nominated members were made responsible for various departments of government and, as Members, they had a semi-ministerial status. This move provided a valuable preparation for the practice of ministerial responsibility under self-government.

In the following year, amendments were made to the citizenship laws. The conditions relating to birth and residence, and to the definition of 'subjects of the Ruler', were made a little easier. The general effect was to improve the immediate position of non-Malays and to open the citizenship door to perhaps another 250,000.

In 1952 also, the beginning of local government through elected councils was authorized. This was thought to be, as in Britain, a training for parliamentary democracy, but the degree of independent action allowed to the councils in towns and New Villages was at first a very limited one. The local government elections in Malaya were, however, important for another reason. They provided the occasion for co-operation between the Malay and Chinese parties, U.M.N.O. and M.C.A. as against candidates from other parties. In the Kuala Lumpur municipal elections in February 1952 U.M.N.O. and M.C.A. candidates won nine of the twelve seats contested. Within the space of a year U.M.N.O. and M.C.A. gained similar successes at Johore Bahru, Muar, and Malacca. During this period co-operation had been extended into a more permanent arrangement of alliance between the two parties, and by early 1953 the term 'UMNO-MCA Alliance', or — more briefly — the 'Alliance party', had come into regular use.

Between U.M.N.O. and M.C.A. there were wide differences of outlook, notably, for instance, on the subject of education and citizenship. They proceeded to work together, however, as an effective political partnership for the gaining of electoral seats in elections to be held for the Federal Legislative Council. A joint council provided a medium through which their own differences could be discussed and possible compromises reached. The partnership was joined in 1953 by a third member, the Malayan

Indian Congress (M.I.C.), which was promised proportional representation in future Alliance successes.

In August 1953 the Alliance included in its aims the establishment of a sovereign and independent state within the Commonwealth, and urged the holding of elections for the Legislative Council, asking for three-fifths of the seats to be open for election. A government-appointed Federal Elections Committee did not go so far as to meet this request, but proposed 52 electoral seats out of 98. This gave the Council an elected majority, although, of course, not necessarily represented by one political group.

In June 1954 General Templer left Malaya, to be succeeded in office by Sir Donald MacGillivray. The Emergency was much less a military affair by this time. The first Federal elections were held in July 1955, and the Alliance party won 51 out of the 52 elected seats in the Legislative Council. This striking success gave the Alliance a clear majority in the Council, and the Alliance now began to plan for self-government. Tengku Abdul Rahman, leader of the Alliance, became Chief Minister of the new government, and both he and the Rulers had talks with the British Secretary of State for the Colonies who visited Malaya in August 1955. It was agreed that a conference should be held in London early in 1956 to discuss future relations between Malaya and Britain. For the Alliance, 'Merdeka' had become the slogan.

The Alliance now took the initiative in an attempt to settle the Communist war. A meeting was arranged in December 1955 in northern Kedah, between Tengku Abdul Rahman, Sir Cheng Lock Tan, and Mr. David Marshal, Chief Minister of Singapore, for the government, and the Secretary-General of the Communist party, Chin Peng. An amnesty was offered for a limited period to all Communists who would surrender, and the surrender conditions were defined. Those willing to abandon Communism would be allowed to return to normal life. Those who remained Communists would be held in detention. Those who wished to go to China would be allowed to do so. Chin Peng was only willing to consider an end to the fighting on terms which would have been very favourable from the Communists' point of view. He wanted the Communist party to be legalised and allowed complete freedom of activity. He made it clear that, while he would co-operate with the government for the time being, especially for the purpose of gaining independence, his ultimate aim was a Communist republic. On this note, the talks ended in a deadlock.

The Alliance was now all the more anxious to secure independence at an early date in order to counter the Communists' claim to represent Malayan nationalism. The Communists carried out some reorganisation to give the appearance of a united front with a Malay and an Indian as second and third in command of the party. They also started rumours to damage the prospects of the London Conference, and they formally requested Communist China to mediate for peace in Malaya.

The London Conference was attended by representatives of the Sultans, the Chief Minister of the Federation, and three other Alliance leaders, as well as the High Commissioner, Sir Donald MacGillivray, members of his staff, and advisers of the Colonial Office. Talks lasting three weeks ranged over a long list of topics, including Defence and Internal Security, Financial and Economic Matters, the Civil Service, and the Constitution.[1] It was agreed that Independence within the Commonwealth should be proclaimed by August 31st, 1957, and principles were established to indicate how this would be achieved. An increase of ministerial responsibility in the existing Executive and Legislative Councils was one type of decision to prepare the way for 'Merdeka'. Subject to the approval of the Crown, and of the Conference of Rulers in Malaya, a commission was to be appointed to draft the details of a constitution for an independent Malaya.

The Constitutional Commission was duly approved. A chairman, Lord Reid, and one other member were appointed by the United Kingdom, and Canada, Australia, India, and Pakistan, nominated one member each. The Reid Commission held its meetings in Malaya between May and October, 1956, and completed a long and detailed Report in February 1957.[2] This Report,

---

[1] *Report by the Federation of Malaya Constitutional Conference held in London in January and February*, 1956 (H.M.S.O., February 1956).

[2] *Report of the Federation of Malaya Constitutional Commission* (H.M.S.O., 1957).

although modified in some ways by a Working Party representing the Alliance and the Rulers, provided the basis for Malaya's new government on August 31st, 1957.

Briefly, there was to be a constitutional Head of State (Yang di-Pertuan Agong, or Paramount Ruler) elected from among their number by the Sultans for a five-year period. The Conference of Rulers was to remain. A Cabinet of Ministers, presided over by a Chief Minister, would be the executive body in the government. The Chief Minister would be appointed by the Yang di-Pertuan Agong, and would normally be the leader of the party with a majority in the House of Representatives or Lower House. The other Ministers would be nominated from the Lower House by the Chief Minister.

There were to be two Houses of Government, a Senate, and a House of Representatives. Legislation, other than Money Bills, could originate in either House and would require the assent of both Houses. The Senate, however, could only delay for a period of one year Bills which had been passed by the House of Representatives, and could virtually not delay Money Bills at all. The Senate was a small House, originally of 33 members, of whom each State (including Penang and Malacca) elected 2, and the Yang di-Pertuan Agong nominated 11. The House of Representatives was to have 104 members elected in single member constituencies by citizens who had reached the age of twenty-one. This House could sit for a maximum of five years, after which a new mandate from the electors must be sought.

In the State governments, the Ruler became a constitutional Head with a Mentri Besar as Chief Minister. Provision was made for an Executive Council of Ministers, responsible to a mainly-elected Legislative Council which would sit for a maximum of four years. The States held powers in Muslim law and custom, land, agriculture, forestry, and local government, and shared responsibility with the Federal government for social welfare and public health.

It was recommended that no new quotas or preferences be granted to Malays, but that existing special rights should be continued with some modifications for a period of fifteen years,

MODERN SINGAPORE

after which the whole position might be reviewed. Land remained a State matter, and was therefore not directly a subject for the Federal government. Emphasis was placed on the aim of a common nationality and a democratic form of government.

Elections were postponed for a period of about two years in order to allow the new citizenship qualifications outlined in the Report to take effect. These proposals went further than existing ones to extend citizenship rights to non-Malays.

At a ceremony held in Kuala Lumpur on August 31st, 1957, Malaya's Independence was proclaimed. The Ruler of Negri Sembilan, Tunku Abdul Rahman, was installed as the first Paramount Ruler; Tengku Abdul Rahman, who had played the greatest part in the 'Merdeka' movement, continued as Chief Minister.

The Communist war was not ended, but increasingly it was becoming less of an armed conflict and more a danger of infiltration and subversion. The new Malaya had defence treaties with Britain. 'Merdeka' had been achieved at an earlier date than had seemed likely two or three years before, and much remained to be done. Most important among the future tasks of government was the formation of a truly Malayan nation. In this sense, Tengku Abdul Rahman's words at the time of 'Merdeka' had a special importance. Independence, the Tengku said, was not the end; it was the beginning.

Independence in Malaya has not been followed by sensational moves or radical changes. In the post-Merdeka elections, held in 1959, the Alliance party gained a convincing victory, tantamount to a vote of confidence. Malayanisation of the public services has proceeded smoothly and without harshness. In international affairs, the new Malaya has gained respect. International conferences have been held very successfully in Malaya, and Malayan representatives have made statesmanlike contributions to the debates of the United Nations. The traditional inter-racial tolerance and harmony amongst Malayans continued.

The campaign against the Communists continued unabated, and July 31st, 1960, was fixed as the target date for ending an Emergency which would by then have lasted for twelve years.

T

This would practically symbolise the end of a shooting war, and would enable irksome regulations to be withdrawn. At the same time, since it would still be necessary to guard against Communist attempts to use methods of subversion, the government retained powers of preventative detention.

Meanwhile, in the post-war period, political developments had been taking place in Singapore. Pre-war Singapore had been the headquarters of the British colony of the Straits Settlements[1] which included Penang with Province Wellesley, Malacca, the Cocos Islands, Christmas Island, and Labuan. The last three had been placed under the administration of Singapore in 1883, 1903, and 1906, respectively. Government of the colony was vested in a Governor appointed by the Colonial Office, who was assisted by an Executive and a Legislative Council. The Executive Council had a majority of official members; in the Legislative Council, from 1924 onwards, the numbers of official and unofficial members were equal. All unofficial members were nominated by the Governor or by groups such as the Chambers of Commerce at Penang and Singapore. The Governor held, in theory, considerable authority, and he could rely on the support of the official members of the councils. In practice, he took note of the opinions of the unofficials, and sought, when necessary, to reach a compromise.

The colonial government was swept away by the Japanese, and they, in turn, were followed by a short period of British Military Administration, as in mainland Malaya. Civil government was resumed on April 1st, 1946.

Under the Malayan Union plan, Penang and Malacca were separated from Singapore, and, at the same time, Labuan became part of North Borneo. Singapore, together with Christmas Island and the Cocos Islands, was constituted a Crown colony. The separation of Singapore both from the old partners, Penang and Malacca, and from mainland Malaya, did not pass without criticism in the former Straits Settlements. When the Malayan Union was replaced by the Federation plan, Singapore's position

[1] Singapore also had an important British naval base built on the north side of the island in the 1920s and 1930s.

remained unchanged. The Federation Agreement did not exclude the possibility of other territories being included later, but this hardly met the wishes of critics in Singapore.

Two main reasons accounted for the division between the Federation and Singapore. One lay in their contrasting economies. The territory of the Federation paid its way largely by the revenues from import and export duties; Singapore traditionally maintained a free-trade policy as an essential stimulus for its *entrepôt* trade. The other reason concerned the balance between the main races. By 1947 the inclusion of Singapore in a Malayan Union or Federation would have meant a slight overall Chinese majority in the population, with Malays in second place. Leading Malay opinion would not have been prepared to accept this situation. In the pre-war Malay States, political offices held by Malayans had been largely filled by Malays. Until the 1930s a great number of the Chinese in Malaya were only temporary residents. Even in 1947, about 40 per cent of Malayan Chinese had been born outside Malaya.[1] Moreover, in the immediate post-war period, apart from the activities of the M.C.P., it was Malay political consciousness which first found its voice through political parties. Thus, in 1946 or in 1948, Malay leaders were not ready to accept a union on equal terms between Peninsular Malaya and Singapore, and this cautious attitude was not dispelled by a number of subsequent events which occurred in Singapore.

British post-war policy for Singapore, as for the rest of Malaya, was aimed at the eventual achievement of self-government. New Executive and Legislative Councils were established. The Legislative Council now had a majority of unofficial members, and nine of its members were to be elected — three by the Chinese, European and Indian Chambers of Commerce, and six by direct election through the votes of all British subjects over the age of twenty-one. These first elections in Singapore were not a great success. From a variety of motives, including apathy, unfamiliarity, and positive opposition to a separate constitution for Singapore or to the citizenship clauses of the Federation, the great majority of eligible voters failed to register and claim their vote.

[1] T. E. Smith, *Population-Growth in Malaya*, p. 64.

In June 1948 the Singapore government followed the example of the Federation and declared a state of Emergency. Communist tactics on the island took a different form from those in the Federation. There were some political murders and occasional riots, but the main moves were directed towards trade-union leadership and the recruitment and organisation of youth cadres from Chinese schools. Singapore also served as a source of supplies for the armed Communists in Johore.

In 1950–1 more unofficial members were added to the two councils, and the number of seats open to general election was increased from six to nine. Two of the unofficial members of the Executive Council were elected from among themselves by the unofficials in the Legislative Council, thus helping to link the two councils together. Out of a potential electorate of 250,000 in 1951, less than 50,000 registered, and only half this number voted. The main political parties which had arisen at this stage were the Progressives and the Labour party. The Progressives stood for the gradual development of self-government, the Labour party took some of its programme, notably for social welfare, from its namesake in Britain, but also urged self-rule and union with the Federation.

The municipal government was also placed on a wider footing. Singapore's local government dated back to 1856, and was in the hands, originally, of five commissioners who were authorised to raise local taxation for public services and amenities in the town. The number of commissioners increased with the scope of the work, but the practice of appointment by the Governor's nomination continued until 1948. In that year the number of commissioners was increased from twenty-five to twenty-seven, and eighteen of these were to be elected. In 1951 Singapore received by Royal Charter the status of a city, and its local government became a City Council.

A government-appointed commission under the chairmanship of Sir George Rendel met in 1953 to consider the failure of electors to use or even claim their vote, and to recommend further changes in the Singapore constitution. Its report, published in February 1954, recommended that those who were qualified to vote should be automatically registered as electors. It rejected any suggestion of a separate Singapore citizenship which might create the possibility of a dual citizenship. A new legislature, to be known as the Legislative Assembly, was proposed with a membership of thirty-two, of whom twenty-five would be elected. This Assembly would sit for a four-year term of office. Instead of the Executive Council, a new Council of Ministers was recommended, to include the Governor and three officials together with six members of the majority party in the Legislative Assembly. These six members would include the leader of the majority party, who would have the title of Chief Minister, together with five other members nominated by him for the ministerial posts.

The new constitution became effective in February 1955, and the election was held in April. The constitution was admittedly and intentionally transitional in character. Its purpose was to pave the way for complete self-government by providing the opportunity for a political party to hold a majority in the elected Assembly and strong representation at ministerial level. To some extent, the Council of Ministers represented a Cabinet in which major policy-planning could take place. At the same time the three officials in this council controlled finance, foreign affairs, defence, and internal security, and they were directly responsible to the Governor. The Rendel commission expressed the hope that this constitution would last for some years and provide valuable experience in parliamentary democracy.

The election of 1955 brought a result which was hardly expected. The main political groupings in the election campaign were the Progressives, who held a majority of the small number of elected seats in the old Legislative Council; the Democrats, a new Chinese party, representing business interests and urging the use of Chinese as one of the official languages of the legislature; the UMNO-MCA Alliance, an off-shoot from Federation politics, but a proportionally much smaller group in Singapore than it was in the Federation; a Labour Front, with trade-union support, which was a coalition of small socialist groups, following a split in the earlier Labour party, and the People's Action Party (P.A.P.), newly formed and comprising various shades of left-wing opinion, and with a fair measure of support in the trade unions which were independent of the Trade Union Congress.

With the exception of the Democrats, all these parties were non-communal. The Progressives the Democrats, and the Alliance stood, politically speaking, to the right, whilst the Labour Front and the P.A.P. stood to the left. The Progressives almost certainly lost ground to the Democrats, and perhaps also to the Alliance, and this worked to the advantage of the Labour Front, who gained a clear victory with ten of the twenty-five seats. As this was not quite sufficient to give an overall majority, the Labour Front, under its leader Mr. David Marshall, a Singapore lawyer, chose to form a coalition in a right rather than a left direction, and made a government party with the Alliance. The Progressives and the Democrats united to form a Liberal Socialist party in February, 1956, representing opposition to the government, but the more militant opposition came from the P.A.P. which had three members in the Assembly as a result of this election. The fact that the Progressives were in a controlling position in the municipal government gave an additional piquancy to Singapore politics at this time.

The P.A.P. and Chief Minister Marshall were, however, the most prominent features in the political scene. The P.A.P. led a vigorous campaign in Singapore labour circles and in the Chinese Middle Schools, and this was accompanied, intentionally or otherwise, by a series of strikes and demonstrations. Mr. Marshall pressed for the appointment of assistant Ministers, to which the Governor, Sir Robert Black, would only partially agree, and this led to a constitutional dispute as to whether the Governor was entitled to reject any or part of the advice given to him by the Chief Minister. In the Assembly, Mr. Marshall successfully put a resolution calling for the immediate grant of a new constitution providing for self-government.

The dispute between Mr. Marshall and the Governor was referred to the Secretary of State for the Colonies (Mr. Lennox-Boyd), who was due to visit Singapore about this time. The Secretary of State's decision, in August, 1955, to amend the constitution so that the Governor was clearly obliged to take the Chief Minister's advice, healed the breach, and Mr. Marshall was invited to come to London with a delegation in the following Spring to discuss self-government.

Mr. Marshall visited London in December 1955 for preliminary talks about the forthcoming conference, and he led an all-party delegation to the conference in April, 1956. From the British point of view, the Labour Front's position was now weaker, because two of its members in the Legislative Assembly had joined the opposition, and recent strikes and riots in Singapore had cast serious doubts upon the party's ability to keep law and order, or even to remain in office.

The Colonial Office agreed to many of the Chief Minister's proposals, including an enlarged and totally elected Legislative Assembly, and the principle of citizenship by registration. The controversial questions concerned foreign defence and internal security, which both sides recognised as interrelated topics. In view of the danger of Communist subversion, and doubts about Singapore's ability to defend itself against either internal or external attack, the Colonial Office wished to retain, for use in an emergency, a controlling interest in the proposed defence and security council on which both Britain and Singapore would be represented. Mr. Marshall would not accept this and, despite further proposals and counter-proposals, the talks broke down on this issue. When the delegation returned to Singapore, Mr. Marshall resigned from the office of Chief Minister and was succeeded by Mr. Lim Yew-Hock.

Internal security had been the main point at issue in the 1956 conference, and Mr. Lim Yew-Hock proceeded to take measures aimed both at reducing the threat of public disorder and at winning confidence by his government's ability to take a firm attitude towards unlawful opposition. He dissolved several organisations in which Communist influence was prominent, including the Middle School Students' Union, and he ordered a number of arrests and detentions on charges of subversive activities. This government campaign was met by strikes and riots from students and some of the trade unions and in September 1956 police and troops had to be called in from the Federation to suppress the disturbances.

So far as constitutional advance was concerned, the net result of Mr. Lim's policy was the arrangement of a second conference in London, which was held in March–April 1957. The Singapore delegation was led by Mr. Lim Yew-Hock and included leaders of the other parties. At this conference agreement was reached on a new constitution. There was to be a Malayan Head of State (Yang di-Pertuan Negara), an elected Legislative Assembly of fifty-one members, and an internal security council including three members from Britain, three from Singapore, and one representative, of ministerial rank, from the Federation of Malaya, by agreement with the Federation's Chief Minister. In the event of deadlock between the Singapore and British points of view, the Federation member would have a deciding vote. Britain, in consultation with the Singapore government, was to be responsible for defence and foreign policy, and British interests would be represented by a Commissioner, who would be also the chairman of the internal security council. Trade and cultural relations would be matters for the Singapore government, but consultations with Britain would take place.

This agreement was accepted by all parties in the Singapore government, but Britain attached to it one condition which caused much controversy. British agreement was based on the proviso that persons who were known to have engaged in subversive activity should not be eligible for election in the first elections to be held for the 'Legislative Assembly of the new State[1] of Singapore'. The Colonial Office replied to Singapore protests on this point by stressing the need for some temporary check on subversion in the interests of truly democratic government. Despite this controversial proviso, the Singapore government proceeded to prepare and pass the citizenship legislation for the new constitution, while the Chief Minister organised further campaigns against political agitators in schools and trade unions. More significant still was the government's round-up (in August 1957) of the leaders of the extreme left faction of the P.A.P., which was

[1] The new title used for Singapore in this agreement.

alleged to be taking control of the party's central executive committee from the more moderate Mr. Lee Kuan-Yew and his supporters. In all, thirty-nine arrests were made on charges of subversive activities, and these included five members of the executive of the P.A.P. and eleven other P.A.P. branch officials. Shortly after this a number of Chinese students were arrested on similar charges and a Chinese school headmaster was deported.

In May 1958 the same all-party delegation from Singapore took part in further detailed talks in London on the new constitution. Again, the only point of disagreement concerned the Colonial Office's insistence on disqualifying those who had been arrested for subversive activities from candidature for the forthcoming elections. The British government proceeded to give assent to the Bill for the new constitution and this was done by 1st August. Orders for the elections were published in November.

Meanwhile the City Council of Singapore had been reorganised in 1957 to consist of thirty-two elected councillors, who elected the Mayor from among their own number. At the first elections in December 1957 the P.A.P. was returned as the largest single party with thirteen of the thirty-two seats, and Mr. Ong Eng-Guan, treasurer of the party, became the first Mayor of Singapore.

The Rendel constitution was due to expire in April 1959, and it was planned to hold elections as soon as possible after the proroguing of the existing Legislative Assembly. The P.A.P. became particularly active in preparations for the elections, declared itself to be non-Communist and to be working for a merger with the Federation. In this latter respect, it urged the adoption of Malay as the national language. In particular, the P.A.P. concentrated on efficient party organisation and close contact with the electorate. It also made good use of any opportunities to discredit the existing coalition government.

At the elections held on May 30th, 1959, the P.A.P. won a sweeping victory with forty-three out of the fifty-one seats. The new citizenship laws had extended the electorate to over half a million voters, which made the P.A.P. success appear very convincing. During the election campaign the P.A.P. leaders had stated that, if elected, they would not take office until eight former party leaders were released from detention under the terms of the Preservation of Public Security Ordinance. Six of the eight had been detained after riots in October 1956, and the other two after the attempt by the extreme left-wing of the party to gain the leadership in August 1957. When Mr. Lee Kuan-Yew, as leader of the majority party, was asked by the Governor to form a government, he formally requested the release of the eight members. The request was granted on the following day, June 2nd, and the date of release was to be June 4th. On June 3rd the new constitution was brought into force with the former Governor, Sir William Goode, as Yang di-Pertuan Negara for a transitional period of about five months, after which he would hand over office to a Malayan-born Head of State. Mr. Lee Kuan-Yew became the first Prime Minister in a Cabinet which totalled nine Ministers.

Thus, in less than two years after Independence in the Federation, Singapore became, to a great extent, a self-governing City-State. The policy of its first government contained promises of social and cultural measures as well as a broad pattern of trade and industrial expansion. The idea of a merger with the Federation was kept very much to the fore. It was the government's stated intention to 'create and bring about conditions favourable to an early re-unification with the Federation'. The Federation government was more cautious. Apart from the older issues of economics and racial groups, the Federation was understandably anxious to avoid trade-union and student troubles of the kind which had disturbed Singapore in 1955 and 1956. For Singapore, even more than for the Federation, the essential nation-building task was to create a general Malayan outlook and loyalty.

DATES OF EVENTS: FEDERATION OF MALAYA

1946 (Jan.)   Malayan Union proposals.
1946   U.M.N.O. founded.
1946–7   Discussions for new constitution.
1948 (Feb.)   Federation of Malaya.
1948 (June)   State of Emergency proclaimed.
1949   M.C.A. founded.
1950–1   Resettlement and New Villages.
1952–3   Municipal elections.

1953   U.M.N.O. — M.C.A. — M.I.C. Alliance.
1955   Federal elections for Legislative Council.
1956 (Jan.–Feb.)   London conference ('Merdeka Mission').
1957 (Aug. 31st)   Independence Day.

High Commissioners

[1] Sir Edward Gent   1946–8   (Killed in air-crash, July, 1948.)
Sir Henry Gurney   1948–51   (Assassinated, Oct., 1951.)
General Sir Gerald Templer   1952–4
Sir Donald MacGillivray   1954–7

Chief Minister   Tengku Abdul Rahman, 1955.

DATES OF EVENTS: SINGAPORE

1946 (Apr.)   Civil government resumed.
              New Executive and Legislative Council.
1948 (June)   State of Emergency proclaimed.
1951   Further elections for Legislative Council.
       City status for Singapore.
1953–4   Rendel Commission.
1955 (Apr.)   Elections for Rendel constitution.
1956 (Apr.)   London conference (Mr. Marshall).
1957 (Mar.–Apr.)   London conference (Mr. Lim Yew-Hock).
1957   City Council made entirely elective.
1958 (May)   London conference (Mr. Lim Yew-Hock).
1959 (May)   Elections for new government.
1959 (June 3rd)   Internal Self-government under new constitution.

Governors of Singapore
Sir Franklyn Gimson   1946–52
Mr. J. F. Nicoll   1952–5
Sir Robert Black   1955–7
Sir William Goode   1957–9

Chief Ministers   Mr. D. Marshall, 1955–6
                    Mr. Lim Yew-Hock, 1956–9
Prime Minister   Mr. Lee Kuan-Yew, 1959–.

[1] Originally, Governor under the Malayan Union plan.

SELECT BIBLIOGRAPHY

Abbreviations
JRASMB — *Journal of the Malayan Branch, Royal Asiatic Society*
JRASSB — *Journal of the Straits Branch, Royal Asiatic Society*

BIBLIOGRAPHIES

Cheeseman, H. R., *Bibliography of Malaya*, Longmans, Green and Co., London, 1959

Embree, John F. and Lillian O. Dotson, *Bibliography of the people and cultures of mainland Southeast Asia*, New Haven, 1950

Hobbs, Cecil, *Southeast Asia: an annotated bibliography of selected reference-sources*, Washington, 1952

Pelzer, Karl J., *Selected Bibliography on the Geography of Southeast Asia, Part III, Malaya*, Human Relations Area Files, Inc., New Haven, 1956

SOUTH-EAST ASIA: GENERAL

Dobby, E. H. G., *South-East Asia*, University of London Press, London, 1957

East, W. G. and O. H. K. Spate (editors), *The Changing Map of Asia*, Methuen, London, 1953

Emerson, R., *Malaysia. A Study in Direct and Indirect Rule*, Macmillan, New York, 1937

    Representative Government in Southeast Asia, Cambridge: Harvard University Press, 1955

Emerson, R., L. A. Mills and V. Thompson, *Government and Nationalism in South-East Asia*, Institute of Pacific Relations, New York, 1943

Hall, D. G. E., *A History of South-East Asia*, Macmillan, London, 1955

Harrison, B., *A Short History of South-East Asia*, Macmillan, London, 1954

Mills, L. A., *The New World of South-East Asia*, Oxford University Press, London, 1949

Robequain, C., *Malaya, Indonesia, Borneo and the Philippines* (trans. by E. D. Laborde), Longmans, Green and Co., London, 1955

MALAYA: GENERAL

Buckley, C. B., *An Anecdotal History of Old Times in Singapore (1819–1867)*, 2 vols., Fraser and Neave, Singapore, 1902

Federated Malay States, *Annual Reports*, Kuala Lumpur

Ginsburg, N. and C. F. Roberts, *Malaya*, University of Washington Press, Seattle, 1958

Harrison, C. W. (editor), *An Illustrated Guide to the Federated Malay States*, The Malay States Development Agency, London, 1910

Linehan, W., 'A History of Pahang', *JRASMB*, Vol. 14, pt. 2, 1936

Malaya, Federation of, *Annual Reports*, Government Press, Kuala Lumpur.

Maxwell, W. G. and W. S. Gibson, *Treaties and Engagements affecting the Malay States and Borneo*, Truscott, London, 1924.

Mills, L. A., 'British Malaya 1824–1867', *JRASMB*, Vol. 3, pt. 2, 1925

 British Rule in Eastern Asia, Oxford University Press, London, 1942

Purcell, V., *The Chinese in Malaya*, Oxford University Press, London, 1941

 The Chinese in South-East Asia, Oxford University Press, London, 1951

 The Colonial Period in South-East Asia, Institute of Pacific Relations, New York, 1953

 Malaya, Outline of a Colony, Nelson, Edinburgh, 1946

Rentse, Anker, 'History of Kelantan', *JRASMB*, Vol. 12, pt. 2, 1934 and Vol. 14, pt. 3, 1936

Sheppard, M. C., 'A Short History of Trengganu', *JRASMB*, Vol. 22, pt. 3, 1949

Singapore, Colony of, *Annual Reports*, Government Press, Singapore

Song Ong Siang, *One Hundred Years' History of the Chinese in Singapore*, Murray, London, 1923

Straits Settlements. *Annual Reports*, Singapore

Swettenham, Sir F., *British Malaya*, Allen and Unwin, London, 1948

Wilkinson, R. J. and Sir R. O. Winstedt, 'A History of Perak', *JRASMB*, Vol. 12, pt. 1, 1934

Winstedt, Sir R. O., *History of Malaya*, Malayan Branch, Royal Asiatic Society, Singapore, 1935

 Britain and Malaya, 1786–1941, Longmans, Green and Co., London, 1944

 Malaya and its History, Hutchinson's Universal Library, London, 1951

 The Malays. A Cultural History, Routledge and Kegan Paul, London, 1950

 'A History of Johore', *JRASMB*, Vol. 10, pt. 3, 1932

 'A History of Perak' (with R. J. Wilkinson, above)

 'A History of Selangor', *JRASMB*, Vol. 12, pt. 3, 1934

 'Negri Sembilan. The History, Polity and Beliefs of the Nine States', *JRASMB*, Vol. 12, pt. 3, 1934

 'Notes on the History of Kedah', *JRASMB*, Vol. 14, pt. 3, 1936

Wright, A. and H. A. Cartwright (editors), *Twentieth Century Impressions of British Malaya*, Lloyd's Greater Britain Publishing Co., London, 1908

Wright, A. and T. H. Reid, *The Malay Peninsula*, Fisher and Unwin, London, 1912

CHAPTERS 1–4

Albuquerque, Braz de, *The Commentaries of the Great Afonso d'Alboquerque*, 4. vols., Hakluyt Society, London, 1875–84

Barbosa, Duarte, *The Book of Duarte Barbosa*, Vol. 2 (trans. by M. L. Dames), Hakluyt Society, London, 1921

Boxer, C. R., *Fidalgos in the Far East*, The Hague, 1948

Bort, Balthasar, 'Report on Malacca' (trans. by Miss M. J. Bremner, ed. by C. O. Blagden), *JRASMB*, Vol. 5, pt. 1, 1927

Brown, C. C., 'Sejarah Melayu (Malay Annals)', *JRASMB*, Vol. 25, pts. 2 and 3, 1952

Cardon, Rev. R., 'Portuguese Malacca', *JRASMB*, Vol. 12, pt. 2, 1934

Danvers, F. C., *The Portuguese in India*, 2 vols., W. H. Allen, London, 1894

Furnivall, J. S., *Netherlands India: a study of Plural Economy*, Cambridge, 1944

Gibson-Hill, C. A., 'Johore Lama and other Ancient Sites on the Johore river', *JRASMB*, Vol. 28, pt. 2, 1955

'The Fortification of Bukit China (Malacca)', *JRASMB*, Vol. 29, pt. 3, 1956

'On the Alleged Death of Sultan Ala'ud'din at Acheh in 1613', *JRASMB*, Vol. 29, pt. 1, 1956

Hamilton, Capt. Alexander, *A New Account of the East Indies*, 2 vols, Mosman, Edinburgh, 1727

Howe, Sonia F., *In Quest of Spices*, Jenkins, London, 1946

Hughes, T. D. (trans.), 'A Portuguese Account of Johore (A.D. 1718)', *JRASMB*, Vol. 13, pt. 2, 1935

Leupe, P. A., 'Siege and Capture of Malacca from the Portuguese' (trans. by Mac Hacobian), *JRASMB*, Vol. 14, pt. 1, 1936

Leur, J. C. van, *Indonesian Trade and Society*, The Hague, 1955

Linschoten, J. H. van, *The Voyage of J. H. Linschoten to the East Indies*, 2 vols., Hakluyt Society, London, 1885

MacGregor, I. A., 'Notes on the Portuguese in Malaya', *JRASMB*, Vol. 28, pt. 2, 1955

'Johore Lama in the 16th century', *JRASMB*, Vol. 28, pt. 2, 1955

'A Sea-Fight near Singapore in the 1570s', *JRASMB*, Vol. 29, pt. 3, 1956

Mills, J. V., 'Two Dutch-Portuguese Sea-fights', *JRASMB*, Vol. 16, pt. 1, 1938

(trans.) 'Eredia's Description of Malacca, 1613', *JRASMB*, Vol. 8, pt. 1, 1931

Overbeck, H., 'Silsilah Melayu dan Bugis dan Sakalian Raja-raja-nya' (abridged English version), *JRASMB*, Vol. 4, pt. 3, 1926

Pires, Tomé, *Suma Oriental (1512–1515)* (trans. by A. Cortesao), 2 vols., Hakluyt Society, London, 1944

Prestage, E., *Afonso de Albuquerque*, Watford, 1931

Resende, Baretto de, 'Account of Malacca' (1646) (trans. by W. G. Maxwell), *JRASSB*, Vol. 60, pt. 1, 1911

Wilkinson, R. J., 'The Malacca Sultanate', *JRASMB*, Vol. 13, pt. 2, 1935

Winstedt, Sir R. O., 'Kingship and Enthronement in Malaya', *JRASMB*, Vol. 20, pt. 1, 1947

CHAPTERS 5–7

Abdullah bin Abdul Kadir, 'Hikayat Abdullah' (annotated trans. by A. H. Hill), *JRASMB*, Vol. 28, pt. 3, 1955

Clodd, H. P., *Malaya's First British Pioneer (Francis Light)*, Luzac, London, 1948

Coupland, R., *Raffles of Singapore*, Oxford University Press, London, 1946

Cowan, C. D., 'Early Penang and the Rise of Singapore 1805-1832', *JRASMB*, Vol. 23, pt. 2, 1950

Crawfurd, J., *Journal of an Embassy from the Governor-General of India to the Courts of Siam and Cochin-China*, 2 vols., Colburn, London, 1828

Fielding, K. J. (editor), 'The Settlement of Penang' by James Scott, *JRASMB*, Vol. 28, pt. 1, 1955

Hahn, Emily, *Raffles of Singapore*, Aldor, London, 1948

Irwin, G., 'Governor Couperus and the Surrender of Malacca. 1795', *JRASMB*, Vol. 29, pt. 3, 1956

Stevens, F. G., 'Early History of Prince of Wales Island (Penang)', . . . a contribution to the *JRASMB*, Vol. 7, pt. 3, 1929

Tan Soo Chye, 'A Note on Early Legislation in Penang', *JRASMB*, Vol. 23, pt. 1, 1950

Tarling, N., 'British Policy in the Malay Peninsula and Archipelago. 1824-1871', *JRASMB*, Vol. 30, pt. 3, 1957

Vella, W., *Siam under Rama III. 1824-1851*, Association for Asian Studies, New York, 1957

Wurtzburg, C. E., *Raffles of the Eastern Isles*, Hodder and Stoughton, London, 1954

CHAPTERS 8–10

Abdullah bin Abdul Kadir, *Pelayaran Abdullah* (trans. by A. E. Coope), Malaya Publishing House, Singapore, 1949

Bird, Isabella (Mrs. Bishop), *The Golden Chersonese and the Way Thither*, Murray, London, 1833

Blythe, W., 'Historical Sketch of Chinese Labour in Malaya', *JRASMB*, Vol. 20, pt. 1, 1947

Comber, Leon, *Secret Societies in Malaya*, Donald Moore, Singapore, 1957

Cowan, C. D. (editor), 'Sir Frank Swettenham's Perak Journals, 1874-1876', *JRASMB*, Vol. 24, pt. 4, 1951

Gullick, J. M., *Indigenous Political Systems of Western Malaya*, University of London, 1956
  'Kuala Lumpur 1880–1895', *JRASMB*, Vol. 28, pt. 4, 1955
  'Captain Speedy of Larut', *JRASMB*, Vol. 26, pt. 3, 1953
  'Sungei Ujong', *JRASMB*, Vol. 22, pt. 2, 1949
McNair, F., *Perak and the Malays. Sarong and Keris*, Tinsley Bros., London, 1878
Middlebrook, S. M., 'Yap Ah Loy', *JRASMB*, Vol. 24, pt. 2, 1951
Newbold, T., *Political and Statistical Account of the British Settlements in the Straits of Malacca*, 2 vols., Murray, London, 1839
Parkinson, C. Northcote, *British Intervention in Malaya, 1867–1877*, University of Malaya, 1960
Sadka, Emily (editor), 'The Journal of Sir Hugh Low, Perak, 1877', *JRASMB*, Vol. 27, pt. 4, 1954
Wallace, A. R., *Malay Archipelago*, Macmillan, London, 1869

CHAPTERS 11–12

Allen, G. C. and A. G. Donnithorne, *Western Enterprise in Indonesia and Malaya*, Allen and Unwin, London, 1957
Bauer, P. T., *The Rubber Industry*, Longmans, Green and Co., London, 1948
Burkhill, I., *A Dictionary of Economic Products of the Malay Peninsula*, 2 vols., Crown Agents, London, 1935
Dobby, E. H. G., *Agricultural Questions of Malaya*, Cambridge University Press, 1949
Fermor, L., *Report upon the Mining Industry of Malaya*, Government Press, Kuala Lumpur, 1939
Furnivall, J. S., *Educational Progress in South-East Asia*, Institute of Pacific Relations, New York, 1943
Grist, D. H., *An Outline of Malayan Agriculture*, Dept. of Agriculture, Kuala Lumpur, 1936
Gullick, J. M., 'The Negri Sembilan Economy of the 1890s', *JRASMB*, Vol. 24, pt. 1, 1951
India Government (Economic Adviser), *Indians in the Malayan Economy* (Report), New Delhi, 1950
International Bank Mission, *The Economic Development of Malaya*, Baltimore, 1955
Jones, S. W., *Public Administration in Malaya*, Royal Institute of International Affairs, London, 1952
King, F., *Money in British East Asia*, H.M.S.O., London, 1957
Malayan Agricultural Journals, Kuala Lumpur
Medical Research Studies, Kuala Lumpur
Medical Research Bulletins, Kuala Lumpur

Mills, L. A., *Malaya. A Political and Economic Appraisal*, Oxford University Press, London, 1958

Parkinson, C. Northcote, *Tin-Plate — An Outline History* (in 'Malaya in History', Vol. 3, no. 2, Kuala Lumpur, 1957)

Silcock, T. H., *The Economy of Malaya*, Donald Moore, Singapore, 1956

Smith, T. E., *Population-Growth in Malaya*, Royal Institute of International Affairs, London, 1952

Thompson, V. and R. Adloff, *Cultural Institutions and Educational Policy in Southeast Asia*, Institute of Pacific Relations, New York, 1948

Tufo, M. V. del, *Malaya 1947 Census Report*, Crown Agents, London, 1949

Watson, Dr. M., *Prevention of Malaria in the Federated Malay States*, Murray, London, 1921

CHAPTERS 13–15

Bartlett, V., *Report from Malaya*, Verschoyle, London, 1954

Chapman, F. Spencer, *The Jungle is Neutral*, Chatto and Windus, London, 1949

Chin Kee Onn, *Malaya Upside Down*, Singapore, 1946

Corry, W., *Malaya Today* (British Commonwealth Affairs No. 9), Longmans, Green and Co., London, 1955

Federation of Malaya Agreement, 1948, Government Press, Kuala Lumpur, 1952

Graham, W., *Kelantan. A State of the Malay Peninsula*, MacLehose, Glasgow, 1908
   Siam, 2 vols., Moring, London, 1924

Malayan Union and Singapore, H.M.S.O., London, 1946

Miller, H., *Menace in Malaya*, Harrap, London, 1955

Morrison, I., *Malayan Postscript*, Faber, London, 1942

Percival, A., *The War in Malaya*, Eyre and Spottiswoode, London, 1949

Purcell, V., *Malaya. Communist or Free?*, Gollancz, London, 1954

Report of the Federation of Malaya Constitutional Commission (Lord Reid, Chairman), H.M.S.O., London, 1957

Robinson, J. B. Perry, *Transformation in Malaya*, Secker and Warburg, London, 1953

Silcock, T. and Abdul Aziz Unku, *Nationalism in Malaya*, Institute of Pacific Relations, New York, 1950

Wood, W., *History of Siam*, Unwin, London, 1926

Wyatt, Woodrow, *Southwards from China*, Hodder and Stoughton, London, 1952

INDEX

A

Abdul Jalil, 51–2, 55
Abdul Jalil Muadzam Shah, 56
Abdul Jalil Rahmat Shah, *see* Raja Kechil
Abdul Jalil Riayat Shah III, 56
Abdul Jamil, 44
Abdullah, (Kampar), 29–30, 32
Abdullah, (Kedah), 76
Abdullah, Munshi, 126, 135
Abdullah, (Perak), (1) 110, 114 (2) 139, 143, (3) 139, 144, 148–54, 158–9, 168, 170–9
Abdu'l Rahman, Sultan, 92, 94–5, 120
Abdu'l Rahman, Temenggong, 92, 101, 136, 249
Abdul Said, 118
Abdul Samad, 140–4, 161, 166, 222 n
Aborigines, 128
Abu Bakar, 136, 184, 215, 249–50, 254
Acheh, 30–6, 39–43, 46–50, 73–6, 82, 90–4, 124, 156, 209, 212
Achinese, 31, 35–6, 42–3, 47, 49–50, 55, 68, 127, 192
Adviser(s), British, 245, 247–8, 251, 253–4, 268
Afghanistan, 243
Africans, 128
Agriculture, 182–3, 187, 201–9, 238–239, 240–1
Agriculture, School of, 233
Ahmad, (Kedah), 142
Ahmad, (Malacca), 26
Ahmad, (Pahang), *see* Wan Ahmad
Ahmad Riayat Shah, 56
Ahmad Taj'ud'din, 105–8, 111–12, 116

Ahmadin, 138
Ala'ud'din, (Johore), 45 n, 46–7, 55
Ala'ud'din, (Malacca), 12–14, 18
Ala'ud'din Riayat Shah II, 55
Albuquerque, Afonso de, 24–8, 34, 42
Aleppo, 22
Alexandria, 22
Ali, (Johore), 136, 249–50
Ali, (Perak), 139, 143
Ali Jalla Abdul Jalil Riayat Shah, 55
Alliance party, 277–81, 285–6, 291
Alliance government, 234
Almeida, Francisco de, 22–4
Amboina, 31
America, United States of, (U.S.A.), 94, 156, 205, 208, 215–17, 256, 258–9
American Independence, War of, 73 n, 76
American Methodist Church, 231
Amiens, Peace of, 85
Amoy, 215
Ampang, 140, 143, 193–4, 201, 225, 227
Andamans, 82
Anderson, John, 110
Anderson, Sir John, 239
Anderson Treaties (1825), 110, 114, 122, 145
Anglo-Burmese War, First, 108–9, 111, 113
Anglo-Dutch Treaty (1824), 98–102, 117, 155
Anglo-Siamese agreement (1902), 204–5, 254

308 *Index*

PRINTED IN GREAT BRITAIN BY ROBERT MACLEHOSE AND CO. LTD
THE UNIVERSITY PRESS, GLASGOW

959.5-K35h   96204

AUTHOR
Kennedy, Joseph

TITLE
A history of Malaya

DATE DUE	BORROWER'S NAME
EE25'63	J Montagus
10 29 8	
	WELCH DOUGLAS A
	LIN GAVIN C
2 11 2	11

DATE DUE	BORROWER'S NAME